Praise for *The More Beautiful World Our Hearts Know Is Possible*

"God damn this is good! This version of the big story by Charles Eisenstein is one of the best I have ever heard. Charles, you are speaking for millions of us and we so know what you are saying to be true. We will absolutely tell the whole fucking world about it."

—BRAD BLANTON, author of *Radical Honesty*

"The more beautiful world I inhabit accords with Charles Eisenstein's vision: a world where we embrace the shadow and give it name so that the healing can begin. Take this book and let it seep into your very being."

—POLLY HIGGINS, author of *Eradicating Ecocide,*
barrister and earth lawyer

"This book will change your world. It is beautiful because Charles Eisenstein has the courage to be vulnerable and it is in acknowledging our vulnerability that we will realize our greater humanity."

—REVD PETER OWEN-JONES, presenter of
Around the World in 80 Faiths, author, and priest

Other books by Charles Eisenstein:

The Ascent of Humanity
Sacred Economics
The Yoga of Eating

THE More Beautiful World Our Hearts Know IS Possible

CHARLES EISENSTEIN

North Atlantic Books
Berkeley, California

Published by
North Atlantic Books
Berkeley, California

Cover image: *Italiaans landschap met parasoldennen,* by Hendrik Voogd (1807)
Cover and book design by Mary Ann Casler
Printed in the United States of America

The More Beautiful World Our Hearts Know Is Possible is sponsored and published by the Society for the Study of Native Arts and Sciences (dba North Atlantic Books), an educational nonprofit based in Berkeley, California, that collaborates with partners to develop cross-cultural perspectives, nurture holistic views of art, science, the humanities, and healing, and seed personal and global transformation by publishing work on the relationship of body, spirit, and nature.

North Atlantic Books' publications are available through most bookstores. For further information, visit our website at www.northatlanticbooks.com or call 800-733-3000.

Library of Congress Cataloging-in-Publication Data
Eisenstein, Charles, 1967–
The more beautiful world our hearts know is possible / Charles Eisenstein.
    pages cm
ISBN 978-1-58394-724-1
1. Consciousness. 2. Humanity. I. Title.
BF311.E416 2013
158.1—dc23   2013013696

5 6 7 8 9 SHERIDAN 20 19 18 17
Printed on recycled paper

North Atlantic Books is committed to the protection of our environment.
We partner with FSC-certified printers using soy-based inks and
print on recycled paper whenever possible.

To the humble,
whose invisible choices are healing the world.

Contents

Acknowledgments

*I*t was just four years ago that my work was nearly unknown, and I was bankrupt, working part-time in construction, writing in whatever moments single fatherhood allowed. It is through the generosity of countless friends and supporters that my life has changed so radically since then.

In the last three years I have spoken at least three hundred times in over a hundred cities. None of these events did I organize myself or pay anyone to organize—each was a gift from people who donated their time, energy, networks, and organizational abilities. Nor did I instigate any of the podcasts, interviews, and films that I've been part of. I am able to be of effective service only because so many others serve the same thing. My work is truly a collective effort.

The people who have played this role are too numerous to mention. The same goes for the hundreds who have welcomed me into their homes, fed me, and driven me around everywhere I visit. Dear hosts, your generosity has sustained me in more ways than you know, reminding me of the truth of what I write about. Likewise the thousands of people who have given me money online or at events, validating the gift principle by which I make my work freely available. Thanks to your generosity, I am able to continue writing and speaking as I support four children.

In addition to all these people, who will have to remain nameless here, I do want to name some who have had a direct impact on the present book. I want to thank Ken Jordan and Daniel Pinchbeck for their total editorial license in publishing the essays in which I developed many of the ideas herein; Andrew Harvey, for our spirited conversations that pushed me into new territory in my thinking about "evil," as well as for his unstinting enthusiasm for my work; Joshua Ramey, for his friendship at a key moment of doubt; Patsy, my ex-wife, for staying with me in the crucible of healing; North Atlantic Books, for indulging my unusual demands around copyright, cover art, and editing; and Marie Goodwin, who appeared out of nowhere to assist me with scheduling, logistics, communication, research, and sanity. I would also like to mention with appreciation the following: Glenn Baumgartner, O.J. Haugen, Brad Laughlin, Cynthia Jurs, Polly Higgins, Satish Kumar, Mark Boyle, Manish Jain, Ian MacKenzie, Filipa Pimenatal, Trenna Cormack, Jeff Dardozzi, Filiz Telek ... ah, now that I've gotten going I want to list hundreds more. Many I have not listed have been just as important as those I have.

Finally and most of all I want to thank my wife, Stella, whose presence in my life has changed everything.

Separation

Sometimes I feel nostalgic for the cultural mythology of my youth, a world in which there was nothing wrong with soda pop, in which the Super Bowl was important, in which America was bringing democracy to the world, in which the doctor could fix you, in which science was going to make life better and better, and they just put a man on the moon.

Life made sense. If you worked hard you could get good grades, get into a good college, go to grad school or follow some other professional path, and you would be happy. With a few unfortunate exceptions, you would be successful if you obeyed the rules of our society: if you followed the latest medical advice, kept informed by reading the *New York Times*, got a good education, obeyed the law, made prudent investments, and stayed away from Bad Things like drugs. Sure there were problems, but the scientists and experts were working hard to fix them. Soon a new medical advance, a new law, a new educational technique would propel the onward improvement of life. My childhood perceptions were part of a narrative I call the Story of the People, in which humanity was destined to create a perfect world through science, reason, and technology: to conquer nature, transcend our animal origins, and engineer a rational society.

From my vantage point, the basic premises of this story seemed unquestionable. My education, the media, and most of all the normality of the routines around me conspired to say, "Everything is fine." Today it is increasingly obvious that this was a bubble world built atop massive human suffering and environmental degradation, but at the time one could live within that bubble without need of much self-deception. The story that surrounded us was robust. It easily kept anomalous data points on the margins.

Nonetheless, I (like many others) felt a wrongness in the world, a wrongness that seeped through the cracks of my privileged, insulated childhood. I never fully accepted what I had been offered as normal. Life, I knew, was supposed to be more joyful than this, more real, more meaningful, and the world was supposed to be more beautiful. We were not supposed to hate Mondays and live for the weekends and holidays. We were not supposed to have to raise our hands to be allowed to pee. We were not supposed to be kept indoors on a beautiful day, day after day.

And as my horizons broadened, I knew that millions were not supposed to be starving, that nuclear weapons were not supposed to be hanging over our heads, that the rainforests were not supposed to be shrinking, or the fish dying, or the condors and eagles disappearing. I could not accept the way the dominant narrative of my culture handled these things: as fragmentary problems to be solved, as unfortunate facts of life to be regretted, or as unmentionable taboo subjects to be simply ignored.

On some level, we all know better. This knowledge seldom finds clear articulation, so instead we express it indirectly through covert and overt rebellion. Addiction, self-sabotage, procrastination, laziness, rage, chronic fatigue, and depression are all ways that we withhold our full participation in the program of life we are offered. When the conscious mind cannot find a reason to say no, the unconscious says no in its own way. More and more of us cannot bear to stay in the "old normal" any longer.

This narrative of normal is crumbling on a systemic level too. We live today at a moment of transition between worlds. The institutions that have borne us through the centuries have lost their vitality; only with increasing self-delusion can we pretend they are sustainable. Our systems of money, politics, energy, medicine, education, and more are no longer delivering the benefits they once did (or seemed to). Their Utopian promise, so inspiring a century ago, recedes further every year. Millions of us know this; more and more, we hardly bother to pretend otherwise. Yet we seem helpless to change, helpless even to stop participating in industrial civilization's rush over the cliff.

I have in my earlier work offered a reframing of this process, seeing human cultural evolution as a story of growth, followed by crisis, followed by breakdown, followed by a renaissance: the emergence of a new kind of civilization, an Age of Reunion to follow the Age of Separation. Perhaps profound change happens only through collapse. Certainly that is true for many on a personal level. You may know, intellectually, that your lifestyle isn't sustainable and you have to change your ways. "Yeah, yeah. I know I should stop smoking. Start exercising. Stop buying on credit."

But how often does anyone change without a wake-up call, or more often, a series of wake-up calls? After all, our habits are embedded in a way of being that includes all aspects of life. Hence the saying, "You cannot change one thing without changing everything."

On the collective level the same is true. As we awaken to the interconnectedness of all our systems, we see that we cannot change, for example, our energy technologies without changing the economic system that supports them. We learn as well that all of our external institutions reflect our basic perceptions of the world, our invisible ideologies and belief systems. In that sense, we can say that the ecological crisis—like all our crises—is a spiritual crisis. By that I mean it goes all the way to the bottom, encompassing all aspects of our humanity.

And what, exactly, is at the bottom? What do I mean by a "transition between worlds"? At the bottom of our civilization lies a story, a mythology. I call it the Story of the World or the Story of the People—a matrix of narratives, agreements, and symbolic systems that comprises the answers our culture offers to life's most basic questions:

- Who am I?
- Why do things happen?
- What is the purpose of life?
- What is human nature?
- What is sacred?
- Who are we as a people?
- Where did we come from and where are we going?

Our culture answers them more or less as follows. I will present a pure articulation of these answers, this Story of the World, though in fact it has never dominated completely even as it reached its zenith in the last century. You might recognize some of these answers to be scientifically obsolete, but this obsolete nineteenth- and twentieth-century science still generates our view of what is real, possible, and practical. The new physics, the new biology, the new psychology have only barely begun to infiltrate our operating beliefs. So here are the old answers:

Who are you? You are a separate individual among other separate individuals in a universe that is separate from you as well. You are a Cartesian mote of consciousness looking out through the eyes of a flesh robot, programmed by its genes to maximize reproductive self-interest. You are a bubble of psychology, a mind (whether brain-based or not) separate from other minds and separate from matter. Or you are a soul encased in flesh, separate from the world and separate from other souls. Or you are a mass, a conglomeration of particles operating according to the impersonal forces of physics.

Why do things happen? Again, the impersonal forces of physics act upon a generic material substrate of fundamental particles. All phenomena are the result of these mathematically determined interactions. Intelligence, order, purpose, and design are illusions; underneath it all is merely a purposeless jumble of forces and masses. Any phenomenon, all of movement, all of life, is the result of the sum total of forces acting upon objects.

What is the purpose of life? There is no purpose, only cause. The universe is at bottom blind and dead. Thought is but an electrochemical impulse; love but a hormonal cascade that rewires our brains. The only purpose of life (other than what we manufacture ourselves) is simply to live, to survive and reproduce, to maximize rational self-interest. Since we are fundamentally separate from each other, my self-interest is very likely at the expense of your self-interest. Everything that is not-self is at best indifferent to our well-being, at worst hostile.

What is human nature? To protect ourselves against this hostile universe of competing individuals and impersonal forces, we must exercise as much control as possible. We seek out anything that furthers that aim; for example, money, status, security, information, and power—all those things we call "worldly." At the very foundation of our nature, our motivations, and our desires, is what can only be called evil. That is what a ruthless maximizer of self-interest is.

What, therefore, is sacred? Since the blind, ruthless pursuit of self-interest is antisocial, it is important to overcome our biological programming and pursue "higher things." A holy person doesn't succumb to the desires of the flesh. He or she takes the path of self-denial, of discipline, ascending into the realm of spirit or, in the secular version of this quest, into the realm of reason and the mind, principles and ethics. For the religious, to be sacred is to be otherworldly; the soul is separate from the body, and God lives high above the earth. Despite their superficial opposition, science and religion have agreed: the sacred is not of this world.

Who are we as a people? We are a special kind of animal, the apex of evolution, possessing brains that allow the cultural as well as the genetic transfer of information. We are unique in having (in the religious view) a soul or (in the scientific view) a rational mind. In our mechanical universe we alone possess consciousness and the wherewithal to mold the world according to our design. The only limit to our ability to do so is that amount of force we can harness and the precision with which we can apply it. The more we are able to do so, the better off we are in this indifferent or hostile universe, the more comfortable and secure.

Where have we come from and where are we going? We started out as naked, ignorant animals, barely hanging on to survival, living lives that were nasty, brutish, and short. Fortunately, thanks to our big brains, science replaced superstition and technology replaced ritual. We ascended to become the lords and possessors of nature, domesticating plants and animals, harnessing natural forces, conquering diseases, laying bare the deepest secrets of the universe. Our destiny is to complete that conquest: to free ourselves from labor, from disease, from death itself, to ascend to the stars and leave nature behind altogether.

Throughout this book I will refer to this worldview as the Story of Separation, the old story, or sometimes outgrowths from it: the Story of Ascent, the program of control, and so forth.

The answers to these questions are culturally dependent, yet they immerse us so completely that we have seen them as reality itself. These answers are changing today, along with everything built atop them—which basically means our entire civilization. That is why we sometimes get the vertiginous feeling that the whole world is falling apart. Seeing the emptiness of what once seemed so real, practical, and enduring, we stand as if at an abyss. What's next? Who am I? What's important? What is the purpose of my life? How can I be an effective agent of healing? The old answers are fading as the Story of the People that once answered them crumbles around us.

This book is a guide from the old story, through the empty space between stories, and into a new story. It addresses the reader as a subject of this transition personally, and as an agent of transition—for other people, for our society, and for our planet.

Like the crisis, the transition we face goes all the way to the bottom. Internally, it is nothing less than a transformation in the experience of being alive. Externally, it is nothing less than a transformation of humanity's role on planet Earth.

I do not offer this book as someone who has completed this transition himself. Far from it. I have no more authority to write this book than any other man or woman. I am not an avatar or a saint, I am not channeling ascended masters or ETs, I have no unusual psychic powers or intellectual genius, I have not passed through any remarkable hardship or ordeal, I have no especially deep spiritual practice or shamanic training. I am an ordinary man. You will, therefore, have to take my words on their own merits.

And if my words fulfill their intention, which is to catalyze a next step, big or small, into the more beautiful world our hearts know is possible, my very ordinariness becomes highly significant. It shows how close we all are, all of us ordinary humans, to a profound transformation of consciousness and being. If I, an ordinary man, can see it, we must be almost there.

Breakdown

The kingdom of God is for the broken hearted.

—FRED ROGERS

*I*t is frightening, this transition between worlds, but it is also alluring. Have you ever gotten addicted to doom-and-gloom websites, logging on every day to read the latest evidence that collapse is coming soon, feeling almost let down when Peak Oil didn't start in 2005, or the financial system didn't collapse in 2008? (I'm still worried about Y2K myself.) Do you look toward the future with a mixture of dread, yes, but also a kind of positive anticipation? When a big crisis looms, a superstorm or financial crisis, is there a part of you that says, "Bring it on!" hoping it might free us from our collective entrapment in a system that serves no one (not even its elites)?

It is quite normal to fear what one most desires. We desire to transcend the Story of the World that has come to enslave us, that indeed is killing the planet. We fear what the end of that story will bring: the demise of much that is familiar.

Fear it or not, it is happening already. Since my childhood in the 1970s, our Story of the People has eroded at an accelerating rate. More and more people in the West no longer believe that civilization is fundamentally on the right track. Even those who don't yet question its basic premises in any explicit way seem to have grown weary of it. A layer of cynicism, a hipster self-awareness has muted our earnestness. What was once so real, say a plank in a party platform, today is seen through several levels of "meta" filters that parse it in terms of image and message. We are like children who have grown out of a story that once enthralled us, aware now that it is only a story.

At the same time, a series of new data points has disrupted the story from the outside. The harnessing of fossil fuels, the miracle of chemicals to transform agriculture, the methods of social engineering and political science to create a more rational and just society—each has fallen far short of its promise, and brought unanticipated consequences that, together, threaten civilization. We just cannot believe anymore that the scientists have everything well in hand. Nor can we believe that the onward march of reason will bring on social Utopia.

Today we cannot ignore the intensifying degradation of the biosphere, the malaise of the economic system, the decline in human health, or the persistence and indeed growth of global poverty and inequality. We once thought economists would fix poverty, political scientists would fix social injustice, chemists and biologists would fix environmental problems, the power of reason would prevail and we would adopt sane policies. I remember looking at maps of rainforest decline in *National Geographic* in the early 1980s and feeling both alarm and relief—relief because at least the scientists and everyone who reads *National Geographic* are aware of the problem now, so something surely will be done.

Nothing was done. Rainforest decline accelerated, along with nearly every other environmental threat that we knew about in 1980. Our Story of the People trundled forward under the momentum of centuries, but with each passing decade the hollowing-out of its core, which started perhaps with the industrial-scale slaughter of World War I, extended further. When I was a child, our ideological systems and mass media still protected that story, but in the last thirty years the incursions of reality have punctured its protective shell and eroded its essential infrastructure. We no longer believe our storytellers, our elites.

We have lost the vision of the future we once had; most people have no vision of the future at all. This is new for our society. Fifty or a hundred years ago, most people agreed on the general outlines of the future. We thought we knew where society was going. Even the Marxists and the capitalists agreed on its basic outlines: a paradise of mechanized leisure and scientifically engineered social harmony, with spirituality either abolished entirely or relegated to a materially inconsequential corner of life that happened mostly on Sundays. Of course there were dissenters from this vision, but this was the general consensus.

Like an animal, when a story nears its end it goes through death throes, an exaggerated semblance of life. So today we see domination, conquest, violence, and separation take on absurd extremes that hold a mirror up to what was once hidden and diffuse. Here are a few examples:

- Villages in Bangladesh where half the people have just one kidney, having sold the other in the black-market organ trade. Usually this is done to pay off debts. Here we see, literalized, the conversion of life into money that drives our economic system.
- Prisons in China where prisoners must spend fourteen hours a day playing online video games to build up character experience points. The prison officials then sell these characters to teenagers in the West. Here we see, in extreme form, the disconnect between the physical and virtual worlds, the suffering and exploitation upon which our fantasies are built.
- Old people in Japan whose relatives have no time to see them, so instead they receive visits from professional "relatives" who pretend to be family members. Here is a mirror to the dissolution of the bonds of community and family, to be replaced by money.

Of course, all of these pale in comparison to the litany of horrors that punctuates history and continues, endemic, to this day. The wars, the genocide, the mass rapes, the sweatshops, the mines, the slavery. On close examination, these are no less absurd. It is the height of absurdity that we are still manufacturing hydrogen bombs and depleted uranium munitions at a time when the planet is in such peril that we all must pull together, and soon, for civilization to have any hope of standing. The absurdity of war has never escaped the most perceptive among us, but in general we have had narratives that obscure or normalize that absurdity, and thus protect the Story of the World from disruption.

Occasionally, something happens that is so absurd, so awful, or so manifestly unjust that it penetrates these defenses and causes people to question much of what they'd taken for granted. Such events present a cultural crisis. Typically, though, the dominant mythology soon recovers, incorporating the event back into its own narratives. The Ethiopian famine became about helping those poor black children unfortunate enough to live in a country that still hasn't "developed" as we have. The Rwandan genocide became about African savagery and the need for humanitarian intervention. The Nazi Holocaust became about evil taking over, and the necessity to stop it. All of these interpretations contribute, in various ways, to the old Story of the People: we are developing, civilization is on the right track, goodness comes through control. None hold up to scrutiny; they obscure, in the former two examples, the colonial and economic causes of the famine and genocide, which are still ongoing. In the case of the Holocaust, the explanation of evil obscures the mass participation of ordinary people—people like you and me. Underneath the narratives a disquiet persists, the feeling that something is terribly wrong with the world.

The year 2012 ended with a small but potent story-piercing event: the Sandy Hook massacre. By the numbers, it was a small tragedy: far more, and equally innocent, children died in U.S. drone strikes that year, or by hunger that week, than died at Sandy Hook. But Sandy Hook penetrated the defense mechanisms we use to maintain the fiction that the world is basically okay. No narrative could contain its utter senselessness and quell the realization of a deep and awful wrongness.

We couldn't help but map those murdered innocents onto the young faces we know, and the anguish of their parents onto ourselves. For a moment, I imagine, we all felt the exact same thing. We were in touch with the simplicity of love and grief, a truth outside of story.

Following that moment, people hurried to make sense of the event, subsuming it within a narrative about gun control, mental health, or the security of school buildings. No one believes deep down that these responses touch the heart of the matter. Sandy Hook is an anomalous data point that unravels the entire narrative—the world no longer makes sense. We struggle to explain what it means, but no explanation suffices. We may go on pretending that normal is still normal, but this is one of a series of "end time" events that is dismantling our culture's mythology.

Who could have foreseen, two generations ago when the story of progress was strong, that the twenty-first century would be a time of school massacres, of rampant obesity, of growing indebtedness, of pervasive insecurity, of intensifying concentration of wealth, of unabated world hunger, and of environmental degradation that threatens civilization? The world was supposed to be getting better. We were supposed to be becoming wealthier, more enlightened. Society was supposed to be advancing. Is heightened security the best we can aspire to? What happened to visions of a society without locks, without poverty, without war? Are these things beyond our technological capacities? Why are the visions of a more beautiful world that seemed so close in the middle twentieth century now seem so unreachable that all we can hope for is to survive in an ever more competitive, ever more degraded world? Truly, our stories have failed us. Is it too much to ask, to live in a world where our human gifts go toward the benefit of all? Where our daily activities contribute to the healing of the biosphere and the well-being of other people? We need a Story of the People—a real one, that doesn't feel like a fantasy—in which a more beautiful world is once again possible.

Various visionary thinkers have offered versions of such a story, but none has yet become a true Story of the People, a widely accepted set of agreements and narratives that gives meaning to the world and coordinates human activity toward its fulfillment. We are not quite ready for such a story yet, because the old one, though in tatters, still has large swaths of its fabric intact. And even when these unravel, we still must traverse, naked, the space between stories. In the turbulent times ahead our familiar ways of acting, thinking, and being will no longer make sense. We won't know what is happening, what it all means, and, sometimes, even what is real. Some people have entered that time already.

I wish I could tell you that I am ready for a new Story of the People, but even though I am among its many weavers, I cannot yet fully inhabit the new vestments. As I describe the world that could be, something inside me doubts and rejects, and underneath the doubt is a hurting thing. The breakdown of the old story is kind of a healing process that uncovers the old wounds hidden under its fabric and exposes them to the healing light of awareness. I am sure many people reading this have gone through such a time, when the cloaking illusions fell away: all the old justifications and rationalizations, all the old stories. Events like Sandy Hook help to initiate the very same process on a collective level. So also the superstorms, the economic crisis, political meltdowns . . . in one way or another, the obsolescence of our old mythology is laid bare.

What is that hurting thing, that takes the form of cynicism, despair, or hate? Left unhealed, can we hope that any future we create won't reflect that wound back at us? How many revolutionaries have re-created, in their own organizations and countries, the very institutions of oppression they sought to overthrow? Only in the Story of Separation can we insulate outside from inside. As that story breaks down, we see that each necessarily reflects the other. We see the necessity of reuniting the long-sundered threads of spirituality and activism.

Bear in mind, as I describe the elements of a new Story of the People in the next chapter, that we have a rugged territory to traverse to get to it from where we are today. If my description of a Story of Interbeing, a reunion of humanity and nature, self and other, work and play, discipline and desire, matter and spirit, man and woman, money and gift, justice and compassion, and so many other polarities seems idealistic or naive, if it arouses cynicism, impatience, or despair, then please do not push these feelings aside. They are not obstacles to be overcome (that is part of the old Story of Control). They are gateways to our fully inhabiting a new story, and the vastly expanded power to serve change that it brings.

We do not have a new story yet. Each of us is aware of some of its threads, for example in most of the things we call alternative, holistic, or ecological today. Here and there we see patterns, designs, emerging parts of the fabric. But the new mythos has not yet formed. We will abide for a time in the "space between stories." It is a very precious— some might say sacred—time. Then we are in touch with the real. Each disaster lays bare the reality underneath our stories. The terror of a child, the grief of a mother, the honesty of not knowing why. In such moments our dormant humanity awakens as we come to each other's aid, human to human, and learn who we are. That's what keeps happening every time there is a calamity, before the old beliefs, ideologies, and politics take over again. Now the calamities and contradictions are coming so fast that the story has not enough time to recover. Such is the birth process into a new story.

Interbeing

I am not sure that I exist, actually. I am all the writers that I have read,
all the people that I have met, all the women that I have loved;
all the cities I have visited.

—JORGE LUIS BORGES

A recognition of alliance is growing among people in diverse arenas of activism, whether political, social, or spiritual. The holistic acupuncturist and the sea turtle rescuer may not be able to explain the feeling, "We are serving the same thing," but they are. Both are in service to an emerging Story of the People that is the defining mythology of a new kind of civilization.

I will call it the Story of Interbeing, the Age of Reunion, the ecological age, the world of the gift. It offers an entirely different set of answers to the defining questions of life. Here are some of the principles of the new story.

- That my being partakes of your being and that of all beings. This goes beyond interdependency—our very existence is relational.
- That, therefore, what we do to another, we do to ourselves.
- That each of us has a unique and necessary gift to give the world.
- That the purpose of life is to express our gifts.

- That every act is significant and has an effect on the cosmos.
- That we are fundamentally unseparate from each other, from all beings, and from the universe.
- That every person we encounter and every experience we have mirrors something in ourselves.
- That humanity is meant to join fully the tribe of all life on Earth, offering our uniquely human gifts toward the well-being and development of the whole.
- That purpose, consciousness, and intelligence are innate properties of matter and the universe.

Much of this book will flesh out the Story of Interbeing. The more we share with each other this kind of knowledge, the stronger we are in it, the less alone. It needn't depend on the denial of science, because science is undergoing parallel paradigm shifts. It needn't endure the denial of livelihood, because from a trust in gift we find unexpected sources of sustenance. It needn't withstand rejection by everyone around us, because more and more people are living from the new story, each in his or her own way, inducing a growing feeling of camaraderie. Nor is it a turning away from the world that is still mired in Separation, because from the new story we access new and powerful ways to effect change.

The fundamental precept of the new story is that we are inseparate from the universe, and our being partakes in the being of everyone and everything else. Why should we believe this? Let's start with the obvious: This interbeing is something we can feel. Why does it hurt when we hear of another person coming to harm? Why, when we read of mass die-offs of the coral reefs and see their bleached skeletons, do we feel like we've sustained a blow? It is because it is literally happening to our selves, our extended selves. The separate self wonders, "How could this affect me?" The pain is irrational, to be explained away, perhaps, as the misfiring of some genetically coded empathy circuit meant to protect those who share our DNA. But why does it extend so easily to strangers, even to other species? Why do we desire so strongly to serve the good of all? Why, when we achieve a maximum of personal security and comfort, are we still dissatisfied? Certainly, as a little introspection will reveal, our desire to help is not coming from a rational calculation that this injustice or that ecological disaster will somehow, someday, threaten our personal well-being. The pain is more direct, more visceral than that. The reason it hurts is it is literally happening to ourselves.

The science of Separation offers another explanation of what it calls "altruistic behavior." Maybe it is a kind of mating display, which demonstrates one's "phenotypic quality" to prospective mates (i.e., it shows that one is so "fit" that he can afford to squander resources on others). But this explanation takes as an unexamined premise another assumption of the worldview of Separation: a scarcity of mating opportunities and a competition for mates. As anthropology, reviewed in books like *Sex at Dawn*, has discovered though, this view of primitive life is more a projection of our own social experience onto the past than it is an accurate description of hunter-gatherer life, which was communal.[1] A more sophisticated explanation draws on game theoretic calculations of the relative advantages of being a strong reciprocator, weak reciprocator, etc., in situations of mutual dependency.[2] Such theories are actually a step closer to an evolutionary biology of interbeing, as they break down the idea that "self-interest" can ever exist independently of the interest of others.

The desire to serve something transcending the separate self and the pain we feel from the suffering of others are two sides of the same coin. Both bespeak our interbeingness. The emerging science that seeks to explain them, whether it invokes mirror neurons, horizontal gene transfer, group evolution, morphic fields, or something further out, doesn't explain them *away*, but merely illustrates a general principle

---

1. Christopher Ryan and Cacilda Jethá, *Sex at Dawn: How We Mate, Why We Stray, and What It Means for Modern Relationships* (New York: HarperCollins, 2010).
2. For a good example of this kind of reasoning, see Ernst Fehr and Urs Fischbacher, "The Nature of Human Altruism," *Nature* 425 (October 23, 2003): 785–791.

of connection or, dare I say it, oneness. The science is beginning to confirm what we have intuitively known all along: we are greater than what we have been told. We are not just a skin-encapsulated ego, a soul encased in flesh. We are each other and we are the world.

Our society runs in large part on the denial of that truth. Only by interposing ideological and systemic blinders between ourselves and the victims of industrial civilization can we bear to carry on. Few of us would personally rob a hungry three-year-old of his last crust or abduct his mother at gunpoint to work in a textile factory, but simply through our consumption habits and our participation in the economy, we do the equivalent every day. And everything that is happening to the world is happening to ourselves. Distanced from the dying forests, the destitute workers, the hungry children, we do not know the source of our pain, but make no mistake—just because we don't know the source doesn't mean we don't feel the pain. One who commits a direct act of violence will, if and when she realizes what she has done, feel remorse, a word that literally means "biting back." Even to witness such an act is painful. But most of us cannot feel remorse for, say, the ecological harm that the mining of rare earth minerals for our cell phones does in Brazil. The pain from that, and from all the invisible violence of the Machine of industrial civilization, is more diffuse. It pervades our lives so completely that we barely know what it is like to feel good. Occasionally, we get a brief respite from it, maybe by grace, or through drugs, or being in love, and we believe in those moments that this is what it is supposed to feel like to be alive. Rarely, though, do we stay there for very long, immersed as we are in a sea of pain.

Our situation is much like that of a little girl who was taken by her mother to visit a chiropractor friend of mine. Her mother said, "I think something is wrong with my daughter. She is a very quiet little girl and always well behaved, but never once have I heard her laugh. In fact, she rarely even smiles."

My friend examined her and discovered a spinal misalignment that, she judged, would give the girl a terrific headache all the time. Fortunately, it was one of those misalignments that a chiropractor can correct easily and permanently. She made the adjustment—and the girl broke into a big laugh, the first her mother had ever heard. The omnipresent pain in her head, which she had come to accept as normal, was miraculously gone.

Many of you might doubt that we live in a "sea of pain." I feel pretty good right now myself. But I also carry a memory of a far more profound state of well-being, connectedness, and intensity of awareness that felt, at the time, like my birthright. Which state is normal? Could it be that we are bravely making the best of things?

How much of our dysfunctional, consumptive behavior is simply a futile attempt to run away from a pain that is in fact everywhere? Running from one purchase to another, one addictive fix to the next, a new car, a new cause, a new spiritual idea, a new self-help book, a bigger number in the bank account, the next news story, we gain each time a brief respite from feeling pain. The wound at its source never vanishes though. In the absence of distraction—those moments of what we call "boredom"—we can feel its discomfort.

Of course, any behavior that alleviates pain without healing its source can become addictive. We should therefore hesitate to cast judgment on anyone exhibiting addictive behavior (a category that probably includes nearly all of us). What we see as greed or weakness might merely be fumbling attempts to meet a need, when the true object of that need is unavailable. In that case the usual prescriptions for more discipline, self-control, or responsibility are counterproductive.

Notice whether, when I described people "running from one purchase to another," you felt any contempt or smugness. That too is a kind of separation. The transition we are entering is a transition to a story in which contempt and smugness no longer have a home. It is a story in which we cannot see ourselves as better than any other human being. It is a story in which we no longer use fear of self-contempt to drive our ethics. And we will inhabit this story not in aspiration to an ideal of virtuous nonjudgment, forgiveness, etc., but in sober recognition of the truth of nonseparation.

In *Sacred Economics* I made the point that what we perceive as greed might be an attempt to expand the separate self in compensation for the lost connections that compose the self of interbeing; that the objects of our selfish desires are but substitutes for what we really want. Advertisers play on this all the time, selling sports cars as a substitute for freedom, junk food and soda as a substitute for excitement, "brands" as a substitute for social identity, and pretty much everything as a substitute for sex, itself a proxy for the intimacy that is so lacking in modern life. We might also see sports hero worship as a substitute for the expression of one's own greatness, amusement parks as a substitute for the transcending of boundaries, pornography as a substitute for self-love, and overeating as a substitute for connection or the feeling of being present. What we really need is nearly unavailable in the lives that society offers us. You see, even the behaviors that seem to exemplify selfishness may also be interpreted as our striving to regain our interbeingness.

Another nonscientific indication of our true nature is visible in yet another apparent manifestation of greed: the endless pursuit of wealth and power. What are we to make of the fact that for many of the very rich, no amount of money is enough? Nor can any amount of power satisfy the ambitious. Perhaps what is happening is that the desire to serve the common good is being channeled toward a substitute, and of course, no amount of the substitute can equal the authentic article.

Upon each of us, the wound of Separation, the pain of the world, lands in a different way. We seek our medicine according to the configuration of that wound. To judge someone for doing that would be like to condemn a baby for crying. To condemn what we see as selfish, greedy, egoic, or evil behavior and to seek to suppress it by force without addressing the underlying wound is futile: the pain will always find another expression. Herein lies a key realization of interbeing. It says, "I would do as you do, if I were you." We are one.

The new Story of the People, then, is a Story of Interbeing, of reunion. In its personal expression, it proclaims our deep interdependency on other beings, not only for the sake of surviving but also even to exist. It knows that my being is more for your being. In its collective expression, the new story says the same thing about humanity's role on Earth and relationship to the rest of nature. It is this story that unites us across so many areas of activism and healing. The more we act from it, the better able we are to create a world that reflects it. The more we act from Separation, the more we helplessly create more of that, too.

Cynicism

I would like to speak to those of you who feel triggered by the principles of interbeing I laid out earlier, which I admit smack of New Age puffery. Actually, let me be brutally honest here: I only use the phrase "New Age puffery" as a way to implicitly assure you that I am no dupe of such a thing; that I am on the side of the hardheaded realists. See, here I am joining you in derision.

This is a common tactic. Liberals take special pleasure in criticizing more radical leftists; nuts-and-bolts UFOlogists are vehement in their derision of abduction claims; the kid who is bullied turns on someone still weaker. The unpopular kids in school take pains not to be tainted by association with the *very* unpopular kids. By doing this, though, we attempt to borrow legitimacy from the very system we hope to subvert, and indirectly enhance its legitimacy by associating our own with its. We commit the same error when we overrely on the academic or professional credentials of our allies to persuade those who are impressed by such things. If I appeal to Dr. Eben Alexander's status as a professor of neurosurgery to get you to believe in extrasomatic near-death experiences, then implicitly I am affirming that you should trust that status generally, along with the edifice of academic science surrounding it.[1] But generally, those of that status and of that edifice deny his arguments. Appeals to authority will only strengthen authority. What implicit message is encoded in "See, this professor, that Republican, this businessman, that mainstream pundit agree with me"? It is that these people carry the legitimate stamp of approval, and not those outsiders, hippies, the uncredentialed, the unpublished. Using this tactic, we might win the battle, but we will lose the war. Audre Lorde said it well: The master's tools will never dismantle the master's house.

Similar logic applies to utility-based arguments for environmentalism. Have you ever heard arguments that we must practice conservation because of the economic value of "ecosystem services"? Such arguments are problematic because they affirm the very assumption we need to question, that decisions in general should be made according to economic calculations. They also fail to persuade. Are you an environmentalist because you are moved by all the money we'll save? Well, no one else will become an environmentalist for that reason either. We have to appeal to what moves us: the love of our beautiful planet.[2]

Knowing all this, why was I still tempted to deploy the disparaging term "New Age puffery" to disclaim the very principles I have enumerated, in an effort to maintain my credibility? Like you, dear reader, I still inhabit two conflicting stories, an old and a new. Even as I tell a Story of Interbeing, part of me remains in the world of separation. I am not some enlightened being trying to guide you on a journey he has already completed. That too is an old model, partaking of a kind of spiritual hierarchy based on a linear conception of the evolution of consciousness.

---

1. I am referring here to Alexander's book, *Proof of Heaven: A Neurosurgeon's Journey into the Afterlife.*
2. This is not to dismiss the idea of aligning economic incentives with ecological well-being. Green taxes and similar measures are important ways of bringing ecological values into our economic system. They have their limit, however; we must understand that no measure, no quantity, can encompass the infinite. When we attempt to reduce the infinitely precious to a number, monstrosities result. For example, if we value a rainforest's ecosystem services at $50 million, that implies that if we can make $51 million by cutting it down, we should.

In the present transition, each of us is pioneering a unique part of the territory of Reunion. In keeping with that, I must offer you my doubt and conflict along with my insight. Those spiritual truths—and I feel squeamish about that phrase—trigger me too, nearly as much, I daresay, as they trigger the most splenetic defender of scientific orthodoxy. The only difference is that my derision is turned inward.

It is not only that I am adopting the vocabulary of the skeptic in order to defuse accusations of naiveté. What motivates my inner cynic? The principles above are frightening, because they foster a tender, vulnerable hopefulness that might easily be crushed, as it has been so many times before. People ask me at talks, "Back in the '60s we were saying similar things about a dawning new age, but it didn't happen. Instead, the course of violence and alienation proceeded apace, proceeded indeed to new extremes. How do we know the same won't happen this time?" It sounds like a reasonable objection. I argue in this book that the 1960s are significantly different from today, but my argument can be rebutted, and counter-rebutted. Underneath it all something is hurting, and as long as that wound festers, no argument will be persuasive to the cynic.

Remember this when you encounter a harsh, cynical critic (whether inside yourself or outside). If you remember that the cynicism comes from a wound, you might be able to respond in a way that addresses that wound. I can't tell you in advance exactly how to respond. That wisdom comes directly from hearing with compassionate ears and being present to the hurting. Perhaps there is some act of forgiveness or generosity that calls to you that might allow healing. When that happens, the intellectual beliefs, which are really just expressions of a state of being, often change spontaneously. Beliefs that were once appealing are no longer so.

The derision of the cynic comes from a wound of crushed idealism and betrayed hopes. We received it on a cultural level when the Age of Aquarius morphed into the age of Ronald Reagan, and on an individual level as well when our youthful idealism that knew a more beautiful world is possible, that believed in our own individual destiny to contribute something meaningful to the world, that would never sell out under any circumstances and would never become like our parents gave way to an adulthood of deferred dreams and lowered expectations. Anything that exposes this wound will trigger us to protect it. One such protection is cynicism, which rejects and derides as foolish, naive, or irrational all of the expressions of reunion.

The cynic mistakes his cynicism for realism. He wants us to discard the hopeful things that touch his wound, to settle for what is consistent with his lowered expectations. This, he says, is realistic. Ironically, it is in fact cynicism that is impractical. The naive person attempts what the cynic says is impossible, and sometimes succeeds.

If you are thinking, "All this stuff about oneness is a lot of garbage," if you feel disgust or contempt, I ask you to look honestly at where the rejection is coming from. Could it be that there is a lonely, timid part of you that wants to believe? Are you afraid of that part? I know I am. If I allow it to grow, if I allow it to guide my life, if I trust all those statements of the new story I listed above, I open myself to the possibility of immense disappointment. It is an exquisitely vulnerable position to believe, to trust in purpose, in guidance, and that I will be okay. Better stay cynical. Better stay safe.

If you respond to this talk of oneness not with cynicism but rather a feeling of vindication, that doesn't mean you do not bear the same wound as the cynic. Perhaps instead of exercising it like the cynic does, you are ignoring it. Could it be that whenever the doubt creeps in, you assuage its pain by picking up the latest book on angel healing, crop circles, or reincarnation? Are you committing spiritual bypass? One way to tell whether your belief in oneness and its associated paradigms conceals an unhealed wound is whether the derision of the skeptic provokes outrage or personal defensiveness. If so, then something beyond a mere opinion is being threatened. Skeptic and believer are not so different, as both are using belief to shelter a wound. So, whether you feel indignant at my mention of UFOs, or feel indignant toward the skeptic's doctrinaire rejection of them, I encourage you to reflect on where this emotion comes from. We want to see what is hidden inside us, so that we won't blindly replicate it again and again in what we create.

I cringe to think what a no-nonsense realist like James Howard Kunstler (someone I admire) would say if he read this book. No matter—my inner critic can do him one better. "You imagine that some magical 'technologies of interbeing' are going to save us?" it snorts. "This is just the kind of wishful thinking that keeps us complacent and paralyzed. You just can't face up to the truth. There is no way out. The situation is hopeless. Barring some miracle, where everyone wakes up tomorrow and suddenly gets it, humanity is doomed. Prattling on about a 'purpose' or 'intelligence' in the universe, for which there is no scientific evidence, only makes matters worse."

I have found, though, that it is the opposite of what my inner cynic says. The doom and gloom is what is paralyzing, and the naive hope is what inspires me to take action. Either one can be a self-fulfilling prophecy. What happens when millions or billions of people begin acting from the Story of Interbeing, in which no action is insignificant? The world changes.

Equally paralyzing is the belief that a nefarious evil cabal controls the world. Why try to create anything, when meaningful change will be crushed by an all-seeing diabolical power? I've dabbled in these theories, which bring me into a heavy, burdened state that feels like I'm suffocating in a pool of molasses. Yet I am told I am naive and impractical to deny it. If only I would open my eyes and see!

Nonetheless, these conspiracy theories do express a psychological truth. They give voice to a feeling of helplessness and rage, the primal indignation of being cast into a world ruled by institutions and ideologies that are inimical to human well-being. The "evil cabal" also represents a shadow aspect of ourselves, driven to dominate and control—an inevitable outgrowth of the separate self in an indifferent or hostile universe. The endless drive to prove conspiracy theories is a kind of protest. It says, "Please believe me. It isn't supposed to be this way. Something awful has taken over the world." That something is the Story of Separation and all that arises from it.

Does that mean the new story is a motivational subterfuge, a device to trick us into acting as if what we did mattered? The last resort of my inner cynic is to say, "Well, I suppose the Story of Interbeing might be useful as a way to deceive people into taking action, but it isn't true." I would be like the preacher exhorting people to pious acts while secretly being an unbeliever himself. Underneath this particular cynicism I find again pain, an anguished loneliness. It wants *proof* that the Story of Interbeing is true, proof that life has purpose, the universe is intelligent, and that I am more than my separate self. I wish I could rely on evidence to choose my belief. But I cannot. Which story is true, Separation or Interbeing? I will in this book offer evidence that fits the latter, but none of it will constitute proof. No evidence is ever enough. There is always an alternate explanation: coincidence, fraud, wishful thinking, etc. Absent conclusive evidence, you will have to decide on some other basis, such as "Which story is most aligned with who you truly are, and who you truly want to be?" "Which story gives you the most joy?" "From which story are you most effective as an agent of change?" To make such a choice on something other than evidence and reason is already a huge departure from the Story of Separation and its objective universe.

So, am I tricking you? Surely, if I offered the new story from a place of secret disbelief, I would be an ineffective storyteller. My duplicity would show in one form or another and mar the integrity of the narrative. That is not to say that I have fully stepped into the Story of Interbeing and the total faith and trust it implies. Far from it. Fortunately, my ability to tell the story doesn't depend on my faith alone. I am surrounded by many, many other people who themselves, imperfectly as I do, hold the same story. Together we move deeper and deeper into it. Enlightenment is a group activity.

Insanity

I became insane, with long intervals of horrible sanity.

—EDGAR ALLAN POE

Contrary to the doctrine of the cynic, the Story of Interbeing is (as we shall see) not actually less rational or evidence-based than the Story of Separation. We like to think that we base our beliefs on evidence, but far more often we arrange the evidence to fit our beliefs, distorting or excluding what won't fit, seeking out evidence that will, surrounding ourselves with others who share them. When these beliefs immerse us as part of a Story of the People, and when financial self-interest and social acceptance are tied to them, it is all the more difficult to accept anything radically different.

That is why to live in the new story can be at times arduous and lonely. In particular, the money system is not aligned with the Story of Interbeing, enforcing instead competition, scarcity, alienation from nature, dissolution of community, and the endless, nonreciprocal exploitation of the planet. If your life's work does not contribute to the conversion of nature into products and relationships into services, you may often find that there isn't much money to be made doing it. There are exceptions—glitches in the system, as well as the halting attempts by benevolent people and organizations to use some of their money in the spirit of the gift—but by and large, money as it is today is not aligned with the more beautiful world our hearts know is possible.

By the same token, neither are our systems of social status, education, or the dominant narratives presented in the media. Immersed in what some call "consensus reality," one's very sanity comes into question for believing the principles of interbeing. We are permitted to entertain them as a kind of spiritual philosophy, but when we start making choices from them, when we start living them even ten percent, people begin to question our sanity. We may even question our own. Alongside the self-doubt comes a profound feeling of alienation. Just this morning I heard ten seconds of a news segment on immigration reform. An image sprang to mind of a vast apparatus of fences, checkpoints, ID cards, paperwork, interviews, borders, security zones, and official "status," and I thought, "Wait a minute—isn't it obvious that Earth belongs to everyone and to no one, and that there should be no borders? Isn't it hypocritical to make life unlivable somewhere through economic and political policies, and then to prevent people from leaving that place?" The two sides of the debate don't even mention that viewpoint, so far outside the bounds of respectable thought it lies. The same is true of practically every issue of public controversy. Isn't it insane to think that I am right and everyone else is wrong?

In a way, it is insane—insofar as sanity is a socially constructed category that serves the maintenance of dominant narratives and power structures. If so, it is time to be insane together! It is time to violate consensus reality.

Human beings are social animals, and it is unrealistic and perilous to carry an alternative story on one's own. Let us pause for a moment of humility here. A number of years ago I came to be acquainted with a man whom I'll call Frank. Frank was highly intellectual, with more than a cursory knowledge of several scientific fields, but his life's work, on which he spent eight or ten hours a day, was to cut out words from product packaging and magazines. From these clues he teased out a vast, all-encompassing conspiracy theory. He believed that by rearranging the words with scissors and glue, he could disrupt the conspiracy and change reality on behalf of all beings.

He brought the most fascinating connections to light. A cereal box might have "General Mills" on the front. "Mills" contains "mil," short for "military," and look, the text on the back of the box has sentences of nineteen and thirteen words respectively. That comes to 1913, the year the Federal Reserve was established. Aha! The pattern begins to emerge. This example barely hints at the labyrinthine complexity of Frank's theories, which tie together packaging, logos, numerology, and more.

Everybody thought Frank was deranged, but I seriously considered, "How am I different from him?" It seems like a trivial question, but I found it fruitful. Both of us uphold an explanation for the workings of the world that seriously violates consensus reality. Both of us are rearranging words drawn from an existing linguistic and conceptual substrate, hoping thereby to alter reality. Both of us are seen by many as deviant, and therefore must persevere indefinitely without much financial support or social affirmation (at the time, I was as broke and unknown as he was).

Sometimes I titillate my brain with the thought that maybe this guy Frank really is right; that he is the greatest and bravest genius in history, working on a magical symbolic level to save the world. Maybe, if only I took the time to delve into his work, I would see it too.

Don't you sometimes wish that your friends and relatives would just take the time to read so-and-so's book, watch such-and-such a documentary, open their minds, and stop dismissing your worldview out of hand? If only they'd look into it, then they'd get it!

I haven't kept in touch with Frank, but I have little doubt that he continues his obscure labors to this day. Most of us don't have that kind of hardihood. We are social animals and need at least a little bit of affirmation. We cannot stay in a deviant story by ourselves; in the face of a whole society that pulls us into the Story of Separation, we need allies. This book is meant to be such an ally. I hope that it will awaken or reinforce your understanding that you are not crazy after all, and that if anything it is the world that has gone insane.

You might say I am preaching to the choir. Yes. But as a member of the choir myself, I am grateful for the wonderful preachers whose words have kept me here, kept me believing. Without them I would have quit long ago and found a job greasing the wheels of the world-devouring Machine. That is also why conferences, retreats, and communities for alternative culture are so important. We hold each other in new beliefs. "Yes, I see it too. You are not crazy." We, the choir, gather, and we learn to sing together.

As things fall apart and the old story releases its thralls into the space between stories, the beautiful music of our choir will beckon, and they will come join us in song. We have been doing important work, first in loneliness, then in small, marginal groups. The time is upon us for the new Story of the People to leave the incubator. When things fall apart, the hopelessly radical becomes common sense.

Force

*T*he state of interbeing is a vulnerable state. It is the vulnerability of the naive altruist, of the trusting lover, of the unguarded sharer. To enter it, one must leave behind the seeming shelter of a control-based life, protected by walls of cynicism, judgment, and blame. What if I give and do not receive? What if I choose to believe in a greater purpose, and am deluded? What if the universe is an impersonal melee of forces after all? What if I open up, and the world violates me? These fears ensure that ordinarily, no one enters the new story until the old one falls apart. It is not something we attain; it is something we are born into.

The same interbeingness that makes us so immensely vulnerable also makes us immensely powerful. Remember this! Indeed, the vulnerability and the power go hand in hand, because only by relaxing the guard of the separate self can we tap into power beyond its ken. Only then can we accomplish things that are, to the separate self, impossible. Put another way, we become capable of things that we don't know how to "make" happen.

To make something happen is to use some kind of force. I can ask you to give me money, but how could I *make* you? Well, I could, if you are frail, physically force your hand into your pocketbook. Or I could put a gun to your head—any threat to your survival is also a form of force. The threat to survival can be quite subtle. Legal force, for example, rests ultimately on physical force: if you ignore the directives of the court, sooner or later a man with handcuffs and a gun will show up at your house. Similarly, economic force rests on the association of money with comfort, security, and survival.

Then there is psychological force, a term that is more than mere metaphor. It refers to the leveraging of motivations tied to basic security, in particular the desire to be accepted by the group and by the parent. Our training in the use of psychological force begins in childhood with conditional approval and rejection by the parent, which taps into perhaps the deepest fear of any young mammal: abandonment by the mother. A baby mammal left alone too long will cry piteously for its mother, attracting every predator within earshot—a risk preferable to the certain death of separation from the nursing mother. To engage that mortal fear is tantamount to a gun to the head. Many modern parenting practices leverage that fear: the accusatory "How could you?" "What's wrong with you?" "What were you thinking?" and, perhaps even more pernicious, the manipulative praise that says, "I accept you only if you do what I approve of." We learn to strive to be a "good boy" or "good girl," the word "good" here meaning that Mommy or Daddy accepts you. Eventually we internalize the rejection as self-rejection—guilt and shame—and we internalize the conditional acceptance as conditional self-acceptance. To allow oneself that acceptance feels deeply gratifying; to deny it is deeply uncomfortable. That feeling of gratification is core to what we really mean by the word "good." It is worth exploring: repeat to yourself, "I am good. Good boy. I am a good person. Some people are bad people but not me—I am a good person." If you think these words to yourself in earnest, you might find that there is something deeply childish about the gratification that they evoke.

Conditional self-approval and self-rejection are powerful mechanisms of self-control: the application of psychological force upon

oneself. We are deeply conditioned to it; it is perhaps the most fundamental of what I will call the "habits of separation." So conditioned,
we are also vulnerable to any authority figure or government that can
take over the role of parent: the arbiter of good and bad, the grantor or
withholder of approval.

The same conditioning also influences our attempts to change other
people and the world. We invoke guilt with slogans like "Are you part
of the problem, or part of the solution?" We proclaim the complicity of
each and every one of us in the imperialistic depredations of Western
civilization, the ecocide, culturecide, and genocide. We try to manipulate the vanity of the people whose actions we hope to change: if you do
X, you are a good person.

We habitually apply force to politicians and corporations as well.
It could be the threat of public humiliation or the incentive of public
praise and a positive image. It could be the threat of a lawsuit or recall
campaign. It could be a financial threat or incentive. "Engage in environmentally responsible practices because it will ultimately enhance
your bottom line."

What worldview, what story, are we reinforcing when we use these
tactics? It is the worldview in which things happen only through the
application of force. These tactics seem to say, "I know you. You are
a ruthless maximizer of rational self-interest or genetic self-interest."
Assuming that, we attempt to leverage that self-interest. We do it to
other people, and we do it to ourselves.

None of this is to say that we should withhold praise and disapproval, or strive to free ourselves from being influenced by the opinions
of others. As interbeings, the world reflects back to us what we put into
the world. There is nothing wrong with celebrating the brave choices
that move us, or expressing anger or grief over harmful decisions. It is
when these are used with manipulative intent that they draw from the
worldview of force.

The habitual application of various kinds of force draws on deep
roots. In the scientific paradigm that, though obsolete, still generates
our view of practicality today, nothing in the universe ever changes

unless a force is exerted upon it. Power over physical reality, then, accords to the one who is capable of mustering the most force and who has the most complete, accurate information about where to exert that force. It is for this reason that the power-hungry are often obsessed with controlling the flow of information.

In a universe lacking intelligence or will of its own, things never "just happen"; they happen only if something causes them to happen, and "cause" here means force. From this universe we must take, within it we must control, and onto it we must project our own designs, harnessing more and more force, applying that force with greater and greater precision, to become ultimately the Cartesian lords and possessors of nature.

Can you see how the word "practical" smuggles in so much of the mentality underlying the depredations of our civilization?

Do you think that operating from within the belief systems of the Age of Separation, we will create anything but more separation?

Control breeds its own necessity. So, when we treat land with heavy pesticides, the superweeds and superbugs that emerge require new and even stronger doses of pesticides. When someone goes on a diet and attempts to control her urge to eat, at some point the pent-up desire explodes outward as a binge, prompting further attempts to control herself. And when human beings are boxed in, surveilled, scheduled, assigned, classed, and compelled, they rebel in all kinds of ways, sometimes irrational or even violent. Ah, we think, we need to control these people. As with an addiction, these escalating attempts at control eventually exhaust all available resources, whether personal, social, or planetary. The result is a crisis that the technologies of control can only postpone but never solve. And each postponement only depletes what resources are still available even further.

It is apparent that "practical" isn't working as well as it used to. Not only because what was once practical is insufficient to our need, but also because it is increasingly impotent in its native realm: the practical is no longer practical. Like it or not, we are being born into a new world.

This book is a call to surrender control-based thinking, so that we can accomplish things far exceeding the capacity of our force. It is an invitation into a radically different understanding of cause and effect, and therefore a radically different conception of what is practical. Acting accordingly, our choices often seem, to those operating within the old paradigms, to be crazy: naive, impractical, irresponsible. Indeed, they seem that way to that part of ourselves—and I trust that it lives just as much in you as it does in me—that also inhabits the old story. You might recognize its voice, critical, disparaging, doubting, insinuating. It wants us to stay small, safe, protected in our little bubbles of control. My purpose here is not to urge you to fight that voice or purge it; simply recognizing it for what it is already begins to loosen its power.

None of this is to imply that we should never use force, or that we should abandon all forms of acculturation that depend on winning acceptance from parents, elders, and the group. These will always be important parts of the human drama. However, our deep ideologies have blinded us to other ways of initiating change. This book will explore the return of force (and reason, linear thinking, etc.) to its proper domain.

Science

*O*ur conception of what is "practical" harbors a trap. "Practical" encodes the laws of cause and effect that the old world has handed us, and according to those laws, nothing we do can possibly be enough to create a more beautiful world, or even to much ameliorate the awfulness of this one. The crises are too great, the powers-that-be too strong, and you are just one tiny individual. If even the most powerful of our system, the Presidents and CEOs, feel at the mercy of forces greater than themselves, constrained by their roles and job descriptions, so much the more powerless are we.

It is no wonder, then, that so many activists sooner or later come to grapple with despair. They might say, "When I was young and idealistic, I poured limitless energy into tackling problems, but eventually I realized just how big the problems were, and just how powerful the resistance to change. Nothing I can do can possibly be enough." In other words, they have tried and exhausted everything in the category of practical.

The question before us, then, is what do we do when in the big picture, nothing practical is practical? Obviously, we are going to have to do things that are not practical according to our customary understanding.

Here is a crucial point: Our customary understanding of what is practical is grounded in a worldview, a mythos, that is rapidly becoming obsolete. Furthermore, that obsolescing worldview is precisely the one underlying the old world we strive to change. *In other words, the crisis of civilization and the despair over the crisis share a common source.*

You might say that the despair we face when we recognize the futility of the technologies of separation to solve the crisis of separation is a sign of the fulfillment of the Age of Separation. It marks a turning point: we give up in despair and something new becomes available. The old story has finally reached the end of its telling, and the space is clear for a new story to emerge. This cannot happen while the old story still carries hope. If anything in the old world's "practical" still has any hope of succeeding, that means the old story has life in it still. That's why "near term extinction" arguments like those of Guy McPherson are valuable. Irrefutable on their own terms, they vanquish any hope within those terms, which encode the narrow view of the possible implicit in the Story of Separation.

Now, I am not suggesting that we abjure anything that makes sense in the old story just because it is of the old story. The new does not negate the old, but contains and supersedes it. My point is, though, that if we are limited to those things, the task before us is impossible. To those in or nearing the despair state, any effort to change the world seems hopelessly naive.

There is a vast territory on the other side of despair, a new story of the world that births a radically different understanding of cause and effect, but this territory is invisible from the other side, although we may get occasional glimpses of it, premonitions. Within its logic, our situation is not hopeless at all.

Where do our notions of practicality, realism, and causality come from? They are grounded in physics. The Story of Separation and the program of control that stems from it is breaking down, personally and collectively, not only because it is becoming decreasingly effective, not only because our crises are collapsing our confidence in our world-creating myths. While all this is happening, the scientific underpinnings of separation are crumbling as well. These profound paradigm shifts offer a different conception of the nature of self, of the universe, and therefore of how things happen and what is practical. These developments on the cutting edge of physics, biology, and psychology are hugely important for how we behave as social, economic, and political beings. They aren't just interesting curiosities. In fact, I would go so far as to say that no movement to change the world can possibly succeed unless it draws from these deeper paradigm shifts.

First is the breakdown in the neo-Darwinian orthodoxy that says that well-defined sequences of DNA called genes have evolved by random mutation and natural selection, and that these genes essentially program living organisms to maximize reproductive self-interest. Now we are learning that this account holds only in a very narrow realm: macroevolution happens not through random mutation, but rather through symbiotic merger, through acquisition of exogenous DNA sequences, and through organisms' cutting, splicing, and recombining of their own DNA. It also happens through cellular and epigenetic inheritance. The lack of any interest-maximizing discrete and separate self on the genetic level negates a primary metaphoric foundation of our Story of the Self. The genetic self has fluid boundaries. It is a chimera resulting from an ongoing exchange of DNA and information with other organisms and the environment. It is not that there are no boundaries of self; it is that these boundaries are changeable, and that the self within these boundaries is changeable as well.[1]

Moreover, the study of ecology is teaching us that species evolve not only to serve their own genetic self-interest (itself hard to define when organisms can reengineer their own genes), but that they also evolve to serve the needs of other species and the whole. This would

---

1. I lay out some of the scientific foundation for these claims, with extensive references, in Chapter 7 of *The Ascent of Humanity*. An excellent source by a prominent academic biologist is *Evolution: A View from the 21st Century* (Upper Saddle River, NJ: FT Press, 2011), by James Shapiro.

not have been surprising to cultures who were close to nature, who knew that each species had a unique and necessary gift, but science has come to understand that only in the last generation: to understand, for instance, that if one species goes extinct the whole ecosystem is just that much more fragile. It is not that the rest are better off, absent a competitor. The interest of each is the interest of all.

An even deeper challenge to the old Story of the World is the quantum revolution in physics, more than eighty years old now but so foreign to the scientific assumptions of the preceding centuries and to our dominant Story of the World that we find it terribly counterintuitive and "weird" to this day. I hesitate to venture into this territory because the wanton use of the word "quantum" to imbue a scientific cachet into all manner of questionable ideas and products has rendered the word almost meaningless. Nonetheless, quantum phenomena so flagrantly violate the basis of "practicality" as I've described it that a short explanation is in order. Please understand that I am invoking quantum mechanics not as a proof of any assertion in this book, but rather on a mythopoetic level, as a source of intuition and metaphor.

A basic principle, expounded earlier, of the Newtonian universe is that things don't "just happen" without a cause. (You have to make it happen.) But in the quantum world, this is simply not true. Rather than being fully determined by the totality of forces bearing upon them, quantum particles like photons and electrons behave randomly. In aggregate, one may calculate the probable distribution of their behavior, but for any given photon, a complete account of every physical influence upon it is insufficient to predict its behavior. Photon A might go through the slit and end up here; photon B might end up there— why? There is no reason, no cause; physics therefore calls the behavior random. Here, at the very basis of our explanation of physical reality is acausality. Things can happen without any force making them happen.

The above account, though suitably simplified, is beyond dispute; physics has tried and failed to preserve determinism for ninety years. The situation has not improved since Einstein's famous protest, "God does not play dice with the universe." Unable to remove indeterminacy altogether, physics had to settle for burying it safely in the microcosm: random quantum behavior adds up in the aggregate to approximate the determinate, causal behavior of the human world, in which, as before, nothing happens without some force being responsible.

Why does one photon go here and one go there, if not compelled by some force? Well, why do you do one thing rather than another, if not compelled by some force? You choose, so the obvious intuitive answer is that the photon *chooses* its course. Physics, of course, cannot countenance such an answer, so far outside the scope of scientific thought it is as to be beyond laughable. Physics—and remember, physics lies at the foundation of our Story of the World, of what is real, what is practical, how things work—says instead that the behavior is "random," preserving, at the price of acausality, a universe of unconscious, generic building blocks. For indeed, to ascribe choice to something as humble as a photon or an electron would be to acknowledge our universe as intelligent through and through. No longer would the universe be just a bunch of stuff; no longer would we so cavalierly arrogate to ourselves the role of its lords and masters. The core project of our Story of the People would be shaken to its foundation.

Let us pause to note that most people who have ever lived on Earth would have no trouble believing that the universe is intelligent through and through. Premodern people, animists or panentheists, ascribed sentience to all beings, not only plants and animals but even rocks and clouds. Young children in our own society tend to do the same. We call it personification or projection, and think that we know better than children and animists that, actually, the universe is mostly a dead, insensate place.

Maybe you don't want your accessing of expanded creative power to depend on accepting the proposal that even electrons bear sentience. Okay, fine—I won't insist. Here at least is a place where force is not the cause of behavior. Moreover, modern physics offers a second, perhaps even more severe, challenge to the Story of Separation: the breakdown of the basic self/other distinction.

We are accustomed to a universe in which existence occurs against a backdrop of an objective Cartesian coordinate system of space and time. If something exists, it occupies point X, Y, Z, at time T, and this existence is independent of you, me, or any other being in the universe. Even if we know about the quantum measurement paradox or entanglement, the assumption of objectivity is woven so deeply into our perceptions that to deny it is laughable. Say you go to bed before the election results come in. You wake up the next morning. Who won? You may not know yet, but you wouldn't deny that it has already been decided, that there is a fact of the matter that exists independently of your knowledge. Or say that you are investigating a traffic accident. Each party to the accident has a different version of what happened. Would you deny that there is a reality, independent of their stories, consisting of what "actually happened"?[2]

I would not indulge in these ontological musings at all, if it were not for the fact (the fact!) that the old, inaccurate Story of Being, the separate self marooned in an external objective universe, is a recipe for impotence and despair. Separate from the world, nothing we do can matter very much. In the vast, uncoordinated melee of separate selves and impersonal forces that compose the universe, our ability to change the course of events depends on the amount of force we can muster (or inspire, if only others would listen. And being separate from us, their choices are beyond our control—unless we *make* them listen. Back we are again to force). In particular, this story devalues most of the small, personal acts of service that we experience, on the feeling level, as important and that characterize the kind of world we would like to live in.

For example, in the world of separation, if you want to change the world, stop global warming, or save the sea turtles, then it would be a waste of time to volunteer at a hospice, rescue a lost puppy, or give food

---

2. I will not in these pages seek to establish an alternative philosophical position on the nature of reality. I just want to point out that our default belief is inaccurate; that it is part and parcel of the Story of Separation. Because that story infiltrates our very language, it may be impossible to undo it with language. Look at that last sentence: ". . . it may be impossible . . ." You see, I am implying that there is an external fact of the matter. Even words like "actual," "reality," and "is" encode an objective reality. To say, "There isn't an objective reality" already presupposes that there is one (because in what reality does an objective reality exist or not exist?).

to a homeless person. That old lady is going to die anyway. What does it matter if her passing is a little more comfortable? Maybe you should have spent those hours educating the young to imbue them with ecological awareness.

To base our decisions on their calculable, measurable effects is itself part of the Story of Separation. We might call it instrumentalism, and it rests on the belief that our understanding of causality is complete—that we can know with reasonable certainty what the full effects are going to be. But this certainty is increasingly unjustified. Science preserved it for a while by relegating quantum indeterminacy to the microcosm, by ignoring the full significance of nonlinear dynamics with its order out of chaos, and by denying any phenomena that bespeak an intelligent, interconnected universe, but today it becomes harder and harder to hold this edifice together.

Even if the intended effect is something noble, the instrumentalist mindset alienates us from other sources of knowledge and guidance that make sense only within a different Story of Self and World. And it can lead to monstrous results. Who knows who or what we must sacrifice for "the cause"?

Orwell made this point in *Nineteen Eighty-Four* when O'Brien, the Party official, is pretending to recruit Winston into the revolutionary Brotherhood that seeks to topple the Party:

"You are prepared to give your lives?"
"Yes."
"You are prepared to commit murder?"
"Yes."
"To commit acts of sabotage which may cause the death of hundreds of innocent people?"
"Yes."
"To betray your country to foreign powers?"
"Yes."
"You are prepared to cheat, to forge, to blackmail, to corrupt the minds of children, to distribute habit-forming drugs, to

encourage prostitution, to disseminate venereal diseases—to do anything which is likely to cause demoralization and weaken the power of the Party?"

"Yes."

"If, for example, it would somehow serve our interests to throw sulphuric acid in a child's face—are you prepared to do that?"

"Yes."[3]

Winston, it is shown, is really no different from the Party in putting an abstract and unreachable goal ahead of any means. It is significant that the Brotherhood is phony, a fabrication of the Party; it *is* the Party. In the same way, only perhaps more subtly, the social or environmental crusader who sacrifices human values for the cause is no true revolutionary at all, but the opposite: a pillar of the system. We see again and again, within environmental organizations, within leftist political groups, the same bullying of underlings, the same power grabs, the same egoic rivalries as we see everywhere else. If these are played out in our organizations, how can we hope that they won't be played out in the world we create, should we be victorious?

Some groups, recognizing this, devote much of their time to group process, seeking to implement within their own organizations the egalitarian, inclusive goals they are striving to bring to society. The danger is that the group becomes all about itself and fails to accomplish any external goals. Many Occupy groups experienced this tendency. Nonetheless, these efforts to work out new principles of organization and consensus signify a growing realization of the unity of the internal and the external. It isn't simply about demonstrating one's virtue by being egalitarian or inclusive. It is that who we are and how we relate affect what we create.

---

3. George Orwell, *Nineteen Eighty-Four* (New York: Penguin [Signet Classic], 1950), 172.

Climate

What, then, of the climate change activist who says, "Certainly, inclusivity, exposing unconscious racism and classism, giving voice to the marginalized, nonviolent communication, deep listening skills, and so forth are all worthy goals, but we are talking about the survival of our species here. We need to achieve CO_2 reduction by whatever means necessary. These other things can come later. None will matter if we don't stop the six or eight degree temperature rise that our present course entails. Therefore, to devote oneself to these things, or indeed to most social issues, is a bit frivolous."

It may not be obvious, but this view buys in to another version of the Story of Separation, in which the universe comprises a multitude of independent phenomena. In it, an environmental leader's neglect of his family or contracting of minimum-wage janitorial services has no bearing on global climate change. Quantum mechanics, with its collapse of the self/ other, object/universe, observer/observed distinction, offers us a new set of intuitions about how reality works. I won't say that it "proves" that by changing your beliefs or relationships you will remedy climate change. It does, however, suggest a principle of interconnectedness that implies that every action has cosmic significance. But even without sourcing that principle in quantum mechanics, we can get there simply by asking, What is the real cause of climate change? CO_2 emissions and other greenhouse gases, perhaps? Okay, what is the cause of those? Maybe consumerism, technological arrogance, and the growth imperative built in to the financial system. And what is the cause of those? Ultimately it is the deep ideologies that govern our world, the defining mythology of our civilization that I have called the Story of Separation.

Carbon dioxide emissions will not change unless everything else that encourages them changes as well. Simply wanting to reduce CO_2 isn't enough, as the abysmal failure of 1992 Rio climate accords shows. The world solemnly declared its intention to freeze CO_2 emissions; in the twenty years following, they rose by 50 percent. Rising CO_2 is inseparable from every other facet of the Story of Separation. Therefore, any action that addresses any of those facets also addresses climate change.

Sometimes, the web of connections that ultimately implicates climate change is visible through our usual lens of causality. Those whose cause is cannabis legalization could point to the ecological benefits of plant medicine over technology-intensive, energy-intensive, chemical-intensive pharmaceuticals, to the biofuel potential of industrial hemp, or even to the way that marijuana smoking weakens some people's drive to participate fully in the Machine. For other areas of activism, the causal link to climate change is harder to see. How about marriage equality? Ending human trafficking? Giving shelter to the homeless? In the separate self's understanding of causality, it is hard to see how these relate.

Let us ask, "What kind of human being is politically passive, votes from fear and hate, pursues endless material acquisition, and is afraid to contemplate change?" We have all those behaviors written into our dominant worldview and, therefore, into the institutions arising from it. Cut off from nature, cut off from community, financially insecure, alienated from our own bodies, immersed in scarcity, trapped in a tiny, separate self that hungers constantly for its lost beingness, we can do no other than to perpetuate the behavior and systems that cause climate change. Our response to the problem must touch on this fundamental level that we might call spirituality.

It is here where the root of our collective illness lies, of which global warming is but a symptomatic fever. Let us be wary of measures that address only the most proximate cause of that symptom and leave the deeper causes untouched. Already some would justify fracking, nuclear power, and other ecologically destructive activities on the (specious) grounds that they will ameliorate climate change. Technological ideologues propose vast geoengineering schemes that would seed the stratosphere with sulfuric acid or the oceans with iron, actions that might have enormous unintended consequences, and that are an extension of the same mindset of managing and controlling nature that is at the root of our ecological predicament.

For this reason, I am a bit wary of the conventional narrative about global warming, in which reducing CO_2 and other greenhouse emissions is the top environmental priority. This narrative lends itself too easily to centralized solutions and the mentality of maximizing (or minimizing) a number. It subordinates all the small, local things we need to do to create a more beautiful world to a single cause for which all else must be sacrificed. This is the mentality of war, in which an all-important end trumps any compunctions about the means and justifies any sacrifice. We as a society are addicted to this mindset; thus the War on Terror replaced the Cold War, and if climate change loses popularity as a casus belli, we will surely find something else to replace it—say, the threat of an asteroid hitting Earth—to justify the mentality of war.

The mentality of war, which justifies and compels the sacrifice of all things for the sake of Victory, is also the mentality of usury. As I describe in *Sacred Economics*, a money system that like ours is based on interest-bearing debt impels the endless growth of the money realm and the conversion of the many into the one—the diversity of values into a unitary quantity called value. As society becomes increasingly monetized, its members accept that money is the key to the fulfillment of any need or desire. Money, the universal means, becomes therefore a universal end as well. Just like the paradise of technological Utopia or the final victory in the war against evil, it becomes a god with an insatiable demand for sacrifice. The pursuit of it subsumes the small or unquantifiable acts and relationships that make life truly rich, but that the numbers cannot justify. When money is the goal, everything that cannot be translated into its terms gets squeezed out.

The same happens with war, of course, and with any campaign toward a grand unitary goal. If you have ever been a crusader to save the world, you may have noticed how the little things that make life rich get deprioritized and squeezed out. You may wonder, "What kind of revolution am I fomenting here? What experience of life am I upholding as an example?" These are important questions! They cannot be ignored if it is true, as our intuitions tell us, that the crisis we face today goes all the way to the bottom.

There is a danger that the climate change issue occludes other important environmental issues: deforestation, eutrophication, fishery depletion, radioactive waste, nuclear accidents, wetlands destruction, genetic pollution, toxic waste, pharmaceutical pollution, electromagnetic pollution, habitat destruction of all kinds, soil erosion, species extinction, aquifer and freshwater depletion and pollution, and biodiversity loss. Some of the things we need to do to reduce CO_2 emissions would also mitigate these other problems; in other cases, they appear unrelated. If the well-being of, say, a coral reef, or even of just one pond, doesn't implicate the future of civilization via climate change, should we not care about it? Focusing on greenhouse gas emissions emphasizes the quantifiable while making the qualitative—might I even say the sacred?—invisible. Environmentalism is reduced to a numbers game. We as a society are comfortable with that, but I think the shift we must make is deeper. We need to come into a direct, caring, sensuous relationship with *this* forest, *this* mountain, *this* river, *this* tiny plot of land, and protect them for their own sake rather than for an ulterior end. That is not to deny the dangers of greenhouse gases, but ultimately our salvation must come from recovering a direct relationship to what's alive in front of us.

We implicitly devalue that direct relationship when we cite greenhouse gases as our reason for opposing fracking, tar sands excavation, or mountaintop removal. We conform to the mentality that sacrifices the local and concrete for the sake of the global and the abstract. That is perilous. Numbers can be manipulated; data can be misinterpreted. For instance, climate change skeptics point out that atmospheric temperature has remained steady since 1997 (but what about the oceans?). It is likely to rise again soon, but what if we face not continued warming, but increasingly violent climate gyrations as the atmospheric composition changes with unprecedented rapidity at the same time the primary homeostatic control systems in the forests and oceans are degraded? Or what if some geoengineering scheme brought down CO_2 levels, or promised to do so? Then fracking and drilling opponents would have no ground to stand on. That is why, in addition to systems-level measures to address climate change (for example, a fee-and-dividend system for carbon fuels), we need to appeal directly to our love for the real, local, unique, and irreplaceable land and water. No amount of data can obscure a clear-cut. It can obscure "total acres of clear-cutting," but not *this* clear-cut. We need to ground environmentalism on something other than data.

Skeptical as I am about the conventional story of climate change, I am even more skeptical of climate change skepticism. Most of the skeptics seem to dismiss every environmental concern with the same blithe confidence that Earth can withstand anything we do to it. The issue of climate change is coming from an important realization that is relatively new for our civilization: that we are not separate from nature; that what we do to the world, we do to ourselves; that we are a part of the dynamic balance of Gaia and must act as responsible members of the community of all life on Earth. Many climate change skeptics seem to long for a simpler time, a story in which we lived on Earth and not as part of it.

In the Story of Interbeing, we should expect that any imbalance in our own society and collective psychology would be mirrored in analogous imbalances in Gaian processes. CO_2 and other greenhouse gases surely contribute to the instability of the climate. Even more dangerous, though, is deforestation, because the forests are so crucial in maintaining planetary homeostasis (in many ways, not only as carbon sinks).[1] With healthy forests, the planet is much more resilient. Forests, in turn, are not merely collections of trees: they are complex living beings in which every species contributes to their health, which means that biodiversity is another factor in climate regulation. Clear-cutting aside, the decline of one after another species of trees all over the world is something of a mystery to scientists: in each case, there seems to be a different proximate culprit—a beetle, a fungus, etc. But why have they become susceptible? Acid rain leaching free aluminum from soil silicates? Ground-level ozone damaging leaves? Drought stress caused by deforestation elsewhere? Heat stress due to climate change? Understory damage due to deer overpopulation due to predator extermination? Exogenous insect species? Insect population surges due to the decline of certain bird species?

Or is it all of the above? Perhaps underneath all of these vectors of forest decline and climate instability is a more general principle that is inescapable. Everything I have mentioned stems from a kind of derangement in our own society. All come from the perception of separation from nature and from each other, upon which all our systems of money, technology, industry, and so forth are built. Each of these projects itself onto our own psyches as well. The ideology of control says that if we can only identify the "cause," we can control climate change. Fine, but what if the cause is everything? Economy, politics, emissions, agriculture, medicine . . . all the way to religion, psychology, our basic stories through which we apprehend the world? We face then the futility of control and the necessity for transformation.

Let me take the argument of interbeing to its extreme. Climate change skeptics often blame climate fluctuations on the sun, which of course is not influenced by human activity—right? Well, I would hazard to bet that most premodern people would disagree that the sun is

---

1. Similar things can be said of the oceans, where overfishing, eutrophication (by fertilizer and sewage), and other forms of pollution may harm the ocean's climate moderating function. Acidification due to CO_2 may also contribute to this problem.

unaffected by human affairs. Many of them had rituals to thank and propitiate the sun, so that it would keep shining. Could it be that they knew something that we do not? Could it be that the sun is recoiling in pain from the ingratitude and violence humanity is perpetrating on Earth? That it will inevitably mirror our own derangement?

Yes, my friends, the conceptual revolution we are beginning goes this deep. We need to rediscover the mind of nature, to return to our original animism and the ensouled universe it perceived. We need to understand nature, the planet, the sun, the soil, the water, the mountains, the rocks, the trees, and the air as sentient beings whose destiny is not separate from our own. As far as I know, no indigenous person on Earth would deny that a rock bears some kind of awareness or intelligence. Who are we to think differently? Are the results of the modern scientific view so impressive as to justify such arrant presumptuousness? Have we created a society more beautiful than they? In fact, as the example of the quantum particle suggests, science is finally circling back toward animism. To be sure, scientific paradigms that countenance an intelligent universe are mostly heterodox today, but they are gradually encroaching on the mainstream. Take the example of water. Emerging from the shadows of homeopathy, anthroposophy, and research by marginal figures like Masaru Emoto and the brilliant Viktor Schauberger, the idea that water itself is alive, or at least bears structure and individuality, is now being explored by mainstream scientists like Gerald Pollack. We still have a long way to go before anything like the sentience of all matter can be accepted, or even articulated, by science. But imagine what that belief would mean when we contemplate mountaintop removal mining, polluting aquifers with fracking fluid, and so on.

Whatever the mechanism—greenhouse gases, deforestation, or solar fluctuations—climate change is sending us an important message. We and Earth are one. As above, so below: what we do to each other, even to the smallest animal or plant, we do to all creation. Perhaps all our small, invisible acts imprint themselves upon the world in ways we do not understand.

Despair

Evil is a talented logic which challenges love and truth
by arguing that since all human beings are by nature selfish and fallible,
any pursuit of virtue must be hypocrisy.

—ROBERT GRAVES

While many people understand that the solution to climate change involves more than a disembedded choice of alternative technologies, few would say that those dedicating their lives to marriage equality for gay people, compassion to the homeless, or care for the autistic are doing something essential for the survival of our species. But that is only because our understanding of interbeing is still shallow. I would like to suggest that anything that violates or disrupts the Story of Separation will heal any and all of the consequences of that story. This includes even the tiny, invisible actions that our rational mind, steeped in the logic of Separation, says cannot possibly make a difference. It includes the kind of actions that get squeezed out by the big crusades to save the world.

I spoke recently with Kalle Lasn, the founder of the radical magazine *Adbusters* and a man who has devoted his entire life to promoting and practicing hands-on activism. He told me that for some time now he hasn't been spending much time on politics or the magazine because he is taking care of his ninety-five-year-old mother-in-law. He said,

"Taking care of her is far more important to me than all my other work put together."

Kalle agreed with me when I said, "Our worldview must accommodate the truth and importance of this." My dear reader, can you countenance a reality in which to save the planet, we have to neglect our ninety-five-year-old mother-in-law? There must be a place in our understanding of how the universe works for the intimate, uncalculated acts of service that are such a beautiful part of our humanity.

Is Kalle to trust his feeling that in taking care of this old woman he is doing something significant?

Do you not know in your bones that any belief system that denies that significance must be part of the problem?

Can you bear to live in a world in which what he is doing doesn't matter?

We only keep performing the tasks that keep the world-devouring machine running by quelling that feeling of significance. We steel ourselves to do what some abstract reasoning tells us we must do, in the interests of practicality. Occasionally, this "practicality" means "what will help heal the ecosystem, bring about social justice, and enable the survival of our species," but for most people, most of the time, practicality involves money or other means of security and comfort. And money, in our current system, generally comes through our participation in the conversion of nature into products, communities into markets, citizens into consumers, and relationships into services. If your heart isn't in all that, you will find that practicality often contradicts the urging of the heart.

The problem goes much deeper than a selfish view of what is practical. It goes to the understanding of cause and effect that underlies it. The urging of the heart might not only contradict the dictates of money, it might contradict instrumentalist logic altogether.

That is not to say we should ignore the mind's logic when attempting to make practical changes in the world, any more than we should abandon technology, literature, or any other fruits of our millennia-long journey of Separation. The tools of control, the application of force and reason, surely have their place. Humanity is not nature's exception: as with all species, our gifts can uniquely contribute to the well-being and development of the whole. We have yet to use our gifts in this spirit; instead we have used them to dominate and conquer, weakening the health of Gaia and all her beings and, therefore, weakening ourselves as well. Now we have the chance to transform our uniquely human gifts from tools of mastery to tools of service.

Specifically, when are the methods of "practicality" appropriate? Quite simply, they are appropriate when we know how to do something from within our current understanding of causality. If your stove is on fire and you have a fire extinguisher, then of course you use the fire extinguisher. You don't ignore it and pray for a miracle instead.

But by the same token, if your house is a roaring inferno and all you have is a puny fire extinguisher that you know is far insufficient to the task, you shouldn't just wave it in front of the flames in a posture of heroism.

The latter situation is a good description of our current predicament. Yes, it is true, our house is on fire. What the environmental alarmists are saying is true. I am not using "alarmist" as a term of disparagement. If anything, the situation is worse than they (fearing the alarmist label) tell us publicly. But what should we do about it? Or more to the point, what should *you* do about it? What, according to the conventional notions of causality that nearly everyone in modern society has deeply internalized, can you do that is practical? Nothing. Therefore, we must learn to follow another kind of guidance, one that leads to an expanded realm of what is possible.

You may think it is dangerous to sow despair, even if what I say is true. But the despair is there whether I sow it or not. Every activist I have asked confirms that they have at one time or another confronted precisely the despair I am evoking. We try to obscure it with reasoning like "Sure, it makes no difference if you are the only one making changes, but if everyone does it then the world will change." True, but is it in your power to make everyone do it? No. What you do would matter if everyone did it; by the same token, since everyone isn't doing it, what you do doesn't matter. I have never found an escape from this logic within its own terms. It is as sound as its premises—the separate self in an objective world. Worse yet, some would say that our individual efforts to buy local or recycle or ride bicycles are even counterproductive, giving us a false complacency, depotentiating more effective revolutionary acts, and enabling the larger mechanisms of ruin to trundle forward. As Derrick Jensen says, don't take shorter showers.

I think it is better not to obscure the despair, because real hope lies only on its other side. Despair is part of the territory we must traverse. Until we reach the other side, despair weighs on our hearts as we soldier on, never fully believing we are doing much good. Eventually, however strong our spirits, our efforts waver, our energy flags, and we give up. Perhaps for a while, personal vanity can keep us going as we uphold a self-image of being ethical, conscious, and a "part of the solution." But that motivation is insufficiently deep to bring us to the courage, commitment, and faith we need.

True optimism comes from having traversed the territory of despair and taken its measure. It is not ignorant of the magnitude of the crisis nor unaware of the forces that stand in the path of healing. Sometimes people confront me at talks to educate me about the power elite and their propaganda machine, their control of finance and politics, or even their mind control technologies, imagining I am unaware or willfully ignorant of the workings of our system. Or they speak of the apathy of the masses, the greed and ignorance of the people who just don't get it and the unlikelihood of their ever changing. All of this is part of the territory of despair, with which I am intimately familiar. It isn't that I have shied away from the bleak truth because I can't take it. Optimism lies on the other side of it, and hope is its herald.

On its own terms, the logic of despair is unassailable. It encompasses more than just the hopelessness of the state of the planet though; it is also woven into our defining mythos, which casts us into an alien universe of force and mass. It is this mythos that at once renders us alone in the universe and at the same time powerless to significantly change it (or to change it at all, given that those same forces determine our actions too). Perhaps this is why the emotional energy behind the case for hopelessness I just described is identical to that behind rejections of alternative scientific paradigms. Readers of my earlier books will forgive me for requoting this passage from "A Free Man's Worship" by Bertrand Russell, one of the great minds of the modern era:

> That man is the product of causes which had no prevision of the end they were achieving; that his origin, his growth, his hopes and fears, his loves and his beliefs, are but the outcome of accidental collocations of atoms; that no fire, no heroism, no intensity of thought and feeling, can preserve an individual life beyond the grave; that all the labors of the ages, all the devotion, all the inspiration, all the noonday brightness of human genius, are destined to extinction in the vast death of the solar system, and that the whole temple of man's achievement must inevitably be buried beneath the debris of a universe in ruins—all these things, if not quite beyond dispute, are yet so nearly certain that no philosophy which rejects them can hope to stand. Only within the scaffolding of these truths, only on the firm foundation of unyielding despair, can the soul's habitation henceforth be safely built.

As I have hinted, the story on which Russell bases his conclusions is no longer so certain. A philosophy that rejects them can indeed hope to stand—on the foundation of the quantum interconnectedness and indeterminacy, the tendency of nonlinear systems toward spontaneous organization and autopoiesis; the capacity of organisms and environments to purposely restructure DNA; and the proliferation of scientific anomalies that promise further paradigm shifts to come. Without attempting to make a rigorous philosophical case for it, I will observe that all these scientific revolutions lend themselves, at least metaphorically, to a very different Story of the World.

Hope

Another world is not only possible, she is on her way.
On a quiet day, I can hear her breathing.

—ARUNDHATI ROY

*H*ope has a bad name these days among certain teachers. On the one hand, it seems to suggest wishful thinking that distracts us from a sober assessment of reality and fosters unrealistic expectations. As Nietzsche put it, "Hope is the worst of evils, for it prolongs the torments of man." Meanwhile, in the language of "spirituality," hope implies a rejection of the present moment, or perhaps a taint of doubt eroding the creative power of one's intentions. But let us not be so quick to dismiss this primal element of the human psyche. What does hope tell us, "springing eternally," as it so often does, like a flower alongside the desolate byways of despair?

Admittedly, people often hope for absurd things that do block their experience of the present truth and their ability to respond wisely to it: the sick woman hoping the lump on her breast will just go away if she ignores it; the child hoping Mommy and Daddy will get back together again; our society hoping the scientists will come up with a solution to climate change. However it is expressed, the emotional energy underneath hope is "It's all going to be okay." In a way, that is true—not because our worst fears won't come to pass, but because we become reconciled to them after they do. The woman will be okay, not because she ignores the lump, but because she acknowledges it and gets it treated, or perhaps because she loses her breast and experiences a love and self-acceptance transcending her appearance, or perhaps because of what happens in the dying process. Likewise, scientists already *have* come up with a solution to climate change, many solutions. They are right in front of our faces: conservation, permaculture, renewable energy, simple living, bicycles, zero-waste manufacturing, and so on. But only when climate change hits us in earnest are we likely to implement these solutions on a significant scale. Hope shows us a destination, but a vast territory, the territory of despair, lies between it and us.

In the darkest despair a spark of hope lies inextinguishable within us, ready to be fanned into flames at the slightest turn of good news. However compelling the cynicism, a childlike idealism lives within us, always ready to believe, always ready to look upon new possibilities with fresh eyes, surviving despite infinite disappointments. Even in the darkest moments of resignation to the old normal, our participation in it has been halfhearted, for part of our energy was seeking something outside the world as we have known it.

From within the logic of the old story, hope is a lie, a hallucination of something impossible. But it comes from our innate idealism, our heart's knowledge of a more beautiful world. The beliefs that tell us that a more beautiful world is not possible conflict with the heart that tells us it is. It is only when the scaffold of those beliefs collapses that hope need no longer clothe itself in the absurd. A new Story of the World gives practical expression to the heart knowing we call hope; then it becomes authentic optimism. Our unreasonable hope is pointing us toward something true. That is why I call it a herald.

This new story, because it embodies a different understanding of reality and of causality, also transforms our understanding of what is practical. From the Story of Interbeing, no longer does the knowledge of the heart that it is important to take care of the ninety-five-year-old mother-in-law conflict with the reason of the mind. The terms of reason have changed. Heart and mind need no longer be at odds. Their rapprochement is part of a greater trend of reunion that is the healing of our world, encompassing the reunion of spirit and matter, discipline and desire, body and soul, money and gift, nature and technology, man and woman, the domestic and the wild, work and play, and life and art. Each of these, we will understand, creates and contains the other. No longer will we live in the illusion that they are separate.

Perhaps most of my readers still have a lot of the territory of despair to navigate before they can be fully grounded in the new story. I know I do. Even so, as we emerge in fits and starts from that territory, we gain the faith and courage to do what the old story told us was futile. This understanding is liberating. So many people squelch the expression of their gifts by thinking that they must do something big with them. One's own actions are not enough—one must write a book that reaches millions. How quickly this turns into a competition over whose ideas get heard. How it invalidates the small, beautiful strivings of the bulk of humanity; invalidates, paradoxically, the very things that we must start doing en masse to sustain a livable planet. Again and again young people ask me something like "I really want to go into permaculture— that's what I love—but don't I have a responsibility to do something bigger than that?" I answer, that choice is only small through the eyes of separation. From the perspective of interbeing, your choice is no more or no less important than any of the president's.

The logic of Separation traps us in a paradox. The world can change only if billions of people make different choices in their lives, but individually, none of these choices makes a difference. The things that make a difference make no difference. What if I do it, and no one else does? It sure looks like almost no one else is. Why do it?

I am not actually suggesting that we do these small acts because they will in some mysterious way change the world (although they will). I am suggesting, rather, that we orient more toward where our choices come from rather than where they are going. The new story validates and clarifies our choices, but the motivation comes from somewhere else. After all, how can we really know what the consequences of our actions will be? Complexity theory teaches us that in the chaotic zone between two attractors, tiny perturbations can have huge, unpredictable effects. We are in such a place today. Our civilization is approaching a phase transition. Who can predict the effects of our actions? A police officer gives a pair of boots to an unshod homeless man, an invisible act of kindness. How could he know that someone was photographing him, and that his act would awaken kindness in millions? The man then sells the boots to buy drugs, inflaming the cynicism of millions more. Whether invisible or not, acts of great faith, acts that come from a stance deep in the territory of reunion, send powerful ripples out through the fabric of causality. One way or another, perhaps via pathways we are unaware of, they surface in the visible world.

When my children were little they attended a Montessori kindergarten. Never before or since have I encountered a school so vibrant with love, laughter, and gentleness. The teachers treated the children with deep, honest respect, never patronizing them, never coercing them, never manipulating them with disapproval or praise, giving them an experience of unconditional love. Those kindergarten days are now but a foggy memory to the children who went on from there into the harsh, degrading world of separation, but in my mind's eye I see a small golden glow inside of them, and within that glow I see a seed. It is the seed of the unconditional love and respect they received there, awaiting the moment to sprout and blossom and deliver the same fruit that my children received to those they touch. Maybe a year or two of kindergarten isn't enough to overcome the brutal apparatus of separation that governs modern childhood, but who knows when and how it might blossom forth? Who knows what effects it will bear? To be in a sanctuary of love and respect every day for one or two years during such a formative stage of life imprints a person with a tendency toward compassion, security, self-love, and self-respect. Who knows how that imprint will alter the child's choices later in life? Who knows how those choices will change the world?

Morphogenesis

Sometimes when I encounter pioneers in a certain domain of alter-native culture, I get the feeling that even if they are doing their work on a small scale, perhaps within a small ecovillage, an isolated prison, a single community in a war zone or gang zone, that they are doing that work on behalf of us all, and that the changes they make in themselves create a kind of template that the rest of us can follow, and do in a short time what took them decades of effort and learning. When I see, for example, how my friend R. has, in the face of near-impossible odds, so profoundly healed from being abused as a child, I think, "If she can heal, it means that millions like her can too; and her healing smooths the path for them."

Sometimes I take it even a step further. One time at a men's retreat one of the participants showed us burn scars on his penis, the result of cigarette burns administered by a foster parent when he was five years old to punish him. The man was going through a powerful process of release and forgiveness. In a flash, I perceived that his reason for being here on Earth was to receive and heal from this wound, as an act of world-changing service to us all. I said to him, "J., if you accomplish nothing else this lifetime but to heal from this, you will have done the world a great service." The truth of that was palpable to all present.

The rational mind, steeped in Separation, doubts that his healing could really make a difference. It says, only if it is somehow made public, for example turned into a motivational story, could it have an effect on the world beyond that man's direct influence. I do not deny the power of story. Maybe J.'s healing is having an influence via my telling of it now. However, story is only one of the possible vectors of manifestation of a more general phenomenon. One of the ways that your project, your personal healing, or your social invention can change the world is through story. But even if no one ever learns of it, even if it is invisible to every human on Earth, it will have no less of an effect.

The principle I am invoking here is called "morphic resonance," a term coined by the biologist Rupert Sheldrake. It holds as a basic property of nature that forms and patterns are contagious: that once something happens somewhere, it induces the same thing to happen elsewhere. One of his favorite examples is certain substances such as turanose and xylitol, which were reliably liquid for many years until suddenly, around the world, they began to crystallize. Chemists sometimes spend years trying to make crystalline forms of a substance; once they are successful, it is henceforward easy, as if the substance has learned how to do it.

Sheldrake discusses the possibility that this phenomenon could be explained by "seed particles"—little bits of crystal blown by the wind or carried in the beard of a visiting chemist that find their way into a supersaturated solution and initiate crystallization. So, he says, let us test the theory of morphic resonance by quarantining a sample in a dust-filtered lab. If crystals still formed more readily there, he says, it would prove the theory of morphic resonance.

I agree with Sheldrake that certain features of the crystallization mystery defy the seed particle explanation, and that his experiment would disprove it. I disagree, however, that the seed particle explanation, if true, invalidates the morphic field explanation. Quite the opposite: the general principle of morphic resonance pertains whether or not the vector of its transmission is crystal dust. If the quarantine experiment works, one might demand it be electromagnetically shielded as well, since the "seed" could be an electromagnetic vibration. And there may be influences that we don't even know about. Sheldrake seems to want to separate morphic resonance from any kind of direct causation, but what if all these causal influences are not alternatives to morphic field induction, but rather examples of how that field operates? Here we have the chance to expand the realm of matter to include the properties of spirit, rather than to appeal to something extra-material in order to bestow intelligence on a dead material world.

In a similar vein, it may very well be through others hearing about it that our personal, relational, or local transformations have global significance. It may also be through the ripple effect of changed people changing other people. These are both mechanisms of transmission, of cause and effect, that our Separation-conditioned minds can accept. What we have trouble accepting, though, is that the effect of our actions doesn't depend on these mechanisms, which are merely means for the implementation of a general metaphysical law. Even if no one ever finds out about your act of compassion, even if the only visible witness is a dying person, the effect is no less than if someone makes a feature documentary about it.

I am not suggesting that we therefore repudiate conventional means for the propagation of our work. I am advocating a kind of confidence in the significance of all that we do, even when our vision cannot penetrate the mysterious, meandering paths through which our actions arrive in the larger world.

There is a kind of senselessness in the most beautiful acts. The acts that change the world most profoundly are the ones that the mind of Separation cannot fathom. Imagine if Kalle Lasn had set out taking care of his mother-in-law with the agenda of making a big public show of his devotion. It would have stunk of hypocrisy. The same is true of, say, peacebuilding projects or ecovillages that, too soon, develop a self-conscious image of themselves as an example. Please don't think that you "have to write a book about it" for your experiences to have a large effect.

The book may come, the peacebuilding project documentary might come, but usually there must first be a latency, a time of doing something for its own sake, a time of inward focus on the goal and not the "meta" goal. The magic comes from that place. From there, the synchronicities flow; there is no sense of forcing, only of participating in a larger happening that seems to have an intelligence of its own. You show up in the right place, at the right time. You respond to practical needs.

Can you believe that changing an old woman's bedpan can change the world? If you do it to change the world, it will not. If you do it because she needs her bedpan changed, then it can.

Many years ago, Patsy, my wife at the time, was a real estate agent. Her client's mother, Mrs. K., was terminally ill and lived in a derelict house outside of town. One day Patsy went to the house to take some measurements and found Mrs. K. lying on the floor in her own urine and excrement, unable to get up. Patsy spent an hour cleaning her up and gave her the egg drop soup she'd bought for her own lunch—the only nourishing food Mrs. K. had had for a long time, as the son was working two jobs and living an hour away. Mrs. K. died soon after; a day later the house caved in, as if it had been held together by Mrs. K.'s habits and memories.

At the time, Patsy never imagined that this basic human response to a woman in need would or could change the world. It didn't cross her mind at all, nor should it have. Her choice to help was a choice between compassion and the practical demands of her busy schedule. Part of her mind was chattering, "Just call the police, you're going to miss your other appointments, this isn't your responsibility, what does it matter . . ." But on some level she knew that it *did* matter. So many voices lobby us to forget love, forget humanity, sacrifice the present and the real for the sake of what seems more practical. Herein lies the medicine of despair: by evacuating our illusions of practicality, it reconnects us to the present needs at hand and allows those senseless, impractical acts that generate miracles.

The principle of morphic resonance justifies our feeling that these senseless, invisible acts are somehow significant. What morphic field does it induce, to trust the promptings of compassion? What morphic field does it induce, to give as best you can of your gifts to meet the needs at hand? Imagine if our politicians and corporate executives were caught up in this field, acting from compassion rather than calculation, from humanity rather than abstract instrumental motives.

No doubt some of you are thinking, "Eisenstein seems to think that if everyone just focuses on taking care of his or her grandmother and picking up litter in the park, that global warming, imperialism, racism, and the rest of the catastrophic problems facing our planet will magically fix themselves. He fosters a dangerous passivity, a complacency that leaves people imagining they are doing something useful, while the world burns." The last few chapters should make it clear that that is not what Eisenstein thinks, but just to be sure, let me address this criticism head-on; after all, I have heard it not only from others but also, with much greater frequency, in my own head.

First, the personal, local, or invisible actions I have been discussing do not preclude other kinds of actions such as writing a book or organizing a boycott. In fact, listening to the call and trusting the timing of the former foster the same disposition toward the latter. I am talking about a wholesale movement into a place of interbeing, and acting from that place in each kind of situation. The universe calls forth different of our gifts at different moments. When the call is for the small and personal, let us heed that, so that we develop the habit of heeding it when it is big and public. Let's cease listening to the logic of Separation, which would devalue the small and personal.

Just as the vectors of morphic resonance may be something quite mundane, so also the actions for creating the impossible might each, on their own, be quite linear and practical. It is their orchestration that is beyond our capacity. Many of us, pressed on by the urgency of the planetary situation, have experienced trying to do big things that amounted to nothing. We write a book and no one publishes it. We shout the truth from our blogs and no one gets it, except the already-converted. Except sometimes it is different. When, and why?

When my elder two children were young I was for several years a stay-at-home dad, immersed in a world of diapers and groceries while trying to write my first book. I often felt terribly frustrated, torturing myself with thoughts like "I have such important things to share with the world, and here I am changing diapers and cooking all day." These thoughts distracted me from the gift at hand and made me less present with my children. I did not understand that those moments when I gave in to my situation, put down my writing, and fully engaged my children had just as powerful an effect on the universe as any book I would write. We don't always have the eyes to see it, but everything has its karmic effect, or as the Western religions say, God sees everything.

Imagine yourself on your deathbed, looking back on your life. What moments will seem the most precious? What choices will you be the most grateful for? For Patsy it will be cleaning up Mrs. K., more than any real estate she sold. For me it will be pushing Jimi and Matthew up the hill in their toy cars, more than any public accomplishment I have recorded. On my deathbed I will be grateful for each choice of connection, love, and service.

Can you countenance a universe in which those deathbed perceptions are wrong? Can you countenance a universe in which we must steel ourselves to neglect those things so that we can more efficiently devote ourselves to the business of planet-saving?

Can you see that steeling ourselves to override our humanity is what has gotten us into this mess to begin with?

That is the old story. We are nearly done with conquering ourselves, just as we are nearly done trying to conquer nature. Thankfully, our entry into the world of interbeing no longer need oppose what science tells us about the nature of reality. We can begin to embrace new scientific paradigms that affirm the understanding that the universe is intelligent, purposive, and whole. These new paradigms arouse the ire of the old guard precisely because they affirm such an understanding.

That is why they are called "unscientific" or "pseudoscientific"—not because they draw on inferior evidence or incoherent thinking, but because they violate the deep, unquestioned premises that the word "scientific" has encoded.[1]

Let's get real here. If everything has consciousness, then what we had believed possible, practical, and realistic is far too limiting. We are on the cusp of an epochal breakthrough, coming into touch with the mind of nature. What can we achieve when we are in harmony with it? I mean "get real" as the opposite of its usual meaning, which would be to ignore the unmeasurable and the subjective in favor of what can be quantified and controlled. That mentality has put vast human capacities out of reach: the technologies of reunion that include much of what we call "alternative" or "holistic" today. All draw in one way or another from the principle of interbeing.

The contradiction between small, personal acts of compassion and steps to save the environment is a straw man, a contrapositive rhetorical device constructed by the cynic to voice his wound of powerlessness. In truth, the habit of acting from love will naturally apply to all our relationships, expanding alongside our understanding. Acts of ecological or social healing, so long as they are in earnest and not secretly designed to establish an identity or prove oneself good, are just as senseless as the small, personal ones. They are senseless because they are a drop in the bucket. What can one person do? As I have said, despair is inescapable in the old story. The alternative, an interconnected, intelligent universe, empowers those acts, but at a price for the activist—it equally empowers the small-scale acts that don't fit into her save-the-world paradigm at all. It makes her climate change awareness campaign no more and no less important than changing the bedpans in the hospice. But again, would you really like to live in any other world?

---

1. These premises also determine what is publishable and what isn't, what will pass peer review easily and what will be subjected to hostile scrutiny, and what research will receive funding and what will not. These are some of the reasons why certain real phenomena remain "scientifically unproven."

A friend recently asked me, "If it is true that we live at a unique juncture in the planet's history, when all great beings have gathered for the crucial moment of humanity's birthing, then why do we not see the great avatars and miracle-workers of yesteryear?" My answer was that they are here, but they are working behind the scenes. One of them might be a nurse, a garbage man, a kindergarten teacher. They don't do anything big or public, nothing that, through our eyes, looks like it is generating the miracles necessary to save our world. Our eyes deceive us. These people are holding the fabric of the world together. They are holding the space for the rest of us to step into. To do the big, public things is important, requiring all our gifts of courage and genius, but it requires not nearly the faith and solidity in the ground of interbeing as the invisible, humble actions of people like those kindergarten teachers.

So, whatever your reasons for choosing to do great things or small, do not let them be the urgent, fearful belief that only the big, public things have any chance of influencing the masses and saving the world. As I will describe later in the book, part of the revolution in which we are participating is a revolution in how we make our choices. To do the possible, the old way works fine. When we have a map from A to B, we can just follow the directions. Now is not that time. The calculable results are not enough. We need miracles. We have caught a glimpse of our destination, the destination that hope foretells, but we have no idea how to get there. We walk an invisible path with no map and cannot see where any turning will lead.

I wish I could say that the new story provides a map, but it does not. It can, however, remove the disorienting fog of habits and beliefs, leftovers of the old paradigms, that obscure our internal guidance system. The principles of interbeing do not, on their own, offer a formula for decision making. Even if you accept that "I and the world are one," you will not be able to distinguish whether it will benefit all sentient beings more to stay home and reduce your carbon emissions, or to drive to the rally to protest fracking. To attempt such a calculation draws from the old story, which seeks to quantify everything, to add up the effects of any action, and to make choices accordingly. That way of making choices is useful only in certain, narrow circumstances—in particular, those in which cause and effect are more or less linear. It is appropriate for many engineering problems and financial decisions. It is the mindset of the actuary, weighing risks and payoffs. The new story is a much bigger change than to revalue the risks and seek new payoffs. It is not going to help you make choices from the calculating mind. But it will provide a logical framework within which our heart-based choices make a lot more sense.

Naiveté

I love those who yearn for the impossible.

—GOETHE

We are entering unknown territory, in which we have glimpsed a beautiful destination but don't know how to get there. It is inaccessible according to what we understand of causality. Things have to happen that we don't know how to make happen. If you don't "make" it happen, and it happens, then how does it happen? Obviously, it happens as a gift. You may have noticed that very generous people themselves attract more gifts. Therefore, if we are giving our lives in service, we will experience more of these fortuitous events. These are key to a creative potency beyond the old conception of causality.

Anything worth devoting a life to today requires some of these miracles, these things that we do not and cannot *make* happen, that come as gifts. Therefore, if you follow your heart's guidance toward any of these worthwhile goals, your choices will seem to many (and sometimes to yourself) a little bit crazy.

Our situation is this: we see the goal but don't know how to get there. That is true of anything genuinely new. To step into the attempt anyway is always an act of courage, at once arrogant and humble: arrogant because our confidence is unwarranted; humble because we put ourselves at the mercy of the unknown. Limited by what we know how to do, we accomplish only what we've been accomplishing. Look at the planet. What we've been accomplishing isn't enough.

In this book, I am calling for a kind of naiveté, which ironically enough is one of the main criticisms of my work. Maybe I should embrace that epithet, and call for even more of it. To be naive is to trust in the goodness of others when there is scant evidence of it, or to trust something might happen when you don't know how it could. Of course, naiveté is a curse when it obfuscates practical actions, but I'm talking about a situation where the practical is insufficient. That is where the planet is right now. And that is where many individuals are right now too as they discover that the things they know how to get, they no longer want.

Paradoxically, the path to achieve the impossible consists of many practical steps, each of them possible. Many pragmatic steps, each of which we know how to do, add up to something we did not. We know how to walk; we just don't have a map. So I am not suggesting we forgo the practical, the doable. It is that the practical is not enough unless put in service to the impractical.

In a similar vein, we cannot abandon the tools, material and cognitive, that defined the Age of Separation. We will not abandon reason in favor of feeling, telecommunications in favor of hugging, symbolic language in favor of song, or money in favor of gift. In each case, though, the former has exceeded its proper domain and usurped the latter. The new story contains the old; to seek the extirpation of the old is itself a thought form of the old story.

Let me share a few stories that illustrate the power of naiveté. Polly Higgins is a barrister and the author of *Eradicating Ecocide*. For the last few years she has been working to establish "rights of nature" and to make ecocide the fifth crime against peace recognized by the United Nations. Early on in this quest, she told me, she realized that the normal channels for trying to amend the U.N. Rome Statute were hopelessly slow and complicated. So, she decided to contact a high-level official directly whom she thought favorably disposed to ideas such as hers.

Let's call him Mr. E. But hundreds of activists and organizations also have ideas that they want to advance through the U.N. How to bypass all the gatekeepers and get into a direct conversation with him?

Polly happened to be in Germany at the time of a major climate summit in Copenhagen that Mr. E. planned to attend. He would be riding a special train along with other officials and specially invited journalists and NGO representatives. "If only I could get on that train," Polly thought, "I might have a chance to talk to him." But she could find no way of finagling an invitation. Maybe she could sneak onto the train? Impossible. Lines of police surrounded it to guard against activists seeking to do just that. So, Polly got on another train, hoping maybe to find Mr. E. in Copenhagen.

Her itinerary involved a transfer to another train in Hamburg. Alighting from her train, she asked a conductor where the train to Copenhagen was. He pointed her to the special U.N. train. "No, that's not my train," she said, knowing she wouldn't be allowed on.

The conductor ignored her. "Ya, ya, it is this train," he said in a thick German accent. She protested a couple more times to no avail ("Ya, ya, you mit me come.") as he took her suitcase and led her onto the train. Escorted by this railroad official and dressed in her lawyerly attire, no one asked to see her invitation. Soon she was seated on the train. She texted an NGO friend who had been invited to ride the train, "I'm on! Coach number two." Her friend texted back, inviting her up to her coach, where she was sitting across from a most interesting gentleman. "I've been telling him about you. There is an empty seat next to him."

You know who it was. It was Mr. E.

This was just one of a long trail of synchronistic events that has brought Polly before the EU Parliament, the Hague, and numerous other high-level bodies and given high visibility to the Law of Ecocide. It is a perfect example of putting the practical in service to the impractical.

Anybody could have told Polly it was naive to think she could get her idea onto the U.N. agenda when so many other organizations, with far more resources and connections, cannot. Anyone could have told her it was naive to expect to have a personal conversation with Mr. E. when so many other activists are kept a hundred meters away behind lines of police. The kinds of coincidences she experiences are not something one can plan out in advance. Often they come as interruptions in whatever plan was in place to begin with. That is not to say we shouldn't plan as best we can, and use whatever practical means are at our disposal, but we should not be limited by what we can plan. We should not limit our ambitions by what we know how to achieve.

Diane Wilson was a shrimp boat operator on the Gulf Coast of Texas.[1] In 1989 she found out that Formosa Plastics, a multibillion-dollar company, was planning to build a huge polyvinyl chloride complex nearby. Determined to stop this project, which she believed would pollute the Gulf, Wilson quite naively launched a campaign against it. Arrayed against this unassuming mother of five was the chamber of commerce, the local government, the legislature, the governor, the State Department of Environmental Protection, and the U.S. Environmental Protection Agency. How could she possibly prevail? What was it about her that enabled her to win against such powerful interests, when most of us seem unable to change the most trivial policy?

Certainly, part of the explanation is that Diane Wilson is an uncommonly brave and stubborn woman who was willing to do anything to accomplish her goal: go on a hunger strike, for example, or chain herself to the company fence. Over time, she also inspired numerous other people, some of them knowledgeable in the workings of the system, to join her cause. And perhaps her personal humility encouraged whistleblowers to seek her out. She had no plan—"I never planned anything: I just had intent, and was willing to put myself at risk"—and she did not through any kind of financial or emotional manipulation "make" these people come to her support. She did not pay them to support her, matching financial force with financial force. These people, like her, had nothing to gain, not even the social benefits of being perceived as heroic, since anyone allied with her was subject to ridicule.

---

1. She tells her story in the book *An Unreasonable Woman*.

Beyond these gifts, which are not unexpected in our conventional understanding of the world, Diane Wilson also was aided by at least one fortuitous coincidence, when an EPA official called her up, mistaking her for another Diane, and divulged key information that led to a breakthrough. Of course, we can easily dismiss this as mere coincidence, but could we also see it as an outcropping of a different kind of cause and effect from the force-based causality we are used to?

Years ago, when I lived in Taiwan, I formed a friendship with some other young American guys, who declared to me one day that they intended to create a three-day outdoor alternative music festival on the southern tip of the island. We guys in our mid-twenties were often declaring big plans over beers that we would forget the next day; the difference was that this event actually came to pass, despite the fact that the band members had no money, spoke only rudimentary Chinese, indeed had been in the country only a few months. "We'll hire buses to transport everyone down. We'll rent tents. We'll work out something with the local police, who knows." And then the hard work—and the gifts—began. For some reason, everyone believed that what these guys said would come to pass, so we all willingly contributed.

No one made any money off this venture; from top to bottom it was done in the spirit of the gift. But aside from the gifts from other people that the organizers' generosity attracted, as with Diane Wilson there were several unusual coincidences that landed as gifts upon the venture. The organizers needed a truck to haul equipment; one day one of their business English students asked, without knowing their need and seemingly out of the blue, "You wouldn't happen to need a truck, would you?" and gave them a truck. This kind of thing happened repeatedly. A kind of magic seemed to surround the event. The local police were no problem—I remember seeing one among the dancers—because for some reason they saw the event outside their usual categories (threat to law and order, opportunity to extort bribes, etc.).

Reader, have you ever been part of something like that, where everything seems to flow, where you find yourself again and again at the right place at the right time to encounter exactly the right person?

Where everything needed shows up, sometimes at the last minute, in completely unanticipated ways? Where an invisible outside power seems to be coordinating everything and everyone?

How and why does this happen? If we could somehow master the technology of being in the right place at the right time, if we could learn to ride the flow of synchronicity, then we would have accessed a power greater than anything the world of force is capable of.

Reality

*H*ow do we do that? This world of miracles, the things we cannot make happen, is a world of the gift. To live in it we must let go of the old ways of controlling, keeping, and holding back. We must learn to see the world through the eyes of the gift. Today most of us live simultaneously in both worlds, the old and the new; therefore our experience of miracles is haphazard. They seem to violate the laws of the physical or social universe, which is to be expected, as those laws are formed from the perceptions of the separate self.

Despite my call for naiveté, I also want to insert a note of caution here, because there is such a thing in this world as pursuing an impossible fantasy. There is such a thing as a delusion distracting one from the work at hand. How can we tell when we are in service to a real possibility, and when we are deluding ourselves, pursuing not a vision but a mirage? I'm not advocating a credulous confidence in whatever fantasy happens to be comforting.

A host of New Age teachings about "reality creation" tell us that in order to "manifest" something in this world, we must align our thoughts and beliefs with it, and it will appear. I use sarcastic quotation marks here, but some of these teachings are actually quite sophisticated. One can think of many situations in which beliefs do, in fact, create reality. For one thing, our beliefs and stories contain within them roles for ourselves that we must play out in order to accomplish anything in the world. Absent, for instance, a belief that it is possible to ride a unicycle, one is unlikely to devote the weeks necessary to learn how. Absent a belief that a music festival can happen, no one will do the things necessary to make it happen. Only when someone believes "I can do it," will they even try. When our beliefs change, so do our motivations and perceptions. We do new things and see new opportunities.

Beyond these mundane vehicles for the translation of belief into reality, I find something more mysterious at work as well. A kind of magic *does* happen when a person undergoes a profound change in worldview. The mundane vehicles I have described are perhaps instantiations of a more general principle. The problem with the New Age teachings about reality creation or the Law of Attraction is not so much in their metaphysics as in their application. I see two key difficulties. First, it is not as easy to alter one's beliefs as we would like to think. Ordinarily, we cannot change a belief through an act of will, for a state of belief is a state of being.[1] A belief isn't just a vapor in the brain. If you have, like me, tried to change your "limiting beliefs" through affirmations and so forth, you might have noticed that even as you repeated to yourself, "I now experience complete financial abundance" or "Every day in every way, life is getting better and better," a part of you is thinking, "Yeah, right. I'll believe it when the results come in." When the results do not, in fact, come in, you might discard the whole reality creation program as a lot of New Age hooey. But really, you have neither proven nor dis-

---

1. Occasionally people do report the experience of having successfully changed a belief as a volitional act. This does not mean they applied superior willpower to banish doubt and negativity, but that the belief was ready to change. When the state of being corresponding to a given belief has run its course, then the belief changes with just a little nudge.

proven the basic principle, because you were entertaining a fake belief, or at best a conflicted belief. Part of you may have believed it, but did it really feel true? Did it really feel possible?

This leads to a second problem: it is not ours to decide what is true or possible. Some teachings ask us to start by creating a vision, but this is mistaken; the proper way to start is to receive a vision. I call it "The vision of that which wants to be born." Not having invented it ourselves, we sense that it has a beingness of its own. Doubts may still assail us, but underneath the doubts there will be a knowing that comes from having seen something. The doubts arise from the wounds I have mentioned herein: the repeated betrayal of our idealism, the crushing of our spirit, the effects of the relentless ugliness of industrial society. We think, "What if I'm just a fool? What if I don't deserve such a blessing? What if humanity doesn't deserve it? What if we missed our chance? What if something beyond my control happens to ruin it?" Indeed, the more beautiful the vision (whether for oneself or the world), the more painful the doubts that arise. The radiance of that which wants to be born illuminates the shadows, bringing them into the light of awareness that they may be healed. I suggest becoming sensitive to the difference between these doubts and the secret, sober knowledge that you are fooling yourself.

The first step in creating change, then, is to receive a vision that feels true. The second step is to heal the wounds and doubts that that vision illuminates. Without doing that, we will be conflicted, simultaneously enacting both the new story and the old one that accompanies the wounds. The third step is to bow into service to that which wants to be born. This process is not linear. Usually, the vision comes more and more into focus as we heal the doubts that obscure it; that, in turn, allows us to enter more deeply into its service. Deeper service, in turn, brings up new dimensions of the vision along with deeper wounds. The path of service is a path of self-realization.

When we are in service to something that is real, when we speak of it our words have power. Others can feel its reality too. That is why some people have the seemingly magical ability to speak things into existence. When they say such-and-such is going to happen, everyone believes it is going to happen, even if its happening depends on everyone believing it will happen.

To be fully in service to something one has experienced as real is the essence of leadership in a nonhierarchical age. A leader is the holder of a story, someone whose experience of its reality is deep enough so that she can hold the belief on behalf of others. Many leaders today are weak, because they don't really believe in what they profess. How can they inspire anyone else to believe, either? Not believing themselves, they quickly capitulate at the slightest pressure, glad to settle for half-measures. If you call for the elimination of all nuclear weapons, but don't really believe it could happen, you will settle for a limited test-ban treaty. If what you want is a halt to all clear-cutting but don't believe it is possible, you will settle for a mere slowdown.

The deeper our service to that which wants to be born, the more it is able to arrange the synchronistic encounters and fortuitous events that allow us to accomplish that which lies beyond our understanding of cause and effect. We might say that the primary "technology" of the Age of Reunion is service. We offer our time, energy, skills, and lives as gifts, stepping into trust, letting go of the habit of looking first and foremost after one's self. Only then can we fully align with the vision. From that alignment, a tremendous force is born. Our expanded selves are far more powerful and less fearful than the discrete, separate individual who, separate from the world, can only manipulate it by force, and looks with wariness and wonder at the amazing coincidences that line up as it lets go and plunges into service. Obviously, since these are not things that we know how to "make" happen, they happen as gifts, confirming the universal principle of the gift: that giving and receiving always come into balance in the end.

This whole process of cocreating change starts not with faith but with honesty. We must first catch a glimpse of something that we recognize as real. One kind of honesty is to recognize our delusions and see what is in front of our faces. This can be painful. It has been humiliating to admit, "I didn't really believe what we've been working on is possible;

all along I was doing it to belong, to appear virtuous to myself and others, and simply to stave off despair." But there is another application of honesty that is braver still: to believe in a true vision that contradicts the consensus view of what is possible or worthwhile. It takes more courage to believe what we know is true than to disbelieve what we know is false. For the visionary, that knowledge is in the beginning a lonely knowledge, surrounded by a welter of doubt both within and without. To trust a moment of clarity and carry it forward, to translate it into belief and act from it amid all the voices that say it is crazy or impossible, is no trivial matter.

Spirit

There is another world, but it is in this one.

—W. B. YEATS

The cynical reader might suppose that I will unveil "spirituality" as an escape from the bleak, dispiriting universe of the Story of Separation. I won't, because unfortunately, spirituality as we typically conceive it is itself a key component of Separation. It concedes that the desolate materialism offered by science is essentially correct: that sacredness, purpose, and sentience cannot inhere in matter itself, cannot be found among the generic subatomic building blocks of the material world. These things, says spirituality, reside instead in another, nonmaterial realm, the realm of spirit.

Given that premise, the goal of spirituality becomes to transcend the material realm and ascend into the spiritual. A kind of antimaterialism infuses such teachings as "You are not your body" as well as aspirations to "raise one's vibrations." Given that our environmental collapse comes from antimaterialism as well (a devaluing and desacralization of the material world), we might want to reconsider these teachings. What is so special about "high" vibrations? Is a bassoon less beautiful than a flute? Is a rock less sacred than a cloud? Is Earth less sacred than Heaven? Is superior better than inferior? Is high better than low? Is abstract better than concrete? Is reason better than feeling? Is pure better than messy? Is man better than woman?

(And, just to throw a monkey wrench into all of it, I might add: Is nondualism better than dualism? Even to critique the idea that one thing is better than another still employs "better than" as a concept, implicitly validating that concept.)

It is no coincidence that the abstraction of spirit from matter, the removal of the abode of the gods into a heavenly realm, and the emergence of patriarchy all happened at about the same time. All arose with the first large-scale agricultural civilizations, with their social classes, division of labor, and need to exert control over natural forces. It was then that the conquest of nature that had started earlier with domestication of plants and animals became an explicit virtue, and the gods became the lords of nature rather than its personification. The builder societies, requiring standardization in their armies and construction projects, developing abstract systems of measure in their accounting and distribution of resources, looked naturally to the sky, with its orderly, predictable movements, as the seat of divinity. Mirroring that, the higher social classes—the priests, nobles, and kings—had less and less to do with the soil and with the messiness of human relationships, but were kept insulated in temples, palaces, and, when they must go out, above the ground on litters. At the same time, the concepts of good and evil were born. Anything that violated the progressive imposition of control onto nature and human nature was evil: floods, weeds, wolves, locusts, etc., as well as fleshly desires, rebelliousness, and indolence. Self-discipline—necessary to raise oneself above the desires of the material world—became a cardinal spiritual virtue.

In distilling an eighty-page chapter of *The Ascent of Humanity* into a one-paragraph synopsis, I hope I haven't reduced a complicated argument into a bunch of clichés. The point here is that our conception of spirituality has very deep roots, and that it shares these roots in common with everything else of our civilization—even, remarkably enough, with science. It should be no surprise then that as our dominant institutions collapse, our spirituality goes through a transition as well.

It is under way already, as the long-buried esoteric core of mainstream religion emerges into mass consciousness.

Enormous energy has gone into attempting to prove the existence of a nonmaterial realm. To take a recent example, Eben Alexander's account of his near-death experience in the recent best seller *Proof of Heaven* asserts that his experience must have happened independently of his brain, which was in a deep coma. This, the book implies, is why his experience was so significant. Critics quickly gathered to refute his conclusions, arguing that there is no way to prove the absence of at least some cortical function, which, together with subsequent false memory and confabulation, offers a materialist, brain-based explanation. But I think the critics and the author himself both miss the book's true significance. What it points to is not an extra-material source of consciousness, but to our shallow understanding of matter itself, which has properties that could not exist in the view of classical physics, chemistry, and biology. The "spirituality" of his experience lies in what it was, not what it proves.

Why are we so desperate to escape the material world? Is it really so bleak? Or could it be, rather, that we have *made* it bleak: obscured its vibrant mystery with our ideological blinders, severed its infinite connectedness with our categories, suppressed its spontaneous order with our pavement, reduced its infinite variety with our commodities, shattered its eternity with our time-keeping, and denied its abundance with our money system? If so, then we are misguided if we appeal to a nonmaterial spiritual realm for our salvation from the prison of materiality.

Activists are right to be wary of such attempts. If the sacred is to be found outside the material, then why bother with the material? If the interests of the soul are opposed to the interests of the flesh, then why seek to improve the world of the flesh, the social and material world? Spirituality becomes as religion was for Marx: the opiate of the masses, a distraction from the very real material problems facing our planet.

On the other hand, it would be arrogant indeed to dismiss thousands of years of sacred teachings as the bumbling fantasies of dreamers, and the last few hundred years of spirituality as the ravings of people who just couldn't handle the bitter truth of a mechanical, purposeless universe. They are seeking to remedy an egregious shortcoming of the scientific worldview, which until recently has had no place for whole dimensions of the human experience. Phenomena that didn't fit into scientific orthodoxy were declared not to exist; to one who accepts science as a more or less complete description of the natural world, the only way to account for these phenomena was to ascribe to them a supernatural explanation.

Put another way, if we agree that the universe of science does not bear inherent intelligence, then whatever intelligence there is must come from outside the material universe. The doctrine of "Intelligent Design" exemplifies this kind of thinking. Such order as life exhibits couldn't just arise spontaneously from dead matter and blind forces; therefore, it must have been designed by an external agency (God). But if we accept intelligence, the movement toward order, beauty, and organization, to be an inherent property of matter, no such external agency is required.

It may sound like I am offering a defense of conventional scientific materialism. Quite the opposite. Instead of taking the route of religion and saying that the intelligence we see has a supernatural origin, science tries to deny it altogether, explaining it away as a kind of illusion, an accidental by-product of those blind forces, not anything inherent. Accordingly, science as an institution is hostile to any paradigm that suggests an inherent intelligence or purpose to matter.

In investigating various heterodox scientific theories and the technologies that derive from them, I've often wondered why some of them provoke such extreme hostility from the establishment. The ones that do, I've found, share something in common: all of them imply that the universe is, as I put it before, intelligent through and through. Consider, for example, water memory. No longer is pure water a mere meaningless jumble of molecules, but any two "samples" of water are unique; they are individuals, carrying as we do a record of all their past influences, and able to transmit those influences onto all they touch. Or consider "adaptive mutation"—the theory that genetic mutation isn't random, but proceeds preferentially toward the mutations that the organism or environment requires. This kind of purposiveness is anathema to scientific orthodoxy. Any theory that implies that the universe has an intelligence or purpose of its own threatens to topple humanity from its privileged position as the masters of nature. Our intelligence becomes instead part of a larger intelligence, which we then seek to understand and cooperate with.

The hostility of science to anything smacking of inherent order and intelligence in matter is now changing. All around the edges of science, new paradigms are growing that are letting the properties once relegated to spirit back into matter. Another way to see it is that spirit and matter are reuniting.

One aspect of this reunion is the coming together of the activism and spirituality. In a workshop a young Occupy activist described how appalled her father, a traditional Marxist, was when she shared her interest in "consciousness" and a spiritual path. Traditionally on the left, anything smacking of spirituality is either a luxury of the privileged class, a distraction from the real work at hand, or a fantasy obscuring the correct analysis of the problem.

I can understand where he was coming from. For a long time now, hands-on activists have derided the so-called spiritual seekers. "Get off your meditation cushion and do something! There is suffering all around you. You have hands, a brain, resources. Do something about the suffering!" If the house were burning down, would you just sit there and meditate, visualizing cool waterfalls to put out the fire through the power of manifestation? Well, the figurative house is burning down around us right now. The deserts are spreading, the coral reefs are dying, and the last of the indigenous are being wiped out. And there you are in the midst of it all, contemplating the cosmic sound OM. In this view, spirituality is a kind of escapism.

To this powerful critique, the spiritual folks offer an equally powerful rejoinder. "Without deep work on yourself, how will you avoid re-creating your own internalized oppression in all that you do?" So often we see the same abuses of power, the same organizational dysfunctions among social change activists as we do in the institutions they seek to change. If these activists were to emerge victorious, why would we expect the society they create to be any different? Unless we have done transformational work on ourselves, we will remain products of the very civilization we seek to transform.

We need to change our habits of thought, belief, and doing as well as change our systems. Each level reinforces the other: Our habits and beliefs form the psychic substructure of our system, which in turn induces in us the corresponding beliefs and habits. That is why political activists and spiritual teachers are equally mistaken when the former say, "It is a frivolous, self-indulgent escape to focus on changing your beliefs around scarcity when the systemic compulsion toward real, life-and-death scarcity continues to oppress billions regardless of your beliefs and lifestyle choices," and the latter say, "Just work on yourself, and the world will change around you. Don't escape the real, personal issue by projecting the problem onto society, the political system, the corporations, etc."

The two camps are meant to be allies, and in fact neither will succeed without the other. The more people who have stepped into gratitude, generosity, and trust and left some amount of fear-based thinking behind, the more receptive the sociopolitical climate will be to radical reform, which will embody the values of interbeing. And the more our systems change to embody these values, the easier it will be for people to make the personal transition. Today, our economic environment screams at us, "Scarcity!"; our political environment screams at us, "Us versus them"; our medical environment screams at us, "Be afraid!" Together, they keep us alone and scared to change.

On the intermediate level, too, that of family, community, and place, our social and physical environment enforces separation. To live in nuclear families in isolated boxes, to procure life's necessities from anonymous strangers, to depend not at all on the land around us for sustenance insinuates separation into our basic perceptions of the world. That is why we might say that any effort to change these circumstances is spiritual work.

By the same token, any effort to change people's basic perceptions of the world is political work. What kind of people take refuge in sprawling suburbs? What kind of people work at jobs that satisfy no desire but the desire for security? What kind of people stand passively by while their nation prosecutes one unjust war after another? The answer is: fearful people. Alienated people. Wounded people. That's why spiritual work is political, if it spreads love, connection, forgiveness, acceptance, and healing.

That doesn't mean that every person "should" address every level. We each have unique gifts that draw us toward the work for which those gifts are best suited. Although a healthy, well-rounded person will generally engage the world on multiple levels, being as she is an individual, a friend, a member of a family, a member of a community and a place, an inhabitant of a bioregion, a citizen of a nation, and a member of the tribe of all life on Earth, even a cosmic citizen, it is also true that we go through phases of relative inward and outward focus, action, and quiet, expression and retreat.

When we no longer hold a rigid self/other distinction, then we recognize that the world mirrors the self; that to work on the self it is necessary to work in the world, and to work effectively in the world, it is necessary to work on the self. Of course, there have always been spiritual practitioners who are politically active and political activists who are deeply spiritual, but now the attraction of each realm to the other is becoming irrepressible. More and more social and environmental activists are rejecting mainstream beliefs in ways that are more personal. The Occupy supporter is also likely to support attachment parenting, practice meditation, use alternative medicine. The hippies and the '60s radicals are converging.

Orthodoxy

That is at bottom the only courage that is demanded of us: to have courage for the most strange, the most singular and the most inexplicable that we may encounter. That mankind has in this sense been cowardly has done life endless harm; the experiences that are called "visions," the whole so-called "spirit-world," death, all those things that are so closely akin to us, have by daily parrying been so crowded out of life that the senses with which we could have grasped them are atrophied.

—RILKE

The convergence of spirituality and activism mirrors a broader reunion of spirit and matter, in which we understand the two realms as one. This is different from the claim of science to have explained away any phenomenon we might call spiritual. More than a reduction of spirit to matter, it is an elevation of matter to spirit.

This reunion is still incomplete. There are still many political activists who will be appalled at this book's reference to phenomena that they label as "scientifically unproven" or causal principles they label as unscientific. They do not realize that scientific orthodoxy is cut from the same cloth and serves the same ends as the rest of our dominant institutions. It contributes to the maintenance of the Story of Separation just as much as economics, politics, or organized religion.[1]

---

1. I should mention here that just as organized religion harbors an esoteric core that does not teach separation, so also we might distinguish between science as an institution, and the Scientific Method itself. While it can be argued that even the Scientific Method is fraught with unexamined assumptions (for example, objectivity: that a hypothesis about reality doesn't alter that reality, and that it is in principle to repeat experiments because the variables of time, place, and the experimenter are independent

Similarly, readers who are knowledgeable about alternative scientific paradigms and technologies may be feeling impatient with my skepticism of the idea that these will save humanity. Although I have firsthand experience with several technologies that conventional science calls impossible, I will not promote them in this book. The reason is, again, if these are to save us, then why haven't they already? Many have been known and suppressed for decades. I have read the literature alleging that this suppression is conscious and systematic; I think it is mostly, rather, unconscious and *systemic*.[2] Through a thousand mechanisms, we have suppressed them because they do not fit into our mythology and identity. Equivalently, one might say, we were not ready for them. We were not ready for technologies that were distributed rather than centralized, that released control from the experts to the people, and that necessitated seeing the interconnectedness of all things. Symptomatic of our unreadiness is inventors' rush to patent each new miracle device, attempting to contain something of the new story within the structures of the old. Perhaps these technologies of abundance—of energy, health, time, and life—will leave the margins and take hold only when we, collectively, exemplify abundance ourselves through generosity, service, surrender, and trust.

We are on the brink of a wholesale metamorphosis. We will never embrace the technologies of interbeing from the mentality of Separation. These technologies are not a magic bullet, though I do think, in the end, they will indeed be part of our healing. But a shift in our perceptions, in our worldview, comes first. At the present juncture, the primary importance of the technologies of interbeing isn't in what they can do. It is that they puncture the reality bubble in which we have lived, showing us that neither we nor the world is what we thought. Their significance is the same as that of any paradigm-busting phenomenon.

---

of the hypothesis being tested), ultimately it encodes a kind of humility, a willingness to change or expand beliefs in response to information coming from outside one's conscious self.

2. See my article "Synchronicity, Myth, and the New World Order" online for further thoughts on the dynamic of unconscious conspiracies.

Now it is easy to believe, when surveying the widespread denial of climate science in my country, that the problem is unscientific attitudes. If only we would listen to the scientists! Unfortunately, the same exhortation is also deployed in the context of genetic engineering of crops, nuclear power, and other questionable technologies that I hesitate to mention lest I too be tarred with the very wide brush of "antiscience." While the two examples above don't enjoy anything like the unanimity that anthropogenic climate change does, advocates like Michael Specter do not hesitate to brand opponents as unscientific. All the more unscientific would they consider my beliefs about holistic medicine, qigong, biodynamic agriculture, water memory, biological nuclear chemistry, crop circles, psi phenomena, over-unity devices, radioactive waste remediation, and Santa Claus. There, I've let the cat out of the bag.

Because of their power to puncture the old story, I encourage people to explore these "unscientific" phenomena. You will discover that they provoke a combination of upliftment and scorn. They relieve the weight of Separation and validate our childlike perceptions of untapped wonders, mysteries, and possibilities. At the same time, they trigger the fear that these perceptions are delusions, and thus the derision of the cynic discussed earlier.

Don't worry—I'm not going to pin my optimism on the hope that some miracle technology is going to save us. If it were up to technology to save us, it already would have. We have long possessed the technologies to live abundantly and sustainably on this planet, but we have used them to other ends. We could live in an earthly paradise using perfectly uncontroversial technologies: conservation, recycling, green design, solar energy, permaculture, biological wastewater treatment, bicycles, designing for reparability, durability, and reusability, and so on.[3] These are technologies that already exist and, by and large, have existed for

3. I purposely left out wind energy here, because I have serious environmental concerns about it as currently implemented, though unorthodox smaller-scale designs show some promise. Ultimately, the solution is not to produce more power in order to sustain our present society. It is to change our society into one that, among other things, uses less power. Most of the ways we use energy don't foster well-being anyway.

decades or centuries. No new, miraculous technologies are necessary. However, another kind of miracle is necessary to redeem the promise of these existing technologies: a social or political miracle. That's what it would take to reverse deforestation, cut greenhouse gas emissions, heal damaged watersheds, and remove all the legal, social, and economic impediments to change. It would doubtless require a different money system, and therefore a radical restructuring of economic power and privilege. It would require a wholesale shift away from militarism and all the belief systems behind it. It would require millions of people going back to the land to engage in small-scale, high-productivity, labor-intensive agriculture. Technologically feasible? Certainly. Politically realistic? Hardly.

There is no denying that one way or another, we are facing a task that we don't know how to accomplish. Any politically realistic proposal today pales into insignificance beside the severity of the crisis at hand. Herein lies the significance of the unorthodox and heterodox technologies that I mentioned before: The worldview that eliminates such things from the realm of possibility also cuts us off from the kinds of actions that are necessary to change the world. In both cases, we face something that cannot happen without violating our Story of the World.

Even though science as we know it is central to the centuries-long or millennia-long program to master nature, even though its approach to gathering knowledge is the very model of "othering" nature and making the world into an object, scientifically oriented people are often fervent environmentalists and supporters of civil rights, equality for gay people, and other compassionate positions. This exemplifies a general principle: our entry into the new story is uneven. In one area of life or thought we may have transcended all vestiges of separation, while being completely blind to it in another. It never ceases to amaze me. Someone might have deep insight into the institutions, both internal and external, of racism, sexism, classism, and colonialism, but have no clue that Western medicine, and to some extent science itself, are among those institutions. I go to a traditional nutrition conference where people thoroughly understand the corruption of our food system, how it destroys land, health, and community, but they are unaware that the school system does much the same. Citing studies that link diet and test scores, they say, "If only children had better nutrition, we would improve school performance," assuming that paying attention in class and doing well on tests are signs of a healthy child. But when we become aware of how the school system is a conditioning agent to instill in children obedience to authority, passivity, and tolerance to tedium for the sake of external rewards, we begin to question school performance as a metric of well-being. Maybe a healthy child is one who resists schooling and standardization, not one who excels at it. Then I go to an educational conference where people do understand that, yet (judging by the food consumed and the health of the participants) have little connection to their bodies or awareness that the food system is just as corrupt as the educational system. And almost anywhere I go, no matter how radical the audience when discussing agriculture or education or sexuality or politics, when push comes to shove concerning their health, they go to a conventional MD.

For a long time, activists in these areas and many others have been operating in their own silos, as if they were addressing a single anomalous malady in a system that, despite a few problems, were fundamentally sound. It was not obvious that someone working for, say, prison reform was devoted to another facet of the same cause as someone working for organic agriculture. Fortunately, this is changing today. A creeping radicalization is taking over, as people recognize the interconnectedness of all our systems and institutions, and the complicity of these in upholding the dominant narratives. The prison system as we know it depends on the same kinds of beliefs that also embed our food system, educational system, and medical system. They all depend on the same political mindsets, the same economic mechanisms, and the same kinds of interpersonal relationships.

They also come from (and contribute to) the same psychology or, one might say, the same state of being. That is why the creeping radicalization I speak of ultimately extends to the spiritual domain as well, by which, again, I mean not something otherworldly, but that which involves the fundamental questions of "Who am I?" "What is the purpose of life?" and so on.

More and more people are entering multidimensionally now into the new story. They are building alliances across previously disconnected areas of activism, and they are entering realms of inquiry that were once the exclusive province of spiritual seekers. They are also striving to apply their discoveries to their own organizations and relationships. No domain of life is irrelevant to the transformation of our world.

There has probably been something in this chapter to tweak nearly everyone. When things fall apart, we look for a redoubt, some familiar institution that we can rely on as a repository of goodness and truth. In this age, there is none: not science, not education, not medicine, not academia. Even our spirituality, as we have seen, is rife with the thought forms of Separation.

It is quite natural to react defensively to the falling apart of the world, to cling to it all the more tightly. If you react emotionally to my aspersions on one of your sacred cows, it probably means that something beyond mere opinion is threatened. Perhaps you disagree with me about the efficacy of acupuncture or the authenticity of crop circles. Is it just an intellectual disagreement, or are you a little bit angry? What emotionally tinged judgments accompany the disagreement? That I am a simpleminded dupe? That I am ignorant of basic science? That I have neglected to examine contrary evidence that would spoil my wishful thinking? That my beliefs are outrageous, contemptible, or shameful? Do you justify the contempt with reasoning like "These beliefs give people false hope and distract them from solutions that might actually work"? If so, is that *really* why you are mad, or is it something else? I have found that when I react emotionally to an idea that contradicts my beliefs, usually it is because it threatens my story of the world or my story of self, creating a kind of existential unease. I feel a sense of violation.

None of this is to imply that if you respond emotionally to my unconventional statements, you are proved wrong and I am proved right. All it implies is that your rejection has little to do with evidence or logic. Evidence and logic are tools we use to justify and flesh out our beliefs, but we are deceiving ourselves to think that they are the source of our beliefs. I will return to this idea, because it is crucial to understanding the process of belief change as well; and clearly, for our world to have a chance of surviving, a lot of beliefs are going to have to change.

Newness

*L*et us pause for a moment to question the newness of the new story. After all, one of the hallmarks of the old story is the glorification of change, of novelty, of constantly discarding the old in favor of something new and better, the latest technological marvel in an endless saga of progress that devalues old relationships, knowledge, and traditions. Fixation on the new can also become a kind of escapism that sees existing problems as inconsequential, since we will leave them behind when we enter the "new" world. Some look to technology to save us, hoping that more novelty can rescue us from the disastrous unanticipated consequences of previous novelty; for example, that nanotechnology will reverse the climate effects of fossil fuel technology. There is nothing new about that ambition. So I would like to preempt that concern by clarifying that the new story is only new in the context of what we in modern "civilized" society are used to.

Many readers will recognize that the Story of Interbeing echoes the worldview of various indigenous tribes and ancient wisdom traditions around the world. None of the principles enunciated herein are new at all. I am wary, however, of appealing to "indigenous wisdom" as a way to legitimize my beliefs, first, because that would imply a uniformity across indigenous belief systems that trivializes their diversity; second, because various elements of indigenous spirituality have oft been ripped from their context and used as sales props for all manner of questionable products and ideas; third, because to draw too sharp a distinction between the civilized and the indigenous obscures our common humanity and perpetuates a kind of inverted racism that superficially valorizes, but ultimately demeans, those labeled as indigenous.

Moreover, even within Western civilization, none of the teachings of interbeing are new. They compose a kind of recessive gene in our culture, never dominant, usually dormant, occasionally reaching a glorious though partial expression during the various golden ages of humankind. Nonetheless, I call it a new story: never before has it generated a civilization. It stands in fresh contrast to the world we are used to, to the Separation embodied in money, school, religion, politics, and the rest of modern life.

Popular interest in native spirituality can be criticized as the ultimate form of cultural murder, in which a culture's stories, rituals, and sacred beliefs are co-opted and debased. But it also comes from a recognition that the indigenous carry important knowledge that has been lost, knowledge that we of the West are finally ready to hear as our own rituals, myths, and institutions break down.

Einstein famously said that our problems cannot be solved at the same level of thinking that created them. True, but how are we to think at a different level? How are we to distinguish what is truly different from what we tell ourselves is different but is really old wine in new skin? Without the infusion of ways of knowing and being that are external to our story, we will remain lost in it forever, reshuffling the same old components. Fortunately, we have, on our journey of Separation, smuggled along with us three seeds of Reunion, three conduits for the influx of wisdom from a once and future time. Well, there could be more than three! But here is how I tell the story:

THE THREE SEEDS

Once upon a time, the tribe of humanity embarked upon a long journey called Separation. It was not a blunder as some, seeing its ravages upon the planet, might think; nor was it a fall, nor an expression of some innate evil peculiar to the human species. It was a journey with a purpose: to experience the extremes of Separation, to develop the gifts that come in response to it, and to integrate all of that in a new Age of Reunion.

But we knew at the outset that there was danger in this journey: that we might become lost in Separation and never come back. We might become so alienated from nature that we would destroy the very basis of life; we might become so separated from each other that our poor egos, left naked and terrified, would become incapable of rejoining the community of all being. In other words, we foresaw the crisis we face today.

That is why, thousands of years ago, we planted three seeds that would sprout at the time that our journey of Separation reached its extreme. Three seeds, three transmissions from the past to the future, three ways of preserving and transmitting the truth of the world, the self, and how to be human.

Imagine you were alive thirty thousand years ago and had a vision of all that was to come: symbolic language, naming and labeling the world; agriculture, the domestication of the wild, dominion over other species and the land; the Machine, the mastery of natural forces; the forgetting of how beautiful and perfect the world is; the atomization of society; a world where humans fear even to drink of the streams and rivers, where we live among strangers and don't know the people next door, where we kill across the planet with the touch of a button, where the seas turn black and the air burns our lungs, where we are so broken that we dare not remember that it isn't supposed to be this way. Imagine you saw it all coming. How would you help people thirty thousand years thence? How would you send information, knowledge, aid over such a vast gulf of time? Maybe this actually happened. So, we came up with the three seeds.

The first seed was the wisdom lineages: lines of transmission going back thousands of years that have preserved and protected essential knowledge. From adept to disciple, in every part of the world, various wisdom traditions have passed down teachings in secret. Wisdom keepers, Sufis, Zen masters, Kabbalists, Taoist wizards, Christian mystics, Hindu swamis, and many others, hiding within each religion, kept the knowledge safe until the time when the world would be ready to reclaim it. That time is now, and they have done their job well. Many spiritual leaders, even the Dalai Lama, are saying that the time of secrets is over. Released too early, the knowledge was co-opted, abused, or usually just ignored. When we had still not covered the territory of Separation, when we still aspired to widening our conquest of nature, when the story of humanity's Ascent was not yet complete, we weren't ready to hear about union, connectedness, interdependency, interbeing. We thought the answer was more control, more technology, more logic, a better-engineered society of rational ethics, more control over matter, nature, and human nature. But now the old paradigms are failing, and human consciousness has reached a degree of receptivity that allows this seed to spread across the earth. It has been released, and it is growing inside of us en masse.

The second seed was the sacred stories: myths, legends, fairy tales, folklore, and the perennial themes that keep reappearing in various guises throughout history. They have always been with us, so that however far we have wandered into the Labyrinth of Separation, we have always had a lifeline, however tenuous and tangled, to the truth. The stories nurture that tiny spark of memory within us that knows our origin and our destination. The ancients, knowing that the truth would be co-opted and distorted if left in explicit form, encoded it into stories. When we hear or read one of these stories, even if we cannot decode the symbolism, we are affected on an unconscious level. Myths and fairy tales represent a very sophisticated psychic technology. Each generation of storytellers, without consciously intending to, transmits the covert wisdom that it learned, unconsciously, from the stories told it.

Without directly contradicting the paradigms of separation and ascent, our myths and stories have smuggled in a very different understanding of reality. Under the cover of "It's just a story," they convey emotional, poetic, and spiritual truth that contradicts linear logic, reductionism, determinism, and objectivity. I am not talking here about moralistic tales. Most of those carry little truth. To transmit the second seed, we must humble ourselves to our stories, and not try to use them for our own moralistic ends. They were created by beings far wiser than our modern selves. If you tell or transmit stories, be very respectful of their original form and don't change them unless you feel a poetic upwelling. Pay attention to which children's literature has the feel of a true story. Most recent kids' literature does not. You can recognize a true story by the way its images linger in your mind. It imprints itself on the psyche. You get the feeling that something else has been transmitted alongside the plot, something invisible. Usually, such stories bear rich symbolism often unknown even to their authors. A comparison of two twentieth-century children's books illustrates my point: compare a *Berenstain Bears* story with *How the Grinch Stole Christmas!* Only the latter has a psychic staying power, revealing the spirit of a true story, and it is rich with archetypal symbolism.

The third seed was the indigenous tribes, the people who at some stage opted out of the journey of separation. Imagine that at the outset of the journey, the Council of Humanity gathered and certain members volunteered to abide in remote locations and forgo separation, which meant refusing to enter into an adversarial, controlling relationship to nature, and therefore refusing the process that leads to the development of high technology. It also meant that when they were discovered by the humans who had gone deeply into Separation, they would meet with the most atrocious suffering. That was unavoidable.

These people of the third seed have nearly completed their mission today. Their mission was simply to survive long enough to provide living examples of how to be human. Each tribe carried a different piece, sometimes many pieces, of this knowledge. Many of them show us how to see and relate to the land, animals, and plants. Others show us how to work with dreams and the unseen. Some have preserved natural ways of raising children, now spreading through such books as *The Continuum Concept*. Some show us how to communicate without words—tribes such as the Hadza and the Pirahã communicate mostly in song. Some show us how to free ourselves from the mentality of linear time. All of them exemplify a way of being that we intuitively recognize and long for. They stir a memory in our hearts, and awaken our desire to return.

><><

In a conversation, the Lakota Aloysius Weasel Bear told me that he once asked his grandfather, "Grandpa, the White Man is destroying everything, shouldn't we try to stop him?" His grandfather replied, "No, it isn't necessary. We will stand by. He will outsmart himself." The grandfather recognized two things in this reply: (1) that Separation carries the seeds of its own demise, and (2) that his people's role is to be themselves. But I don't think that this is an attitude of callousness that leaves the White Man to his just deserts; it is an attitude of compassion and helping that understands the tremendous importance of simply *being who they are*. They are keeping alive something that the planet and the community of all being needs.

By the same token, our culture's fascination with all things indigenous is not merely the latest form of cultural imperialism and exploitation. True, the final stage of cultural domination would be to turn

Native ways into a brand, a marketing image. And certainly there are some in my culture who, sundered from community and from a real identity, adopt Native pseudo-identities and pride themselves on their connections to Native culture, spirituality, people, and so forth. Underneath that, however, we recognize that the surviving First Peoples have something important to teach us. We are drawn to their gift, to the seed that they have preserved until the present time. To receive this seed, it is not necessary to participate in their rituals, take an animal name, or claim a Native ancestor, but only to humbly see what they have preserved, so that memory may awaken. Until recently, such seeing was impossible for us, blinkered by our cultural superiority complex, our arrogance, our apparent success in mastering the universe. Now that converging ecological and social crises reveal the bankruptcy of our ways, we have the eyes to see the ways of others.

Urgency

The Way is calm and wide,
Not easy, not difficult.
But small minds get lost.
Hurrying, they fall behind.

—SENG CAN

A year or two ago a young man confronted me at a talk in Florida. I'd been describing my view that the paradigm of urgency, heroic efforts, and struggle may itself be part of the problem; that it comes from the same place of scarcity and domination as the conquest of nature; that coming from that place, we might blindly create more of the same. Instead, I suggested, we might try slowing down, perhaps even doing nothing sometimes. Instead of holding ourselves to a high standard of revolutionary asceticism, we might approach life in a spirit of ease and play. Perhaps from this place our creative energies can bring about something truly new for civilization.

The man said something to the following effect (embellished here with words from my own inner critic):

How can you propose sitting still even for one moment? Now is a crucial time for action. Don't you know that even as we sit here in comfort, U.S. agents are abducting innocent people and sending them off to be tortured? Don't you know that even as we speak, huge factory farms are slaughtering animals and pumping their wastes into the waterways? It's all very well for you to blather on about changing our cultural stories, but there are children starving out there. What will you say when one of them asks you what you were doing on that Saturday afternoon when the paramilitary killed his family? How can you live with yourself if you haven't devoted every waking moment to justice on Earth? There is no time to waste. There is no time for indulgences. There is no time for sitting around talking, no time for watching films, no time for play. If there were thugs torturing and raping young girls on that lawn over there, we wouldn't be sitting around talking about things, we wouldn't be holding workshops on reclaiming play, and we wouldn't be setting up "compassionate listening posts." We would go stop them. Well, that is happening right now, just a little out of sight, and because it is invisible you act is if it were not happening. I'm sorry, but I'm afraid all of this talk is nothing but rank hypocrisy. Your lifestyle is complicit in every way with the ongoing pillage of the planet, and you imagine that your words somehow excuse you from guilt. Stop pretending, get off your ass, and do something about it.

I would like to contrast this view with that of a Dogon tribal elder whom my friend, Cynthia Jurs, asked about urgency. Cynthia was in Mali to conduct an Earth Treasure Vase ritual for peace and ecological healing. She asked him about the threats to the planet—deforestation, climate change, etc.—as well as threats that encroaching powers were presenting to his tribe and way of life. "Don't you feel urgency to do something about it?" The man understood very well the threats and knew that something is out of balance in the world, but he said, "You don't understand. Urgency isn't something we have here."

My friends, who is the wiser, this "primitive" Dogon elder or the young man in Florida? Is this another case where civilized man with his clocks, calendars, and linear scarcity-based thinking knows better?

Do we need to school the Dogon? Or could it be that the key to our redemption cannot be found among the modes of being in which we, the civilized, are fluent? Could it be that we have something crucial to learn from the indigenous? Could it be that our only path out of this mess is, as Martín Prechtel puts it, to recover our own indigenous soul?

If there were a child being abused in the room next to me, it is true, I would not be writing these words right now. I would be acting bodily, and I would know exactly what to do. But to map that onto our present macroscopic circumstances would be a false analogy, because on a global scale, *we do not know what to do.*

If my house is on fire, I won't stay sitting in front of the computer. The world is on fire! Why am I sitting in front of my computer? It is because I don't have a fire extinguisher for the world, and there isn't a global 911 to call.

If my brother is starving, I will give him food. Millions of my global brothers and sisters are starving, but I don't have enough food to give to them all. And even if I did, I study the economics of food aid and how it sometimes creates dependency, fuels nepotism and warlordism, and destroys local food production, and the right response becomes less clear. A Marxist would say that alleviating hunger through food aid merely obscures the true source of the problem and perpetuates the underlying injustice.

When we know the true cause of a problem and what to do about it, then everything the young man said is true. That is the time to act, and perhaps to act urgently. But when we haven't penetrated to the true cause, or when we don't know what to do, then it might be counterproductive to jump into action. The young man's words might actually apply to himself: the appearance of frenetic action placates the conscience, creating the illusion that one is part of the solution, but are these actions doing any good? Imagine someone heroically waving a fire extinguisher at a giant inferno—maybe at such a moment words and not "actions" are the best action; maybe it is time to gather some help. And what if we don't know what kind of fire it is? Electrical, grease, wood? And what if there are fires everywhere, some more advanced than others? And what if there are children in some of the houses? And what if three-quarters of the people don't even believe that their houses are on fire? What if putting out the fire is hopeless, and it would be more useful to give it up and design better houses instead?

Could it even be that our urgent scurrying to solve one problem after another is stoking the fire? Perhaps global warming is a symptomatic fever of our hurrying.

After all, why is global warming happening? There are the proximate causes: the burning of fossil fuels, and the assault on the forests and biodiversity that maintain climate homeostasis. And why are these happening? It is all in the name of efficiency: labor efficiency (doing more work per unit of labor) and economic efficiency (maximizing the short-term return on capital). And efficiency is just another name for getting it done faster.

One might wish to think that there is good hurrying (to save the planet) and bad hurrying (to use machines to get things done with less work), but maybe the underlying mindset behind both kinds of hurrying is the problem. This mindset is one of the habits of separation, the next theme of this book.

There is a time to act, and a time to wait, to listen, to observe. Then understanding and clarity can grow. From understanding, action arises that is purposeful, firm, and powerful.

But wait. For the Marxist, the understanding might be that hunger is a consequence of capitalism, but the action isn't so obvious. How does one "overthrow capitalism"? Even for the non-Marxist, it is abundantly clear that the financial system is deeply implicated in hunger and, for that matter, in most of the world's ills. So, what "actions" are necessary to change the money system? Furthermore, as I describe in *Sacred Economics*, the money system itself rests on a deeper foundation: the dual myths of Separation and Ascent. How do you change the defining mythology of civilization?

I would like to propose that the reason our actions have been so manifestly unsuccessful in steering the world away from its present collision course is that we have not, generally speaking, been basing them on any true understanding.

I would not be writing this book if the Endangered Species Act, Clean Air Act, and Clean Water Act of the early 1970s had been followed by even more powerful legislation here and around the world. I would not be writing if our awakening to racism and social inequality in the 1960s had transformed our economic system. I would not be writing if the scientific realization of global warming had led to a swift reversal of fossil fuel consumption in 1980 (rather than its continued growth). The ruin of planet and people has not halted nor even slowed down. Whatever strategies and tactics we have used have not worked. The fire extinguisher hasn't put out the inferno, nor has our shouting from the rooftops drawn much of a fire brigade.

It is quite natural to first apply familiar solutions to new problems. Perhaps only their failure awakens us to the idea that the problems are of a different nature than we supposed. In any event, we are arriving, many of us, at that place of not knowing what to do.

I have perhaps oversimplified things a bit. It is not that we spend half our lives in benighted impotence until we awaken to true understanding, purpose, and creative power. Instead, we go through phases when we believe in what we are doing, when life more or less makes sense, and when we hope and expect our efforts to bear fruit. And they do, for a time, but as we grow in that world we begin to question our assumptions. Our tools don't work as well anymore; we cease believing in our goals or in the possibility of achieving them. We approach a resting phase, an empty phase. Immersed in a system that never lets us rest, that condemns laziness and pushes us toward ever-increasing busyness through economic pressure, we have trouble accepting this phase. We tell ourselves we must always be doing something. Time's a-wastin'!

None of this should be taken as a rejection of action or a call for passivity. There is a place in this world for effort, for urgency. What I have described is much like a birth process. From what I've witnessed in the birth of my children, when the time comes to push, the urge to push is unstoppable. Here is the very epitome of urgency. Between contractions the mother rests. Can you imagine saying to her, "Don't stop now! You have to make an effort. What happens if the urge doesn't arise again? You can't just *push when you feel like it!*"

"You can't just do whatever you feel like." "You can't just do anything you want." "You have to learn self-restraint." "You're only interested in gratifying your desires." "You don't care about anything but your own pleasure." Can you hear the judgmentality in these admonitions? Can you see how they reproduce the mentality of domination that runs our civilization? Goodness comes through conquest. Health comes through conquering bacteria. Agriculture is improved by eliminating pests. Society is made safe by winning the war on crime. On my walk today, students accosted me, asking if I wanted to join the "fight" against pediatric cancer. There are so many fights, crusades, campaigns, so many calls to overcome the enemy by force. No wonder we apply the same strategy to ourselves. Thus it is that the inner devastation of the Western psyche matches exactly the outer devastation it has wreaked upon the planet. Wouldn't you like to be part of a different kind of revolution?

Scarcity

The hardest thing of all is to find a black cat in a dark room,
especially if there is no cat.

—CONFUCIUS

*E*ven as the old world comes apart around us, or even as we leave it in disgust, still we carry its conditioning. We have been colonized through and through by the old Story of the World. We are born into its logic, acculturated to its worldview, and imbued with its habits. And all of this is so pervasive as to be nearly invisible. As the comment of the Dogon elder suggests, we take for granted the very things that are at the root of the crisis, helplessly replicating them in all we do.

Wisdom traditions, indigenous worldviews, and sacred stories help to illuminate some of this baggage we carry from the Age of Separation, just like the Dogon elder questioned the operating assumption of scarcity of time. As we become more attuned to a new way of seeing the world, the more we wish to rid ourselves of the burdensome habits of the old. Not only do they no longer resonate with who we are and who we are becoming, but we recognize that trapped by those habits, we cannot help but create the world in their image. To release the habits of separation is therefore more than an issue of self-cultivation; it is also crucial to our effectiveness as activists, healers, and changemakers.

As I will describe, changing these habits of seeing, thinking, and doing is no trivial matter. First, they must be made visible. Second, we must attempt the change in a way that is not itself among those habits—and so many of the ways we conceive and enact change draw from paradigms of conquest, judgment, and force. Third, we must deal with an environment that enforces the old habits, not only through economic and social means, but through a relentless barrage of subtle messaging that takes for granted the very things we are seeking to change.

The debate over debt reduction versus fiscal stimulus takes for granted economic growth as an unquestionable good. The question of immigration reform takes for granted the social conventions of borders and ID. Statistics on Third World poverty take for granted that money is a good measure of wealth. The choice of news stories on television implies that these are the most important, relevant things happening. Signs all over public space saying things like "Emergency brake. Penalty for misuse" imply that it is penalties that maintain social order, just as ubiquitous security cameras imply that people need to be watched. Above all, the normalcy of society's routines tells us that this way of life *is* normal.

For many people, the most powerful enforcer of the habits of separation is money. Usually, the actions that love inspires don't redound to our financial self-interest; to the contrary, it is money that often seems to thwart such actions. Is it prudent? Is it practical? Can you afford to? For other people the enforcer is a religious teaching, or social pressure, or the fear of family and friends. "It won't do any good." "It isn't safe." "It's weird."

You have probably experienced the old story's power to draw you back in. You have a transcendent experience of unity, flow, connection, compassion, or the miraculous, and see with total clarity how you will henceforward live in a different way. It could be the kind of experience people describe as spiritual, or maybe as mundane as fully realizing the impact of high-carbon lifestyles on the planet. It could be an inspirational book or seminar, a training in nonviolent communication, a course on yogic philosophy. In the days and weeks following the experience, you live effortlessly according to what you realized. Maybe you see everyone around you as an emanation of the divine. But after a while, what had been clear and effortless starts to require an effort to remind yourself, to recall the experience. You need discipline where you needed none before. You have to make a practice of seeing the divine in all, whereas it had been obvious and effortless. Or you start driving your car more again, making compromises. Life goes back to normal.

What is happening here is that usually, people cannot hold a new story by themselves. A story can be held only in community, which is why people seek to establish communities dedicated to spiritual ideas, sheltered from the corrosive influences of the dominant Story of the World. To some extent, we can do the same by surrounding ourselves with people who are living similar values.

No matter how strong it is, no external social or economic pressure would be able to keep us in the old story if it did not operate on something internal. More than anything external, it is our own habits that draw us back into the old story after we have glimpsed a new one. These habits run so deep that we are rarely aware of them; when we are, we usually assume them to be human nature. Many of them fall into one of three categories: habits of scarcity, habits of judgment, and habits of struggle. The next few chapters will elucidate some of these habits, their originating cultural and personal state of being, and the new habits of interbeing that can supplant them.

You will notice that many of the habits of separation are familiar. Injunctions against them abound in mainstream religious teachings as well as popular morality. That is because religion and culture both carry seeds of reunion. But we find these teachings hard to live up to because they are inconsistent with the dominant myths and structures of civilization. Thus they become rules: prohibitions, prescriptions, etc., and therefore agents of a prime habit of separation, which is to conquer the self. This is impossible to avoid. Immersed in a story that defines one as a discrete, separate individual in a world of other, surrounded by institutions like money that enact and enforce that story, teachings like the Golden Rule seem indeed to run counter to natural human behavior. For the separate self, selfishness seems to run counter to service.

No wonder, trying to reconcile the rules with the world we have lived in, religious authorities divided the universe into two realms, the earthly and the heavenly, the material and the spiritual. Yes, they conceded, the material world is sinful, and our bodies, being of that world, are sinful as well, but there is something else, another world with different rules. To live according to those, we have to resist the ways of the material world and the flesh.

Please notice any tendency you may have to apply the program of self-conquest to the habits of separation that I will describe. There is a different way.

❧

Scarcity is one of the defining features of modern life. Around the world, one in five children suffers from hunger. We fight wars over scarce resources such as oil. We have depleted the oceans of fish and the ground of clean water. Worldwide, people and governments are cutting back, making do with less, because of a scarcity of money. Few would deny that we live in an era of scarce resources; many would say it is dangerous to imagine otherwise.

On the other hand, it is not hard to see that most of this scarcity is artificial. Consider food scarcity: vast amounts, as much as 50 percent of production by some estimates, is wasted in the developed world. Vast areas of land are devoted to producing ethanol, vaster areas still are devoted to America's number one cultivated species: lawn grass. Meanwhile, land that is devoted to food production is typically farmed by chemical-intensive, machine-dependent methods that are actually less productive (per hectare, not per unit of labor) than labor-intensive organic agriculture and permaculture.[1]

Similarly, scarcity of natural resources is also an artifact of our system. Not only are our production methods wasteful, but much of what

---

1. See Chapter 2 of *Sacred Economics* and my article "Permaculture and the Myth of Scarcity" for a more thorough discussion with references.

is produced does little to further human well-being. Technologies of conservation, recycling, and renewables languish undeveloped. Without any real sacrifice, we could live in a world of abundance.

Perhaps nowhere is the artificiality of scarcity so obvious as it is with money. As the example of food illustrates, most of the material want in this world is due to lack not of anything tangible, but to lack of money. Ironically, money is the one thing we can produce in unlimited quantities: it is mere bits in computers. Yet we create it in a way that renders it inherently scarce, and that drives a tendency toward concentration of wealth, which means overabundance for some and scarcity for the rest.

Even wealth offers no escape from the perception of scarcity. A 2011 study of the superwealthy at Boston College's Center on Wealth and Philanthropy surveyed attitudes toward wealth among households with a net worth of $25 million or more (some much more—the average was $78 million). Amazingly, when asked whether they experienced financial security, most of the respondents said no. How much would it take to achieve financial security? They named figures, on average, 25 percent higher than their current assets.

If someone with $78 million in assets can experience scarcity, it obviously has much deeper roots than economic inequality. The roots are nowhere else than in our Story of the World. Scarcity starts in our very ontology, our self-conception, and our cosmology. From there, it infiltrates our social institutions, systems, and experience of life. A culture of scarcity immerses us so completely that we mistake it for reality.

The most pervasive, life-consuming form of scarcity is that of time. As the Dogon man exemplifies, "primitive" people generally don't experience a shortage of time. They don't see their days, hours, or minutes as numbered. They don't even have a concept of hours or minutes. "Theirs," says Helena Norberg-Hodge in describing rural Ladakh, "is a timeless world." I have read accounts of Bedouins content to do nothing but watch the sands of time pass, of Pirahã fully absorbed in watching a boat appear on the horizon and disappear hours later, of native people content to literally sit and watch the grass grow. This is a kind of wealth nearly unknown to us.

Scarcity of time is built in to the Story of Science that seeks to measure all things, and thereby renders all things finite. It delimits our existence to the boundaries of a single biographical timeline, the finite span of a separate self.

Scarcity of time also draws from the scarcity of money. In a world of competition, at any moment you could be doing more to get ahead. At any moment you have a choice whether to use your time productively. Our money system embodies the maxim of the separate self: more for you is less for me. In a world of material scarcity, you can never "afford" to rest at ease. This is more than a mere belief or perception: money as it exists today is not, as some teachings claim, "just energy"; at least it is not a neutral energy. It is always in short supply. When money is created as interest-bearing debt as ours is, then always and necessarily there will be more debt than there is money. Our systems mirror our collective perceptions.

"More for you is less for me" is a defining axiom of Separation. True in a competitive money economy, it is false in earlier gift cultures in which, because of widespread sharing, more for you was more for me. Scarcity conditioning extends far beyond the economic realm, manifesting as envy, jealousy, one-upmanship, social competitiveness, and more.

The scarcity of money, in turn, draws from the scarcity of love, intimacy, and connection. The foundational axiom of economics says as much: human beings are motivated to maximize rational self-interest. This axiom is a statement of separateness and, I hazard to say, loneliness. Everyone out there is a utility-maximizer, in it for themselves. You are alone. Why does this seem so true, at least to economists? Where does the perception and experience of aloneness come from? In part it comes from the money economy itself, which surrounds us with standardized, impersonal commodities divorced from their original matrix of relationships, and replaces communities of people doing things for themselves and each other with paid professional services. As I describe in *Sacred Economics*, community is woven from gifts. Gifts in various forms create bonds, because a gift creates gratitude: the desire to give in return or to give forward. A money transaction, in contrast, is over and done with once goods and cash have changed hands. Each party goes separate ways.

The scarcity of love, intimacy, and connection is also inherent in our cosmology, which sees the universe as composed of generic building blocks that are just things, devoid of sentience, purpose, or intelligence. It is also a result of patriarchy and its attendant possessiveness and jealousy. If one thing is abundant in the human world, it should be love and intimacy, whether sexual or otherwise. There are so many of us! Here like nowhere else is the artificiality of scarcity plain. We could be living in paradise.

Sometimes I lead a workshop activity that involves prolonged mutual gazing between two people. After the initial discomfort fades and the minutes go by, most people experience an ineffably sweet intimacy, a connection that penetrates through all the superficial posing and pretense that define daily interactions. These pretenses are much flimsier than we would like to think—they cannot withstand more than half a minute of real seeing, which is probably why it is rude to gaze into someone's eyes for more than a couple seconds. That is all the intimacy we typically allow ourselves. That is all the wealth we can handle right now. Sometimes, after the activity, I will observe to the group, "Can you imagine—all that bliss is available all the time, less than sixty seconds away, yet we go for years and years without it. Experiencing it every day, would people still want to shop? Drink? Gamble? Kill?"

How close is the more beautiful world our hearts know is possible? It is closer than close.

What need, beyond basic survival needs, is more important to a human being than to be touched, held, groomed, seen, heard, and loved? What things do we consume in futile compensation for the unfulfillment of these needs? How much money, how much power, how much control over other people does it take to meet the need for connection? How much is enough? As the above-mentioned Boston College study implies, no amount is enough. Remember that the next time you think greed is the culprit behind Gaia's woes.

I could go on to mention many other kinds of scarcity that are so normal in our society as to escape notice. Scarcity of attention. Scarcity of play. Scarcity of listening. Scarcity of dark and quiet. Scarcity of beauty. I live in a hundred-year-old house. What a contrast there is between the regular, factory-perfect commodity objects and buildings that environ us, and the old radiators in my house, clanking and hissing all night, with their curved iron, their irregular valves and connectors, made with a touch more care than they needed to be, that seem to possess a quality of life. I drive past the strip malls and big box stores, the parking lots and auto dealerships, office buildings and subdevelopments, each building a model of cost-efficiency, and I marvel, "After five thousand years of architectural development, we've ended up with *this*?" Here we see the physical expression of the ideology of science: Only the measurable is real. We have maximized our production of the measurable—the square feet, the productivity per labor unit—at the expense of everything qualitative: sacredness, intimacy, love, beauty, and play.

How much of the ugly does it take to substitute for a lack of the beautiful? How many adventure films does it take to compensate for a lack of adventure? How many superhero movies must one watch, to compensate for the atrophied expression of one's greatness? How much pornography to meet the need for intimacy? How much entertainment to substitute for missing play? It takes an infinite amount. That's good news for economic growth, but bad news for the planet. Fortunately, our planet isn't allowing much more of it, nor is our ravaged social fabric. We are almost through with the age of artificial scarcity, if only we can release the habits that hold us there.

From our immersion in scarcity arise the habits of scarcity. From the scarcity of time arises the habit of hurrying. From the scarcity of money comes the habit of greed. From the scarcity of attention comes the habit of showing off. From the scarcity of meaningful labor comes the habit of laziness. From the scarcity of unconditional acceptance comes the habit of manipulation. These are but examples—there are as many responses to each of these missing things as there are individuals.

Doing

*A*ll of these flavors of scarcity share a common root, a kind of existential scarcity for which I cannot find a name. It is a scarcity of being, the feeling "I am not enough" or "There is not enough life." Born of the cutoff of our extended selves that inter-exist with the rest of the universe, it never lets us rest. It is a consequence of our alienation, our abandonment to a dead, purposeless universe of force and mass, a universe in which we can never feel at home, a universe in which we are never held by an intelligence greater than our own, never part of an unfolding purpose. Even more than the scarcity of time or money, it is this existential unease that drives the will to consume and control.

The primary habit that arises from it is the habit of always doing. Here and now is never enough. You might protest that most people in the Western world spend vast amounts of time doing nothing productive at all, watching TV and playing video games, but these are displacements of doing, and not nondoing.

I am not saying that it is bad to do. I am saying that there is a time to do, and a time not to do, and that when we are slave to the habit of doing we are unable to distinguish between them. As I mentioned earlier, the time to do is when you know what to do. When you don't know what to do, and act anyway, you are probably acting out of habit.

Let's not get too caught up in the word "do"—obviously, the distinction between doing and not doing breaks down under close scrutiny. Perhaps an example will make my meaning clearer. I recently participated in a daylong meeting of about thirty activists from around the world, gathered around the issue of localism. We'd all been speakers at a conference. The day started with a conversation that, after an hour or two, started to touch on some deep issues of how to create change. But then some of us were uncomfortable with what we perceived as "just talking" (or was it that we were uncomfortable with the deeper things we were touching?), so we split up into task-centered groups to "do something." Part of our group consciousness believed that if we didn't produce an action plan, a statement, or something tangible from the day, it would have been a waste. As it turned out, it was the afternoon that felt like the waste, and the morning that felt productive—despite the fact that nothing got "done." Perhaps the problem was that we had rushed into an attempt to "do" before the group as an entity was mature. We acted from a habit of urgency. Again, that is not to say we should never make plans, organize task groups, delegate work, or engage in linear, step-by-step thinking. It is that we need to acquire sensitivity to when it is the right time to do these things.

We are like a man lost in a maze. He runs around frantically, hitting the same dead ends again and again, repeatedly circling back to his starting point. Finally he pauses to rest, to breathe, to ponder. Then in a flash he understands the logic of the maze. Now it is time to begin walking. Imagine if instead he says, "No, I cannot pause to rest. Only by moving my feet will I ever get anywhere. So I must not stop moving my feet." We tend to devalue those periods of pause, emptiness, silence, and integration.

How to get out of a maze? Yes, it does help to wander around and explore, but at some point one must stop and reflect. Is there a pattern to my wanderings? What do I remember about how I got lost here in the first place? What is this maze for, anyway? Perhaps the earlier stage of panicked, frantic running around, or of increasingly futile action, is necessary, but many of us are now ready to try another way.

The situation on Earth today is too dire for us to act from habit—to reenact again and again the same kinds of solutions that brought us to our present extremity. Where does the wisdom to act in entirely new ways come from? It comes from nowhere, from the void; it comes from inaction. When we see it, we realize it was right in front of us all along. It is never far away; yet at the same time it is in a different universe—a different Story of the World. A Chinese saying describes it well: "As far away as the horizon, and right in front of your face." You can run toward it forever, run faster and faster, and never get any closer. Only when you stop do you realize you are already there. That is exactly our collective situation right now. All of the solutions to the global crisis are sitting right in front of us, but they are invisible to our collective seeing, existing, as it were, in a different universe.

When we are trapped in a story, we can only do the things that that story can recognize. Often we are aware of being trapped (the old story is ending) but don't have access to any alternative (we haven't yet inhabited a new story). Leaders in social and environmental organizations feel trapped in the confines of the fund-raiser, the membership campaign, the press release, and the white paper. A new outrage looms. What to do? Send out another appeal? On every level, our solutions are less and less effectual, but our story allows no alternative.

The same might be said for the monetary authorities' response to financial crisis, and more generally to governments everywhere. In most places, the political system is frozen into increasingly irrelevant debates, in which real solutions aren't even on the table. In the U.S., amid the wrangling over troop levels, withdrawal timetables, and so on, where is the call to withdraw from all military bases worldwide and dismantle the standing army entirely? It is not part of the conversation.[1] Of course, for it to enter the conversation would require the rejection

---

1. Except of course on the fringes. It is not, as far as I know, one of the options that those in government are talking about.

of deeply held myths about the way the world works, the causes of war and terrorism, the real goals of American foreign policy, and so on, all the way down to our notions of good and evil. If one has not questioned these myths, then a call to disband the military would seem laughably naive.

Similarly, where in the universe of political dialogue on agricultural policy is the idea of a large-scale transition to permaculture, involving big gardens where lawns are today, a repopulation of rural land, humanure composting, and the therapeutic benefits of reconnecting to the soil? This could sequester carbon back into the soil, end the eutrophication of waterways, replenish aquifers, and reverse desertification. It would provide meaningful work to millions who are looking for it, drastically reduce fossil fuel use—and produce more food on less land, allowing wild ecosystem restoration.

It takes some doing to document these claims. Many authorities state categorically, "The only way to feed seven billion people on this planet is with massive fossil fuel inputs." To refute this claim requires deconstructing its basic assumptions about agriculture and diet. How many of them take into account (to use one example of hundreds) crops like the Mayan bread nut, which in the tropics can produce eight times the caloric yield of corn per hectare with superior nutrition and storability, can be collected in vast quantities with minimal labor, requires no pesticides, only needs to be planted once, is drought-resistant, provides fodder for goats and cows, and can be used as an overstory crop with vegetables, aquaculture, etc., underneath? This tree has been cut down all over Central America to make room for corn.[2]

---

2. I have chosen here an example that conflicts with current paradigms only mildly. I could also discuss Schauberger-inspired water practices, homeopathic soil preparations, the methods used at Findhorn, or Machaelle Small Wright's work with nature devas. But then, those of you who are prepared to accept Mayan bread nuts but not water intelligence or nature devas might doubt the rest of what I have to say too—guilt by association. Now, now, I don't really believe in those things, do I? Joking aside, the truth is that I would like to believe them, but still need help to effectively inhabit those stories. When I tried supplicating the nature devas, a groundhog ate every vegetable in my garden anyway.

Clearly, a transition to crops like Mayan bread nuts and hundreds of other underutilized food species cannot happen without accompanying cultural and economic changes. The globalization of food culture, media images that perpetrate an industrial diet, the cultural narrative that holds agricultural work as lowly, the financial system that pushes farmers toward commodity crop production, regulations that take existing agricultural practices for granted, and the pecuniary interests of seed and pesticide companies all contribute to the agricultural status quo. The very notion of a uniform crop growing on a controlled substrate draws from scientific paradigms of a generic material substrate of uniform elements upon which we impose order and design.

That's a lot of stories, layer upon layer, that have to change. Thus I say that our revolution must go all the way to the bottom, all the way down to our basic understanding of self and world. We will not survive as a species through more of the same: better breeds of corn, better pesticides, the extension of control to the genetic and molecular level. We need to enter a fundamentally different story. That is why an activist will inevitably find herself working on the level of story. She will find that in addition to addressing immediate needs, even the most practical, hands-on actions are telling a story. They come from and contribute to a new Story of the World.

Nondoing

The problems we experience in our lives and in the world (whether relationship issues or world hunger) stem from energetic weakness and disconnection, from our lack of capacity to feel ourselves, each other, the earth, and how life seeks to move and evolve through us. The issue is not whether or not to act and "do something," but what actually prompts us to act.

—DAN EMMONS

Before they are able to enter a new story, most people—and probably most societies as well—must first navigate the passage out of the old. In between the old and the new there is an empty space. It is a time when the lessons and learnings of the old story are integrated. Only when that work has been done is the old story really complete. Then, there is nothing, the pregnant emptiness from which all being arises. Returning to essence, we regain the ability to act from essence. Returning to the space between stories, we can choose from freedom and not from habit.

A good time to do nothing is any time you feel stuck. I have done a lot of nothing in the writing of this book. For several days I was trying to write the conclusion, spinning my wheels, turning out tawdry rehashes of earlier material. The more I did, the worse it got. So I finally gave up the effort and just sat there on the couch, a baby strapped to my chest, mentally traveling through the book I had written, but with no agenda whatever of figuring out what to write. It was from that empty place that the conclusion arose, unbidden.

Do not be afraid of the empty place. It is the source we must return to if we are to be free of the stories and habits that entrap us.

If we are stuck and do not choose to visit the empty place, eventually we will end up there anyway. You may be familiar with this process on a personal level. The old world falls apart, but the new has not emerged. Everything that once seemed permanent and real is revealed as a kind of hallucination. You don't know what to think, what to do; you don't know what anything means anymore. The life trajectory you had plotted out seems absurd, and you can't imagine another one. Everything is uncertain. Your time frame shrinks from years to this month, this week, today, maybe even to the present moment. Without the mirages of order that once seemed to protect you and filter reality, you feel naked and vulnerable, but also a kind of freedom. Possibilities that didn't even exist in the old story lie before you, even if you have no idea how to get there. The challenge in our culture is to allow yourself to be in that space, to trust that the next story will emerge when the time in between has ended, and that you will recognize it. Our culture wants us to move on, to do. The old story we leave behind, which is usually part of the consensus Story of the People, releases us with great reluctance. So please, if you are in the sacred space between stories, allow yourself to be there. It is frightening to lose the old structures of security, but you will find that even as you might lose things that were unthinkable to lose, you will be okay. There is a kind of grace that protects us in the space between stories. It is not that you won't lose your marriage, your money, your job, or your health. In fact, it is very likely that you will lose one of these things. It is that you will discover that even having lost that, you are still okay. You will find yourself in closer contact to something much more precious, something that fires cannot burn and thieves cannot steal, something that no one can take and cannot be lost. We might lose sight of it sometimes, but it is always there waiting for us. This is the resting place we return to when the old story falls apart. Clear of its fog, we can now receive a true vision of the next world, the next story, the next phase of life. From the marriage of this vision and this emptiness, a great power is born.

I wrote, "Possibilities that didn't even exist in the old story lie before you, even if you have no idea how to get there." This is a pretty good description of a place we are approaching collectively. Those of us who have in various ways left the old Story of the People are the organs of perception of the collective human body. When civilization as a whole enters the space between stories, then it will be ready to receive these visions, these technologies and social forms of interbeing.

Civilization is not quite there yet. At the present moment most people still tacitly believe that the old solutions will work. A new president is elected, a new invention announced, an uptick in the economy proclaimed, and hope springs anew. Maybe things will go back to normal. Maybe the Ascent of humanity will resume. Today it is still possible, without too strenuous an effort of denial or pretense, to imagine that we are just in a rough patch. We can get through it, if only we discover some new sources of oil, build more infrastructure to ignite economic growth, solve the molecular puzzle of autoimmunity, deploy more drones to protect us from terrorism and crime, genetically engineer crops for higher yields, and put white colorant in cement to reflect the sun's rays and slow global warming.

Given that all of these efforts are likely to produce unintended consequences even worse than the problems they intend to solve, it is not hard to see the wisdom of doing nothing. As I will describe later, this does not imply that the activist should focus on obstruction. Doing nothing arises naturally from the breakdown of the story that had motivated the old doings, calling us therefore to do what we can to hasten that story's demise.

My brother, whose clarity of mind is relatively pristine because he rarely reads anything written after 1900, described to me his vision of how the changeover will finally manifest. A bunch of bureaucrats and leaders will be sitting around wondering what to do about the new financial crisis. All the usual central bank policies, bailouts, interest rate cuts, quantitative easing, and so forth will be on the table, but the leaders just won't be able to bring themselves to deal with it. "Fuck it," they'll say. "Let's go fishing instead."

At some point, we are just going to have to stop. Just stop, without any idea of what to do. As I described with the examples of disarmament and permaculture, we are lost in a hellscape carrying a map that leads us in circles, with never a way out. To exit it, we are going to have to drop the map and look around.

As your old story came to an end, or comes to an end, do you find yourself contracting a case of the fuck-its? The procrastination, the laziness, the halfhearted attempts, the going through the motions—all indicate that the old story isn't motivating you anymore. What once made sense, makes sense no longer. You are beginning to withdraw from that world. Society does its best to persuade you to resist that withdrawal, which, when resisted, is called depression. Increasingly potent motivational and chemical means are required to keep us focused on what we don't want to focus on, to keep us motivated to do that which we don't care about. If fear of poverty doesn't work, then maybe psychiatric medication will. Anything to keep you participating in business as usual.

The depression that makes it impossible to vigorously participate in life as it is offered has a collective expression as well. Lacking a compelling sense of purpose or destiny, our society muddles along, going halfheartedly through the motions. "Depression" manifests in the economic sense, as the instrument of our collective will—money— stagnates. No longer is there enough of it to do anything grand. Like insulin in the insulin-resistant diabetic, the monetary authorities pump out more and more of it, to less and less effect. What would once have sparked an economic boom barely suffices now to keep the economy from grinding to a halt. Economic paralysis could indeed be the way this "stop" appears. But it could be anything that makes us give up our story and its enactments once and for all.

Doing nothing is not a universal suggestion; it is specific to the time when a story is ending and we enter the space between stories. I am drawing here from the Taoist principle of *wu-wei*. Sometimes translated as "nondoing," a better translation might be "noncontrivance" or "nonforcing." It means freedom from reflexive doing: acting when it is time to act, not acting when it is not time to act. Action is thus aligned with the natural movement of things, in service to that which wants to be born.

In this I draw inspiration from a beautiful verse from the *Tao Te Ching*. This verse is extremely dense, with multiple meanings and layers of meaning, and I haven't found a translation that highlights what I'm drawing from here. Therefore, the following is my own translation. It is the last half of verse 16—if you compare existing translations you will be astonished at how much they differ.

All things return to their root.
Returning to the root, there is stillness.
In stillness, true purpose returns.
This is what is real.
Knowing the real, there is clarity.
Not knowing the real, foolish action brings disaster.
From knowing the real comes spaciousness,
From spaciousness comes impartiality,
From impartiality comes sovereignty,
From sovereignty comes what is natural.
What comes naturally, is the Tao.
From the Tao comes what is lasting,
Persisting beyond one's self.

Attention

What most needs attention is the part of us that we seek to avoid feeling.
When we have tended to that, we are changed, and the world changes with us.

—DAN EMMONS

*L*et me offer you an example from my own inner monologue that illustrates nondoing as an active principle. I dropped off my car one morning for state inspection and, rather than ask my then-pregnant wife Stella to wake up early to pick me up, walked the five or six miles home. Now let me be clear that this was no hardship at all—I love walking, I was wearing comfortable shoes, and the weather was cold but clear. But as I walked, I started thinking, "Gee, this is taking a long time. I wonder how I can milk this. I know, when I get home I'll make a little show of being more tired and hungry than I am so that Stella thinks I underwent a hardship for her sake. Then she'll be extra nice to me."

That seemed a bit obvious, so I came up with a better idea. "I can put on a brave face and say I'm not tired or hungry, but subtly signal that I am. Then I will get credit not only for having made a sacrifice for her, but also for valiantly trying to keep it secret."

Recognizing both of these plans as habits of separation (scarcity of love, needing to manipulate and control, exercising psychological force against an "other" who would otherwise just look out for herself), I decided not to implement them. That was when Plan C arose. I would keep my tiredness secret for real. I would bear it in silence and not indulge in puerile machinations. But wait, that's no good: I'd be acting the part of the martyr, still a habit of separation because it valorizes struggle and cuts me off both from Stella and from gratitude. On to Plan D: I would be someone who has gotten past all that. Then I would be able to approve of myself and—would I smugly look down on others who still do such things? No!—I would tolerantly, nonjudgmentally allow others their own journey.

Unfortunately, I quickly realized that that too was coming from Separation. Why am I so anxious to prove myself good, to meet some standard of virtue? That comes from a kind of scarcity too. In Reunion, love and acceptance of self is natural, a default state. Even positive self-judgment is still judgment; it is conditional approval.

That led to Plan E. I would use this opportunity to take a sober inventory of my habits of separation and put them behind me. I would be someone who is seriously working on himself, someone who has no time for self-pity, self-praise, judgment, or any other frivolity that would impede the important work at hand. Oops. Here I am constructing a pretty self-image that I can like. More separation.

Maybe as a last-ditch plan I could feel ashamed of myself for all of these plans, and therefore earn absolution because at least I feel disgusted with myself. Actually I didn't consider that one, but you are welcome to try it if you like.

Such sequences of realizations are, I am told, common among meditators, who will then marvel at how sneaky the ego is in trying to get something for itself. Hey, I have an idea. Having gotten past fighting the ego or being disgusted with it, we can at least shake our heads in rueful bemusement, as if in humility at the enormous task before us about which we have no pretenses. That would be mature, wouldn't it?

All of these plans went through my mind in about fifteen seconds. I ended up implementing none of them. (Well, maybe a bit of Plan A—you'll have to ask Stella.) It wasn't because I came up with a Plan F though, to not implement any of them. I simply didn't implement them. It wasn't a choice at all in the usual sense.

One of the more subtle habits of the old story is the goal-oriented attempt to seek self-improvement by carrying out a plan. We might unconsciously apply that technique even toward the goal of leaving behind the habits of the old story, but if we do, we will continue re-enacting it on a subtle level. Reading over my account above, I see that my description implies that I rejected each plan because it represented a habit of separation, but that is misleading. It isn't as if I go through my day vigilantly parsing my motivations to make sure I winnow out anything coming from separation. Rather, I note their association with separation in order to help clarify how each choice feels and where it is coming from.

Do I then base my choice on that? No! It is almost accurate to say, "I make my choices based on what feels good," but not quite. That makes it look like I am advancing a principle about choice-making: choose what feels good. I have advocated such a principle in earlier books, because of the way it breaks down the habit of self-rejection by embracing pleasure as an ally. Nonetheless, it still implies that the way to choose is to consciously weigh two alternatives, evaluate which feels better, and then through an act of will choose that one.

What if we are fooling ourselves when we think we are making our choices according to one or another principle? What if the choices are really coming from somewhere else, and all the reasons we cite for the choice are actually rationalizations? In fact, there is a lot of social psychology research that demonstrates precisely this. Unconscious motives of social conformity, self-image, coherence with belief systems, valida-tion of group norms and worldviews, and so on demonstrably wield a far greater influence than most people suspect.[1]

These findings conform to certain spiritual teachings about the "automaticity of man," which say that most (though not necessarily all) apparent choices are not really choices, but are the automatic result

---

1. For some examples, see Jon Hanson and David Yosifon, "The Situation: An Intro-duction to the Situational Character, Critical Realism, Power Economics, and Deep Capture," *University of Pennsylvania Law Review* 152 (2003–2004): 129.

of choices made long ago. That does not mean that we should cease attempting to change ourselves or the world—as we shall see, it is quite the opposite—but it does suggest a very different approach to doing so.

So what do we do about it? What if you have habits of separation like mine and you want to change them? So many personal empowerment seminars conclude with some kind of declaration of the new you and affirmation of personal responsibility and choice, but over time many people find that the old habits are much stronger than they seemed at that moment of declaration. You might say, "I choose now and forever to respond with loving patience to my children" or "Who I am is courageous nonjudgment"; you might join a work group where you "hold each other accountable"; and when you find yourself doing the very things you forswore or living from old patterns, you feel deep chagrin or shame, and you resolve anew to hold to your word. And you do, for a while, and feel good about yourself. It really isn't so different from someone on a diet. Willpower, and all the techniques of the motivational arsenal, only work temporarily unless something fundamental has changed. When that fundamental thing has changed we might give ourselves and our willpower the credit, but that is an illusion. We are used to giving the credit to force. That is what willpower encodes: a kind of psychological force to overcome an enemy: yourself.

Before I answer my question "What do we do about it?" I would like to explain why I think it is such an important question. I gave a rather petty example above: if I were in the habit of enacting Plan A, the result would be no worse than Charles Eisenstein having a rather infantile relationship to his wife. You probably know a lot of couples where the wife is a little bit too much like a mommy. Now don't you name names! Not exactly sexy, but not the end of the world either. But consider what it means for a healer, an activist, or anyone with high ideals to be unconsciously subject to petty ego motivations like those I described. Her activism would harbor a secret agenda. Her energy would be working at cross-purposes.

Whom do we serve? Do we truly serve the more beautiful world our hearts know is possible? Or is that just the banner under which we pursue our private agendas of approval-seeking, identity creation, self-approval, vanity, and self-justification? How much political discussion online is like a big game of "Look, I'm right! And they're wrong. How could they? How stupid. Aren't they awful? Aren't I good?" If our energy is divided, with the majority going toward selfish goals, then those are what we will achieve while nothing much else changes.

I want you to reread the last paragraph and see if you can do it from a story that does not generate any shame, indignation, or condemnation. It sounds like I leveled an awful accusation by using words like approval-seeking, vanity, and self-justification. So let us recognize where the need for these things comes from. They are the responses of a wounded person, cut off from the intimate connections that form a robust identity, and conditioned through conditional acceptance and rejection at a tender age to adopt a deep-seated self-rejection that leaves him ever hungry for approval. All of the habits of separation are symptoms, and only secondarily causes, of our present condition.

A second reason this is such an important question is that what is true on the individual level is also true on the collective. Our civilization is stuck in patterns that we seem helpless to alter. One need only look at the stirring pronouncements of the 1992 Rio Summit to see that. Organizations and nations routinely pursue policies that only a small fraction of their members support—or sometimes in the case of organizations, that *no one* supports. How is this possible? Certainly, part of the explanation has to do with the interests of the elites who wield financial and political power, but we must remember that this power comes ultimately from social agreements and not from the super powers of the rulers. Moreover, such things as global warming or the risk of thermonuclear war are not in the interest of the elites either. So we are back into the realm of self-deception. The question I am asking is "How can the body politic, the human species as a whole, change its destructive habits?" I investigate the question on the individual level, therefore, because it might have a metaphorical or more than metaphorical bearing on the collective level—as one would expect in a universe where self and other, macrocosm and microcosm, part and whole mirror each other.

The reason that (in this particular instance—you don't think I'd confess to you the times I *have* acted like a self-centered drama king now, do you?) I did not act from the habits of separation after my walk is not that I tried not to or chose not to. It is because of the attention I gave to the habits themselves and to the feelings underneath them. To give attention to a habit weakens its compulsion. To give attention to the condition underlying the habit robs it of its motivation. The feeling underlying all of my little plans was a kind of tender, helpless loneliness. I gave attention to these things without even having an agenda of stopping myself from acting on them. I trusted the power of attention to do its work. Maybe the result would be that I would adopt Plan A after all. I didn't worry about that.

What would have happened if, instead, I had noticed my secret plan to milk some benefits out of my trek, and then resolved to stop myself at all costs? What would have happened if I'd threatened myself with punishment (guilt, shame, self-castigation, verbal abuse by my inner voice saying, "What's wrong with you!") and motivated myself with rewards (self-approval, telling myself I was mature, better than Uncle Bob, etc.)? I can tell you what would have happened. I would have withheld from Plan A or B in the obvious ways, but I would have done it nonetheless in a way that gave my own conscious mind plausible deniability. Because if my goal is simply to pass the muster of my own inner judge, then that judge and other parts of me will conspire to arrange a verdict of innocent. I need not elaborate on we humans' capacity for self-deception. If the motive is self-approval, then self-approval we will get, even if it comes at the expense of everything beautiful.

That sounds alarming, doesn't it? My purpose here is not to scare you into making a change. Maybe I would if I could, but this is not the kind of change one can be scared into making. I could scare you into trying, perhaps, but the result would be the same as in my scheme of reward and threat above. No, this is the kind of change that happens when it is time for it to happen.

The habits of separation not only succumb to attention; they also seek out the attention they need for their passing, when their time has come. One way they seek attention is by creating situations, which can be quite humiliating, in which they are noticed. Another way is that another person mirrors them: the things in someone else that provoke our judgment often are within us as well. The mirroring might not be direct—for example, someone's constant anxiety about trivial things could mirror my own lack of attention to a big thing—but I have found there is usually something in me calling for attention through the triggering person. Another way a hidden habit reveals itself is through spiritual teachings or, especially, stories, which again hold a mirror up to our selves.

I am hoping that the stories and lists of habits of separation will bring some of you readers to a curious awareness of whichever of those habits resides within you. Please do not try to stop them by force. If you do try, it probably won't work; you will only deceive yourself. Indeed, it would be a habit of separation to respond with shame, chagrin, and the desire to turn over a new leaf when you notice a habit of separation. We are not on a quest here to become better and better people. "Being good" is part of the old story. It reflects an internalized approval-seeking originating in modern parenting, schooling, and religion. The quest to be good is part of the war against the self and the war against nature that it reflects.

Here is another paradox: We become better people only when we give up the quest to become better people. That quest can achieve only the appearance of what it seeks. None are as capable of evil as the self-righteous.[2] One amusing study showed participants packages of organic food or comfort food like brownies. Those shown the organic food displayed less empathy and made harsher moral judgments than those shown the comfort food. When you're honest with yourself that you want that brownie as much as the next person, naturally you'll be less judgmental. Studies like this are often interpreted so as to sound a call for humility. Unfortunately, humility is not something one can attain

---

2. Kendall J. Eskine, "Wholesome Foods and Wholesome Morals? Organic Foods Reduce Prosocial Behavior and Harshen Moral Judgments," *Social Psychological and Personality Science* (March 2013).

through hard work or an act of will. If we could, then we could also rightly take credit for our own humility. Be wary of those who strive for humility—usually what they achieve is a counterfeit of it that, in the end, fools no one but themselves. It might actually be more humble to be cheerfully immodest.

If you do notice the habit of self-righteousness, you know what to do: give it attention. Give attention to any feelings of embarrassment or frustration, *without intending to stop those feelings*. Let the attention you give your habits and the underlying feelings be as gentle as you can make it: loving, forgiving, and peaceful. You can even thank the habit for having done its job for so long, knowing that it is in a late stage of its life span and will soon pass on.

Now you may sometimes experience a very sudden and dramatic release of a habit. There is even a time for declarations and willpower. That would be when the unmistakable feeling arises strongly in you: "It is time for this to stop!" It is not an anguished feeling of wishing it would stop; it is a clear, direct perception that comes with confidence and a kind of finality. If you are blessed with such a feeling, you can put down those cigarettes, or that habit of showing off, or that habit of getting in the last word, and never pick it up again. But please do not imagine that you are therefore made of stronger spiritual fiber than the next person. I take that back—go ahead and imagine it. And notice yourself imagining it. And give attention to all the other ways in which you lobby your inner judge to render a verdict of "good girl" or "good boy," because this is one of the most damaging habits of separation there is.

You may be noticing that my answer to the question "What do we do about it?" is a bit paradoxical. Almost everything we put into the category of "doing" is itself a habit of separation, usually one of self-struggle, or otherwise drawing on some form of judgment. Really, the answer is "You are already doing something about it." This is hard for the mind of separation to grasp. It sounds like I am telling you to do nothing. And there is a time to do nothing, but sooner or later, from nothing doing comes, a natural impulse backed by one's full unconflicted energy. For some of you, I hope, reading this book has set a process in motion, or accelerated a process that began long ago. You will find yourself doing things and not doing things that were invisible to you before, or that seemed beyond your power.

When people ask me at talks for something practical, something to do, I sometimes feel as if they are asking me to insult them. It would be like a smoker asking, "What should I do about my smoking habit that is killing me?" hoping for me to say, "Stop smoking. You're going to have to try harder." We are no longer at a time when people don't know what the problems are. That was the 1970s. Few people knew about global environmental threats then. We are also no longer at a time when people don't know what the solutions are. That was the 1980s or '90s. Today the solutions are legion, on every level from the personal to the global, yet on every level, we are not enacting them. And we are helpless to enact them through the means we are used to. Isn't that obvious by now?

Sit for a moment with the thought "I don't have to do anything. The change I seek is already happening." Does that bring up the same feelings in you as it does in me? Feelings of scorn, a kind of swelling outrage, and a secret longing as for something too good to be true? The scorn and outrage say, "This is a recipe for complacency and therefore for disaster. If I give up my efforts, however feeble they admittedly are, then there is no hope whatever." They also tap into the deep unease that comes from a worldview that casts us into a purposeless, insentient universe. In that world of force, if you don't *make* something happen, nothing will happen. You can never let go and trust. Yet there is that secret longing too, that wants to do just that. Will it be okay? Or will the hostility of the universe that our ideology has taught us and that our society has reified once again exploit our vulnerability?

Yes, it is scary to not do, or rather, to not impose doing. Most of us have grown up in a society that trains us, from kindergarten or even earlier, to do things we don't really want to do, and to refrain from things we do want to. This is called discipline, the work ethic, self-control. Since the dawn of the Industrial Revolution at least, it has been seen as a cardinal virtue. After all, most of the tasks of industry were not anything a sane human being would willingly do. To this day, most of the tasks that keep society *as we know it* running are the same. Lured by future rewards, chastened by punishment, we face the grim necessity of work. This would all be defensible, perhaps, if this work were truly necessary, if it were contributing to the well-being of people and planet. But at least 90 percent of it is not.[3] Part of our revolution is the reunion of work and play, work and art, work and leisure, of have to and want to.

Our discomfort with a teaching like "You don't have to do anything" comes in part from our thorough indoctrination into the work ethic, which holds that without the discipline of doing, nothing gets done. If there were no grades hanging over their heads, no paycheck at the end of the week, and no internalized habit of work such devices have created, then most people wouldn't keep doing what they do. Only those who work for the love of it would continue—only those whose work gave them a palpable sense of service, of contribution, or of meaning. In preparation for such a world, and to prepare such a world, let us cultivate the corresponding habit: in whatever way makes sense, let us practice trusting the impulse to work, and when it is not present, let us hold each other through the panic, uncertainty, and guilt that may arise.

You may have recognized the discomfort underneath "You don't have to do anything" as akin to the cynicism that challenges our belief that a more beautiful world is possible, or our belief that even the warlords and corporate CEOs have a desire to serve that world, or that our personal choices have planetary significance. All come from the same wound of Separation. You can't be trusted. I can't be trusted. They

---

3. As I argue in depth in *Sacred Economics*, discussing how local, peer-to-peer, decentralized, and ecological production methods have an added benefit of involving work that is less tedious and more meaningful. Consider for example the difference between assembly line work to make throwaway goods and repair work for well-designed durable products. Consider the difference between monocrop farming and small-scale gardening. Between being a hotel maid and running a bed-and-breakfast or hosting a couchsurfer. Of course, some tedious tasks will remain, but these take on a different character when they are not an economic necessity, eight hours a day, five days a week, year in and year out.

can't be trusted. What I know in my heart can't be trusted. There is no purpose, no unfolding wholeness, no intelligence in the universe outside ourselves. We are alone in an alien universe.

I will leave this topic with a paradox. You don't have to do anything—why? Not because nothing needs to be done. It is that you don't *have* to do, because you *will* do. The unstoppable compulsion to act, in bigger and wiser ways than you knew possible, has already been set in motion. I am urging you to trust in that. You needn't contrive to motivate yourself, guilt yourself, or goad yourself into action. Actions taken from that place will be less powerful than the ones that arise unbidden. Trust yourself that you will know what to do, and that you will know when to do it.

Because our habits of self-forcing are so deep-seated and often quite subtle, it might help to have a way to distinguish where your actions are coming from. Sometimes it is not clear to me if I have done something out of a direct, uncontrived desire to serve, or if the real motive was to show myself or others that I am good, to confirm my membership in an in-group, to avoid self-censure or the censure of others, or to fulfill my duty as an ethical person. I find, though, that there is a lot more pleasure in the former. Because the desire to give is a primal expression of the life-force, actions taken in the gift bring a feeling of being fully alive. That's the feeling to look for.

In case you think that this advice belongs in a self-help book only, let me share with you a story from my friend Filipa Pimentel, a leader in the Transition Town movement, who has applied this principle in an activist setting. She was involved in a Transition initiative in one of the most depressed regions of Portugal, itself mired in an economic depression with 25 percent unemployment. The group was suffering a lot of pressure, feeling burned out, thinking nothing they were doing was nearly enough, wanting to retreat inward in the face of the overwhelming enormity of the crisis and the need.

One day, she said, they had to admit that the group was collapsing. The main flame holders had a long discussion and after many hours came to the following consensus:

- They would look after each other, caring and protecting, and if one is not doing well, the others would surround this person;
- Their initiatives would have to come from a pure intention, generosity;
- They would continuously look into their personal development, supported by the group; and most importantly,
- That everything they do must come from pleasure, real desire, and their epiphanies. They decided not to engage in sacrifice, nor to prioritize action based on what someone says is most urgent.

This last principle was a response to a situation in which one of the core team was organizing an activity relating to swaps. Maybe it was just a drop in the bucket given the town's huge unmet needs, but she was having fun and really stretching her comfort zone. Then some people in the network began criticizing the project. It was inefficient. It should be a secondhand market, not just trading, because the impact would be much bigger that way. Soon she was questioning, "Is this really going to make a difference?" and became discouraged and paralyzed. In their meeting, they realized, as Filipa puts it, "This town needs a world of things to happen, a gift exchange, a secondhand market, a farmers' market—all these things need to exist. We can't do it all. But just because we can't do everything, doesn't mean we shouldn't do something." So they choose now by what connects them, and what gives them pleasure. She says, "This is the first criterion when we are looking to an enormous list of things that can be done, most probably most necessary. When somebody is showing signs of distress and tiredness in organizing a specific activity we always ask—do you feel connected with what you are doing? Does it make you happy or do you feel that you need to sacrifice for it? If this feels like 'work,' stop it!"

Doing only what makes them feel good, only what makes them feel connected, only what doesn't feel like work . . . does that mean they get less done than when they were driven by urgency and seeking to be more efficient? No. They get more done. Filipa says, "The group is much more cohesive; there is freedom in expressing our feelings without being on the spot or feeling that we are responsible for all the negative stuff. I feel that, in a way, with the people near me and myself, it is much easier to give ourselves to what we do without fear, with true joy and with a feeling of belonging. Somehow, I feel that the others around the group sense that and a lot of 'situations' are unblocked—if the group does not flow, things tend to get stuck at one point. Since then, we do much more, in a much more positive way."

Wouldn't you like to do much more, and in a more positive way? Dare you stop doing what feels like work? How much more effective will you be when you "give yourself to what you do with true joy and a feeling of belonging"?

Not that there is anything wrong with work. Work and play, work and leisure . . . it is time to question these polarities. That doesn't mean indolence. When I worked in construction, the labor was sometimes very strenuous, but it was rarely an ordeal. I didn't have the feeling of fighting myself or forcing myself. There is a time to make great efforts, a time to push one's capacities to the limit. We have after all been given those capacities for a reason. But struggle is not supposed to be the default state of life.

The same applies to spiritual practice. You may have also noticed that my recipe for releasing the habits of separation corresponds quite closely with Buddhist teachings and practices of mindfulness. Ah, finally, something to do! Now we can all embark on a heroic effort at mindfulness. We can admire those (especially ourselves, who if not as mindful as, say, Thich Nhat Hanh are at least more mindful than most people, right?) who are more mindful and look with disdain or patronizing indulgence at those who are less. We can use all the same psychological apparati toward a new goal: mindfulness.

I hope after having read this far you are a bit suspicious of this plan. Could it be that mindfulness too comes as a gift, when circumstances make us newly mindful of what had been beneath the threshold of our awareness? I urge you to see mindfulness as a gift and to cherish it as such. Fully accept that gift, indulge in it. Perhaps the path to mindfulness is not one of a fierce mustering of the will. We cannot will the exercise of will—volition too comes as a gift.

Struggle

When is the right time to do the right thing? No one can offer a formula to answer that question, because the rhythm of the phases of action and stillness has an intelligence of its own. If we tune in, we can hear that rhythm, and the organ of perception is the desire, the nudge of excitement or the feeling of flow, of rightness, of alignment. It is a feeling of being alive. To listen to that feeling and to trust it is a profound revolution indeed. What would the world be, if we all listened to that?

This kind of deep self-trust highlights the common habit of separation that is its opposite: the habit of struggle. In the old story, just as humanity as a whole is destined to conquer and rise above nature, so are we as individuals charged to conquer and rise above that bit of nature that we call the body, including pleasure, desire, and every physical limitation. Virtue comes from self-denial, willpower, discipline, self-sacrifice. Mirroring the war against nature, this war against the self can have only one result: you lose.

A corollary principle of self-struggle is to elevate anything that is hard and devalue anything that comes easy. It is therefore also a habit of scarcity and of ingratitude. Imagine you are a practitioner of meditation and someone asks you, "What do you do?" You reply, "Well, I sit on a cushion and pay attention to my breath." The questioner says, "That's all? What's so hard about that?" "Oh," you say, offended, "it's really hard!" Being hard validates it. To do it, you have to overcome something in yourself; you have to prevail in some kind of struggle.

I realize that the paradigm of struggle is something that quickly falls by the wayside as one pursues the practice of meditation. Maintaining focus on the breath cannot happen through forcing, but only through allowing. In fact, it is extremely easy; our habit of making things hard is what gets in the way. Nonetheless, we often use "easy" as a term of disparagement, as in "She took the easy way out."

The belief that goodness comes through sacrifice and struggle goes back thousands of years—but only thousands of years. It is the defining mentality of agriculture: only if ye sow, shall ye reap. The ancient peasant had to learn to overcome the immediate urges of the body for the sake of a distant future reward. Just as it takes a lot of work to overcome nature (for example by clearing fields, pulling weeds, etc.) so also does it take work to overcome human nature: the desire perhaps to play, to sing, to roam, to create, and to seek food only when hungry. Agricultural life requires sometimes overcoming these desires.

In tracing the deep roots of this programming, I fear I am overstating the case. The transition from hunting and gathering to agriculture was not a sudden rupture, either in lifestyle or in psychology. Foragers are not without forethought; they might move to a food-rich area or go on a hunt even if they are not at that very moment hungry. And small-scale farmers enjoy plenty of leisure, and their work need not be tedious or exhausting or anxiety-driven. Gardening, many of us know, can be a pleasure and a joy. So really the origin of the valorization of self-conquest probably came later, with the first "builder" civilizations. Their high degree of division of labor, standardization of tasks, hierarchy, and other regimentation necessitated the virtues of discipline, obedience, sacrifice, and the work ethic.

These civilizations developed the conceptual and organizational basis for the Industrial Revolution, which took division of labor, standardization of processes, and the attendant degradation, exploitation, and tedium to new heights. It was then as well that the values of the machine achieved their full expression. Society required millions of people to do very hard things indeed. We devised numerous institutions to compel ourselves to sacrifice the present for the future. Religion taught us to do that: renounce and overcome fleshly desires for the sake of a heavenly reward in the afterlife. School taught us to do that, conditioning us to perform tedious tasks we really don't care about for the sake of an external future reward. And, most of all, money taught us to do that, or, more often, compelled us to do that, through the devices of interest and debt. The former tempts the investor to forgo immediate gratification (or generosity) for the sake of even more in the future. The latter *compels* the equivalent of the debtor.

These social institutions reified the struggle contained in our basic scientific paradigms. Not only in Darwinian biology with its struggle to survive, but in physics as well with the doomed and endless struggle against entropy embodied in the Second Law of Thermodynamics, we reside in a hostile universe in which we must overcome natural forces and carve out a realm of security, and apply force to impose our design on a purposeless, disorderly jumble.

You can see how intertwined are the habits of scarcity and the habits of struggle. On the economic level, it is scarcity that motivates and compels sacrifice. On the psychological level, the need to validate oneself through (paradoxically) self-conquest comes itself from another form of scarcity: "I'm not good enough." And both scarcity and struggle are implicit in our basic concept of being. The separate self can never have enough: never enough power to stave off every threat from the arbitrary, merciless forces of nature; never enough money to ensure against every possible misfortune; never enough security to defeat death, which, for the separate self, means total annihilation. At the same time, in striving for money, power, and security at the expense of other beings, the separate self is essentially evil; only by self-conquest, self-sacrifice, can it act in the interests of other beings. In the face of this desolation, it is easy to see the appeal of an otherworldly realm of spirit, a place where our perpetual sacrifice is redeemed.

In this world, the world of Separation, the sacrifice is indeed perpetual. The debtor lives it. The investor leverages it. The schoolboy learns it. When will we wake up from that delusion and enjoy life?

The awakening will be profound, because the habit of struggle is woven so intricately into modern life that we hardly distinguish it from reality itself. We take it for granted that if one doesn't exercise some self-restraint, then both oneself and society will suffer. It sure does seem that if you don't restrain your appetite for food, you will become overweight; that if you don't limit your propensity to lounge around, you will never get anything done; that if you give free rein to your temper, you will yell at people; and so on. Desire is not to be trusted! What if your desire is to eat a dozen donuts? Go on an alcoholic bender? Sleep in every day until noon? Shout and hit and rape and kill? Well, maybe you are better than some people—maybe you don't have a desire to do those things. Or maybe you exercise more self-restraint. More than the obese, the addicts, the criminals, the child abusers, the murderers.

A later chapter will deal with the habit of judgment that, among other things, holds oneself different from and superior to those who are slaves to their desires. Here I want to meet head-on the perception that it is unrestrained desire that destroys our lives and, in the form of consumerism and greed, is destroying the rest of life on Earth. It sure can seem that way. It behooves us to be suspicious of that appearance, though, simply because of how seamlessly it fits in with the internalized War on Nature and the Story of Control. Is there another way to understand it that doesn't invoke a war against the self?

One time after a talk in England a young woman asked me if I flew around giving a lot of speeches. "Yes," I replied.

She then asked, "How do you justify that?"

"What do you mean?"

She began to explain about the carbon footprint of air travel, at which point I interrupted, "Oh, I don't justify it. I do it because it makes me feel alive, it gives me pleasure. I do it because I like it." I went on to say, "Now I could concoct a justification if you like. Maybe I could say that I believe the overall effect of my flying and speaking, which sometimes changes the course of people's lives, outweighs the carbon dioxide produced as a result of my air travel. Maybe some people will hear me and choose a career in permaculture rather than tax law. Maybe they will have the courage to live a life that will contribute to an ecological society. But even though I think this is true, I would be lying to you if I said that is my justification. The real reason, the truth, is that I do it because I like it."

The woman was aghast. "You are completely amoral," she said. "By that logic, you could do anything you like, just because you feel like it. You could justify eating animal flesh, sacrificing the life of a sentient being for the sake of some transitory mouth pleasure. You could justify murder, if you 'felt like doing it.' Surely you can't be serious. You can't be telling people to just *do whatever they want!*"

"Yes, that is exactly what I am doing," I answered. The conversation proceeded no further, but I will continue it now. It will become clear that "Do whatever you want" very quickly leads to the realization that we do not actually know what we want. And, what we have been told about the natural objects of desire is a fiction.

What, exactly, is the problem with doing whatever I want, or doing whatever feels good? Why do we make a virtue of self-restraint?

If what we want is destructive to self and others, then indeed it would be awful to encourage people to just do what they want. If John Calvin was right about the total depravity of man, if human progress is indeed an ascent from a state of bestial savagery, if nature is at bottom a war of each against all and human nature is to win that war by any means necessary, if human beings are ruthless maximizers of rational self-interest, then yes, we must conquer desire, conquer the flesh, and transcend pleasure, conquering inner biological nature just as we conquer the outer, becoming the Cartesian lords and possessors of ourselves as well as of the universe.

That is the old story. In the new story, no longer are we at war with nature and no longer do we seek to conquer the self. We discover that desire has been so destructive because we have been misled. The things we think we want are often substitutes for what we really want, and the pleasures we seek are less than the joy that they distract us from. From the normal vantage point, it certainly seems that only with discipline can we withstand the temptations that surround us: overeating, drugs, video games, mindless internet surfing, and everything else we consume. These things are undeniably destructive to our own lives and beyond; therefore, it would seem, we cannot always trust desire at all. But when we recognize that these are not really what we desire, our goal becomes not to suppress desire but to identify the true want or need, and to fulfill it. That is no trivial task; it is a profound path of self-realization.

Desire comes from unmet needs. That is a fundamental precept of self-trust. One expression of the War against the Self that mirrors the War against Nature and the program of control is to allow the meeting of one's needs while limiting the "selfish" fulfillment of one's desires. That is part of the old story. It leads not only to self-rejection, but also to judgmentality. *I* limit the fulfillment of my desires, but *they* don't. How selfish of them. They should exercise restraint. They should exercise discipline. And if they do not, if they are just plain selfish people and don't have it in them, why, then we will have to force them to behave less selfishly through incentives and rules, rewards and punishments. We will have to impose a program of control.

In the new story, we look for the unmet need that drives the desire. This is a powerful transformative tool not only for personal development, but also, as I will explain, for social change. When we address the unmet need directly, it no longer drives the desire that had been so destructive. Fail to address the need, and the boiler that drives the desire keeps building pressure. Addiction and the gratification of superficial desires are like a release valve. When we clamp down on it with willpower, the pressure builds and eventually explodes out, perhaps as a binge, or, if the old expression of the desire is rendered unavailable, then as a new addictive behavior. This explains the common phenomenon of "addiction transfer" among recipients of bariatric surgery.

Unable to overeat, they often take up drinking, gambling, or compulsive shopping.[1]

The futility of the War against the Self mirrors the futility of war in general, which always leaves the deep causes of the provoking situation untouched. The only exception would be if a nation or its leaders were just plain *bad*. If they are irredeemable, then force is the only solution. Similarly, if your bad behavior comes from an innate badness, an inherent elemental depravity within you, then it would also be true that the only solution would be to subdue it.

That logic leads eventually to despair, because what happens if you try to subdue it and fail? What happens if that depraved part of you is too strong, stronger than any force you can muster to subdue it? What happens when this part of yourself runs your life? What happens when the seemingly bad people run the world? As any addict can tell you, force is insufficient in the face of a much stronger force. The despair of the dieter, trying to overcome the force of desire, and the despair of the activist, trying to overcome the force of the consumptive powers that rule the world, are identical. We all wrestle the same demon in a myriad of different forms. Fortunately, our perception of the origin of the violence, greed, etc., is mistaken, as, therefore, is the remedy of force.[2]

---

1. This phenomenon is controversial; some authorities say it doesn't exist, while others give a rate of 5–30 percent. A bariatric surgeon I know personally and who meets with patient groups post-surgery has told me he thinks the figure is closer to 90 percent.
2. Let me qualify that. Force, like all things, has its proper role. I would not suggest that a recovering alcoholic abandon his disciplined commitment to not drink today. Neither would I suggest that we refrain from using force to stop a gunman on a rampage, or a massacre that is in progress. When we understand that these solutions don't reach the root of the problem, we won't be tempted to apply them in place of real healing.

Pain

So, what exactly are these unmet needs, and how can we discover and satisfy them? A multiplicity of basic human needs go chronically, tragically unmet in modern society. These include the need to express one's gifts and do meaningful work, the need to love and be loved, the need to be truly seen and heard, and to see and hear other people, the need for connection to nature, the need to play, explore, and have adventures, the need for emotional intimacy, the need to serve something larger than oneself, and the need sometimes to do absolutely nothing and just be.

An unmet need hurts, and fulfilling a need feels good. Here lies the connection between need, pleasure, pain, and desire. The deeper the unmet need, the greater the pain we feel, the stronger the desire it generates, and the greater the pleasure in meeting it. Pain and pleasure are the doorways through which we discover what we really want and really need.

One thing that we discover as we enter the space between stories is that we do not want what we thought we wanted, and we do not like what we thought we liked. We look within and question: What do I really want? Why am I here? What makes me feel alive? Because our deeper unmet needs were mostly invisible to us, and because they have been unmet for so long, our physical and mental systems have adapted around them so that the pain becomes subconscious, diffuse, latent. That makes it hard sometimes to identify what the unmet need is. During life transitions, the obscuring stories break down and what's missing in life becomes clearer. We begin to ask ourselves, "What hurts?" and to discover answers. These answers orient us toward meeting our true needs for connection, service, play, and so on. As we do so, we find that our experience of joy and well-being deepens, and that we far prefer this feeling to the pleasures that we now recognize were mere substitutes for it.

Actually, that isn't quite true. Our addictions and superficial pleasures aren't only substitutes for something else—they are also glimpses of that something, promises. Shopping does give many people a fleeting experience of abundance or connection. Sugar does give many people a feeling of loving themselves. Cocaine offers a moment of knowing oneself as a capable, powerful being. Heroin offers a brief surcease from the pain that one had experienced as omnipresent. A soap opera produces the feeling of belonging, which properly comes from being enmeshed in the stories of the people one sees every day. All of these things are palliative medicines that make the state of Separation a bit easier to maintain, but also contain the seeds of Separation's undoing: first, because they sow discontent by contrasting the momentary experience of well-being or connection or animation with the default state of aching, lonely dullness; second, because their effects rend the fabric of life, wealth, and health, hastening the unraveling of the old story. Over time, their palliative efficacy diminishes while their destructive side effects grow. The drug stops working. We up the dose. Eventually that doesn't work either.

The same dynamic currently afflicts our civilization. We constantly up the dose of technology, of laws and regulations, of social controls, of medical interventions. In the beginning, it seemed, these measures brought great improvements, but now they barely suffice to maintain normality and keep the pain at bay. The first pharmaceutical prescriptions vastly improved health; now, when more than four billion prescriptions are written for Americans every year, endless new pills are necessary even to keep people functioning. The first machines vastly increased the productivity and leisure of the people who adopted them; today, people buy one high-tech device after another and still feel unable to keep up with the accelerating pace of life. The first chemical fertilizers brought dramatic increases in crop yields; now, agrochemical companies can barely keep up with declining soil health, pesticide resistance, and other problems. In the early days of science, the reduction of the complexity of observed phenomena to a few elegant laws bestowed upon us an astonishing ability to predict and control reality; today, we find more complexity and more unpredictability as we endlessly elaborate what were once simple laws in a futile quest for the Theory of Everything; meanwhile, the spiraling ecological calamity puts the lie to our pretensions of control.

I could make similar points about military interventions, government bureaucracies, lies and cover-ups, trying to control teenagers, and many other situations where a control-based quick fix brings dramatic short-term results. The kid is shut in his room. The dictator is deposed. Let's do something to feel better. Let's have a drink.

In both cases, the personal and collective, the fix masks an underlying malady. In both cases, when the fix stops working, the underlying condition comes to the surface, and there is no choice but to confront it. That is what is happening to our society today. As I wrote above, the obscuring stories are breaking down, what's missing becomes clearer, and we begin to ask ourselves, What hurts?

In describing personal transformative work, I advocate giving full attention to the pain that arises with the breakdown of an addiction and the story that embeds it. (The "addiction" can be something subtle, a self-image, for example, or thoughts about how ethical or successful one is.) Just as it feels good to meet a need, an unmet need hurts. Pain is its call for attention. When all the substitutes for meeting that need are exhausted, when all the palliatives stop working, finally the pain that had been diffuse and latent leads us to the need.

The same is happening on a collective level. What is the equivalent of attention in a mass social sphere? It is the sharing of stories about what is really happening on our planet. Of course, there have always been activists sharing these stories, trying to make society aware of the human cost of war and civilization, commerce and empire. But the obscuring narratives of progress and growth were too thick. We had not the ears to hear.

That is changing now. The immune system of the old story—all the mechanisms that keep inconvenient truths outside of view—is deteriorating. Each contradictory data point that comes in weakens that story, allowing the ingress of still more in a self-reinforcing process.

Just as attention, by itself, has a power to heal beyond any remedial action one might take, so also does telling the truth about what is happening on Earth have a power to alter the course of events. Again, it is not that no action will result. It is that when we digest the information, who we are changes, and therefore what we do.

We are only able to continue our ravaging of the planet under the cover of pretense. How is it that we as a society take no action, when the awful artifacts of our way of life on this planet lay strewn all around us? How is it that we continue to hurtle toward an obvious abyss? It is only because we have been rendered blind and insensate. Underneath their numbers games, the banks and hedge funds are stripping wealth away from the masses and the planet. Behind every profit statement, behind every executive bonus, is a trail of wreckage: strip mines, debt slaves, pension cuts, hungry children, ruined lives, and ruined places. We all participate in this system, but can do so willingly only to the extent we do not feel, see, or know. To conduct a revolution of love, we must reconnect with the reality of our system and its victims. When we tear away the ideologies, the labels, and the rationalizations, we show ourselves the truth of what we are doing, and conscience awakens. Bearing witness, then, is not a mere tactic; it is indispensable in a revolution of love. If love is the expansion of self to include another, then whatever reveals our connections has the potential to foster love. You cannot love what you do not know.

One role of the changemaker is to be the eyes and ears of the world. Recall the power of the videos taken of police brutality during the Occupy movement. Just as nearly everyone who saw passively seated protesters pepper-sprayed in the face was sickened by what they saw, so also, everyone who sees behind the veil of numbers is sickened by what our financial system is doing to the world. By being antennae for the collective attention, we can tear away the veil. Even if some of the perpetrators retreat more deeply into rationalization and denial, others will have a change of heart. More and more police will refuse to shoot, more and more authority figures will counsel restraint, more and more functionaries of power will quit their jobs, blow the whistle, or try to reform their institutions from the inside.

What is power, after all? Every one of the power elite's overwhelming advantages—military forces, surveillance systems, crowd control technology, control over the media, and nearly all the money in the world—depends on having people obeying orders and executing an assigned role. This obedience is a matter of shared ideologies, institutional culture, and the legitimacy of the systems in which we play roles. Legitimacy is a matter of collective perception, and we have the power to change people's perceptions.

Pleasure

*A*ll right, so if attention is the tool for working with pain on a personal or social level, how do we work with pleasure? Pleasure, remember, is among other things the feeling we get from satisfying a need. The more powerful the need, the greater the pleasure. To follow this principle requires, first, accepting that our needs are valid and even beautiful. And not just our needs, but our desires as well, coming as they do from unmet needs. Hold your breath, and your need for oxygen generates a desire to breathe. Stay too long at a dull job, and your need to grow will generate a desire to break free of limitations. Society tries to confine or divert that urge to break free, channeling it toward something inconsequential like drunkenness, video games, or bungee jumping, but what are these pleasures next to the exuberant expansiveness of real freedom?

To trust pleasure is to controvert norms and beliefs so deep that they are part of our very language. I have already mentioned the equation of "hard" with "good" and "easy" with "bad." The fact that words like "selfish" and "hedonist" are terms of disparagement speaks to the same basic belief. But the logic of interbeing tells us that among our greatest needs are the needs for intimacy, connection, giving, and service to something greater than oneself. Meeting these needs, then, is the source of our greatest pleasure as well.

Pleasure and desire are a natural guidance system that directs organisms toward food, warmth, sex, and other things that meet their needs. Are we to imagine that we are exceptions to nature's way? Are we to imagine that we've graduated past that guidance system, moved on to a higher realm in which pleasure is no longer ally, but enemy? No. That is a thought form of Separation. The guidance system of pleasure works in us too. It does not stop at the basic animal needs of food, sex, and shelter. In all its forms, it guides us toward the fulfillment of our needs and desires, and therefore to the unfolding of our potential.

To trust it again, after all these centuries, is a journey that might begin, for those of us who are most alienated from it, with the conscious, deliberate fulfillment of whatever trivial pleasures are available, building the habit of self-trust. As that muscle of discernment grows stronger, we can use it to choose greater and greater pleasures, which correspond to the fulfillment of deeper and deeper desires. It is for good reason that hedonism has always carried a faintly subversive air. To choose pleasure, even the most superficial, and to embrace and celebrate that choice, is to set in motion a process that upends the Story of the World. Eventually, the superficial pleasures become tedious and unsatisfying, and we move on to the kind of pleasure we call joy.

To follow this path strikes at the heart of the program of control, and outrages the intuitions of anyone affected by that story. Images come to mind of the consequences of the wanton pursuit of pleasure: rape, sexual abuse, overeating, shooting heroin and smoking crack, sports cars and private jets . . . for the sadistic there is even the pleasure of torturing and killing. Surely, Charles, you can't be serious in advocating the pleasure principle. Surely, it must be tempered with moderation, with balance, with self-restraint.

I am not so sure. For one thing, let us ask, how many people ever really pursue the pleasure principle? How often does anyone pause before a decision and honestly consider, "What would really feel good to me? What action right now would truly be a gift to my self?"? I am advocating a dedication to pleasure that is almost unknown to us. Perhaps pleasure isn't quite the right word for it; perhaps I should use the word joy, except that I want to emphasize that pleasure and joy are not two separate things, the first getting in the way of the second, but, rather, are on a continuum. Bring to mind a moment of real joy or connection, a moment at the bedside of a dying loved one, perhaps, or that breakthrough moment of forgiveness melting away a decades-long enmity. I am remembering the time I encountered a doe in the woods, and we stood, just a few feet apart, looking at each other. And I am thinking of my eight-year-old son Philip, looking long and innocently at me this morning as I dropped him off at school, saying out of the blue, "Dad, I love you." You have experienced moments like these: the joy of connection, the momentary dissolution of separation. Bring one to mind, and compare it to the feeling of binging on cookies, looking at pornography, or lashing out in anger. Based on what feels the very best, what would you choose? Which of these is the best gift to your self?

Can you see that our notions of selfishness and restraint have been turned on their heads? Can you see the enormity of the crime that has been perpetrated upon us, cutting us off from our guidance toward Reunion?

The more beautiful world my heart knows is possible is a world with a lot more pleasure: a lot more touch, a lot more lovemaking, a lot more hugging, a lot more deep gazing into each other's eyes, a lot more fresh-ground tortillas and just-harvested tomatoes still warm from the sun, a lot more singing, a lot more dancing, a lot more timelessness, a lot more beauty in the built environment, a lot more pristine views, a lot more water fresh from the spring. Have you ever tasted real water, springing from the earth after a twenty-year journey through the mountain?

None of these pleasures is very far away. None requires any new inventions, nor the subservience of the many to the few. Yet our society is destitute of them all. Our wealth, so-called, is a veil for our poverty, a substitute for what is missing. Because it cannot meet most of our true needs, it is an addictive substitute. No amount can ever be enough.

Many of us already see through the superficial substitute pleasures we are offered. They are boring to us, or even revolting. We needn't sacrifice pleasure to reject them. We need only sacrifice the habit, deeply ingrained, of choosing a lesser pleasure over a greater. Where does this habit come from? It is an essential strand of the world of separation, because most of the tasks that we must do to keep the world-devouring machine operating do not feel very good at all. To keep doing them, we must be trained to deny pleasure.

It was with great difficulty that the workers of the early Industrial Revolution were induced to work in factories. The organic rhythms of biological life had to be sacrificed to the monotony of the machine; the sounds of nature, children, and stillness had to be sacrificed for the din of the mill; the individual's sovereignty over his time had to be sacrificed to the clock. A whole system of education and morality was therefore constructed around self-denial. We still live in it today.

Let us be wary of any revolution that isn't threaded with an element of play, celebration, mystery, and humor. If it is primarily a grim struggle, then it may be no revolution at all. That is not to say that there is never a time for struggle, but to frame the transformative process primarily in terms of struggle reduces it to something of the old world. It devalues other parts of the process: the gestation, the latency, the coming inward, the breathing, the emptiness, the observation, the listening, the nourishing, the reflection, the playful exploration, the unknowing. Aren't these the things we could use a little more of on this earth?

The recovery of sensitivity and discernment in pleasure can be a long process, unique to each individual, that proceeds according to its own pace and rhythm. It is *not* to heroically conquer all fear, disregard restraint, ignore caution, and break through all limitations. That kind of transcendence smacks of the old story. Fear is not Enemy Number One, as some spiritual teachers would have us think: the new evil to conquer in place of the old bogeymen like sin or ego. Fear limits growth, it is true, but it also bounds a safe zone within which growth can happen. Only when the growth is bumping up against those boundaries is it time to break through it. So the feeling to look for is that of a fear that feels a bit obsolete, a new step that you're ready to take. When you contemplate it, whatever fear you feel should have the flavor of exhilaration, not dread.

We might apply the same ideas to our relations with other people as we strive to invite them into the new story. Salesmen understand the power of invoking an unmet need and associating it with some product that appears to meet it. How much more powerful it would be to see the unmet needs, and offer people something that actually met them. We can practice perceiving the unmet needs and unexpressed gifts in other people. Then we can meet those needs or create opportunities for them to be met. Herein lies half of what leadership is in a less hierarchical world: a leader is someone who creates opportunities for others to give their gifts.

Another way to look at meeting the needs of others is that we are serving their pleasure, joy, and happiness. As our understanding of what these are deepens, the needs we seek to meet evolve. Usually, of course, our ability to see those needs depends on having met them within ourselves—as one would expect, in a world of interbeing.

I hope you can see how this philosophy differs from what we ordinarily call hedonism (though I think our reflexive contempt for hedonism is a symptom of our self-rejection). I'm not telling you to indulge in more cigarettes, booze, and casual sex. I am saying, "Feel free to do these things as much as you truly want to." When we do them with full permission and no guilt, we may find they aren't truly what we wanted, or perhaps that the desire evolves with its fulfillment into something else.

Years ago I was (unprofessionally) counseling a woman who was trying to get off Ritalin and her obsessive behavior with the men in her life. She would call and text her ex-boyfriend tens, hundreds of times a day, compulsively. She started to call me more and more often, asking, "You don't think I'm crazy, do you?" "Is it really possible for me to leave this addiction and have a normal life?" And, "Am I calling too much? Maybe I'll drive you away like everyone else."

I told her, "I trust you to call when it truly serves your highest good.

Please do call whenever you truly want to." After that, she stopped calling so much. By giving her permission to call when she wanted to, I was also subliminally giving her permission *not* to call when she did *not* truly want to.

Usually, destructive pleasure-seeking behavior arises as an outburst of pent-up desire, and not as the expression of authentic desire. The Catholic priest pedophilia scandal shows us how healthy sexual desire denied finds another way out. The same applies more generally. What are the consequences of the suppression of our urges toward creativity, service, intimacy, connection, and play? What we call hedonism is a symptom of that suppression. Suppressing the symptom will only channel that desire-energy toward another, even more destructive, outlet, or it will express itself as cancer or some other disease. Instead, we can follow the symptom to the cause. After the binge, the bender, the indulgence in whatever vice, really ask yourself, "How do I feel now?" Did it meet a real need, as a nourishing meal does, leaving a feeling of satiety and well-being? Or is there still a hunger there? A hangover? A wound still throbbing under the narcotic? Give attention to that feeling—not as a trick to make yourself stop, but as a sincere inquiry intended to increase the amount of pleasure in your life. The power of attention integrates the whole experience, so that the behavior includes among its internalized associations the unpleasant aftereffects. It will no longer seem superior to other pleasures, and the craving will diminish. The power of attention is much greater than the force of self-restraint.

Earlier, you may have questioned my somewhat flippant nonjustification of my air travel. I am not dismissing the importance of information about the effects of burning jet fuel, or more broadly, the effects of consumption in general. It is important to know, for instance, that every electronic device we buy uses rare earth minerals mostly taken at horrifying ecological and human cost from places like Congo, Brazil, and Ecuador. We need to integrate the pain of that. When we do so, we begin to make different choices—the results of "Do what you want to" change naturally.

When we expand our scope of attention, we expand ourselves. We are what we eat, and any object of attention becomes a kind of food. Conditioned as we are to a worldview of force, it is new for us to trust that new information alone is enough for someone to change. We want to back it up with some kind of emotional pressure, an accusation, a guilt trip. As I argue throughout this book, these are counterproductive. They provoke resistance to the information. I prefer to use humor and love as a kind of Trojan horse to get the information in. Once it is in, it will have its effect.

Now, please consider the possibility that everything in this chapter is wrong, and I am just weak-willed, justifying my indiscipline through an elaborate psychological rationalization. Certainly there are many venerable spiritual teachings enjoining us to cultivate self-discipline, restraint, and moderation. Who am I, born into the lap of privilege, to question an ancient spiritual tradition of asceticism? On the other hand, the equally venerable tradition of tantra, which has expressions in Buddhism, Hinduism, and Taoism alike, is more or less aligned with everything I am saying. Which is true? I don't think I can offer any logic or appeal to authority that will settle the matter. Perhaps the two, tantra and asceticism, are one. I know that the results in my life of trusting pleasure have often taken me to a place that looks, from the outside, a lot like asceticism. I have witnessed the truth of verse 36 of the Tao Te Ching: "To reduce something, one must deliberately expand it; to weaken something, one must deliberately strengthen it; to eliminate something, one must let it flourish." Very often, it is only by achieving what we thought we wanted that we can realize that we didn't want it. Having gone through that cycle, we quicken it for others. Our stories shorten the time others spend lost in what they do not want. Sometimes our exploration of that territory is enough to prevent others from going there at all. On the collective human journey, each bit of the territory of Separation must be explored before we can, in completion and repletion, make the return journey.

So, by giving myself absolute license to drink as much alcohol as I wanted, I ended up almost never drinking any. By giving myself absolute license to eat as much sugar as I wanted, I ended up eating far less than when I tried to restrain myself. And my unrestrained license to shop leads me mostly to the thrift store. It isn't because I have disciplined myself to stop these behaviors. It is because I have integrated on multiple levels the fact that they actually don't feel very good. Then, it takes no more willpower to stop them than to refrain from poking my thumb in my eye. If my eye had no pain receptors, I might have difficulty refraining, just as it is hard to stop a habit if we don't integrate the full experience of it, before, during, and after.

Our society promulgates a belief that the pain resulting from any act can somehow be avoided. Feel bad? Do something to take your mind off it. Have a cigarette. Feel even worse? Put on a movie. Still feel bad? Have a drink. Got a hangover? Take a pill. The habit of endlessly managing the consequences is analogous to the mentality of the technological fix, which seeks to avoid the consequences of the damage caused by the previous fix. But because the underlying wound is still there, the pain will be waiting there too in the end, when every fix is exhausted. Hence the saying of Ch'an Buddhism: The ordinary person avoids consequences; the Bodhisattva avoids causes. Why? The Bodhisattva would probably try to avoid consequences too, except that she knows it is impossible. The pain is waiting in the end, when every fix is exhausted. That's where our society is today.

From the Bodhisattva's perspective, we might reinterpret certain rule-based religious teachings. Perhaps the Ten Commandments are meant to be the Ten Indications: you will know you are close to God when you find that you do not kill, do not steal, honor your parents, and so forth.

The focus on pleasure, desire, aliveness, and joy offers a guideline for work on the social and political level as well. Amid all the doom-laden exhortations to change our ways, let us remember that we are striving to create a more beautiful world, and not sustain, with growing sacrifice, the current one. We are not just seeking to survive. We are not just facing doom; we are facing a glorious possibility. We are offering people not a world of less, not a world of sacrifice, not a world where you are just going to have to enjoy less and suffer more—no, we are offering a world of more beauty, more joy, more connection, more love, more fulfillment, more exuberance, more leisure, more music, more dancing, and more celebration. The most inspiring glimpses you've ever had about what human life can be—that is what we are offering.

If you can firmly hold the vision of that, you will communicate it as a subtext to your activism. People respond much better to that than to the secret message "You are going to have to sacrifice and live a poorer life. You are too selfish. Your life is too good." They will react as if you are attacking them, and in a sense they will be right. To be effective servants of a more beautiful world, we have to know that the things we will sacrifice aren't nearly as good as the things we will discover. We have to believe that five-thousand-square-foot houses aren't as happiness-inducing as communities with walkable public space. We have to believe that the convenience lifestyle isn't as happy as gardening and cooking our own food. We have to believe that living life faster isn't living life better. We have to believe that civilization's baubles are miserable substitutes for what a human being really needs. If these beliefs are insincere, and if we cannot see the real possibility of the world we seek to create, our words will have little power and our actions will have little motivation. That's also why it is so important to "walk the walk"—to practice what we preach. It is not to avoid hypocrisy (that would be part of the campaign to be good). It is to fully inhabit and embody the new story so we can serve it joyously and effectively.

Judgment

Given how pervasive and deep-rooted the structures of scarcity and struggle are, it is no wonder that we bear their imprint on our own psychology. How do we free ourselves? Their grip is so total that when we try, we risk only strengthening them further. For example, when I asked, "How do we free ourselves?" did you expect that to do so would require some hard effort, some monumental effort of self-transformation? If you think it is going to be hard and began either to steel yourself for the effort or to turn wearily away from it, then you are subject to a habit of struggle.

And do you feel chagrined or defensive about your subjugation to that habit, or are you proud of having "passed the test" at being free of it? Either way, you are in another habit of separation, granting or denying conditional self-approval. If you don't measure up, you are not good enough. Self-judgment, a crucial ingredient of the war against the self, is one of the most common habits of separation.

Many people have little trouble confessing to being hard on themselves, to being "my own worst critic," or to being a perfectionist. They are, after all, merely confessing to something that our culture upholds as a virtue: the struggle against the self. Who would admit to being more harshly critical or judgmental of others than of oneself? That would be tantamount to outing oneself as a hypocrite.

Unfortunately for the image of the self-critic, it is impossible to be judgmental of oneself without being judgmental of others. Suppose each evening you look back over your day and evaluate whether you were truthful, ecologically responsible, wasteful, ethical, or greedy, praising yourself or beating yourself up accordingly. Well then, what about all those other people out there who were less honest, responsible, or ethical than you were? Are they therefore not as good as you are? Whether you accord them patronizing indulgence or condemnation, the implicit belief that "I am better than you are" (or worse than you, but at least better than someone) is inescapable.

What do I mean by judgmentality? To be judgmental is not merely to draw distinctions, to have preferences, or to make comparisons. It carries a moral judgment, an assignment of right or wrong, good or evil, to a person. This assignment can take many forms. Words like "should" and "shouldn't," "responsible" and its opposite, right and wrong, ethical, moral, justifiable, valid, shameful, or other synonyms for good and bad usually appear in articulations of judgment.

Judgment is separation. At bottom, judgment says that you choose differently from me because you *are* different from me. It says, "If I were you, I wouldn't have done what you did." "If I were a corporate CEO, I wouldn't destroy the environment and lie to the public about it." "If I were that wealthy, I wouldn't spend my money on sports cars and McMansions." "If I were that fat, I wouldn't be on my fourth trip to the buffet line." I am better than that. I am not so ignorant. I am not so irresponsible. I am not so lazy. At least I have an open mind. At least I consider the evidence. At least I got an education. I paid my debts. I eat responsibly. I work for it. At the very least, I make an effort. What is wrong with those people?

This is the essence of Separation: If I were in the totality of your circumstances, I would do differently from you.

A substantial body of experimental evidence shows that this statement is false, that in fact if you were in the totality of his circumstances, you would do exactly as he does. As I shall explain, to align ourselves with this truth is perhaps the most powerful way to magnify our effectiveness as agents of change. It is the essence of compassion to put oneself in another's shoes. It says, you and I are one; we are the same being looking out at the world through different eyes, occupying different nexus points in the universal web of relationship.

It is also very hard to accept. I might be able to see how I might resort to theft if my children were hungry or how I might senselessly vandalize public property if my childhood had filled me with rage, but what would it take for me to massacre seventy-seven people like Anders Breivik did, shooting them one by one as they kneeled before me weeping and begging for mercy? What would it take for me to take a chainsaw to a three-hundred-foot-tall redwood? I confess, it is very hard to put myself in the shoes of a torturer, an abuser of toddlers, a trafficker of sex slaves, a murderer. Yet let us not pretend that we are better than these people. Judgment toward them reflects only our lack of understanding, not any fundamental difference in our core being.

I am articulating here a position known in social psychology as "situationism," which says that it is the totality of our internalized and external situation that determines our choices and beliefs. In contrast, most people in our society hold the view of dispositionism, which says that people make decisions by the exercise of free will based on relatively stable dispositions or preferences. If someone does a good thing, says the dispositionist, it is probably because he is a good person. The situationist says no, that is an error—the "fundamental attribution error." A lot of careful research has shown that people (in our society) consistently attribute situational influences to dispositional qualities, and consistently underestimate the effect of conditions on people's behavior. Someone says a mean thing and our first impulse is to think she is a mean person. We might later learn that she had a toothache and change our judgment, but the first impulse is to make a dispositional judgment.

That is no accident. Dispositionism and its attendant judgmentality is encoded into our Story of the World. In your shoes, I would not do as you did, because I am different from you, separate from you. More-over, situationism says that the "I" is bigger than the individual, that the subject, the actor and chooser, is the individual plus the totality of his or her relationships. The self has no independent existence. Abstracted from its relationships to the world, the self is not itself.

Decades of research, going back to the Milgram experiments of the 1960s, belie our sanctimonious belief that if I were that CEO, that poli-tician, that brother-in-law, that ex-spouse, that teacher, that addict, that inexcusable person, then I wouldn't have done what she did. Ask your-self, what kind of person would deliver painful, even life-threatening, electrical shocks to an innocent subject as part of a psychological experi-ment? Surely only a very bad person would do that. Surely *you* wouldn't do that! Well actually, as it turns out, "you" would. Or at least nearly everyone did in Stanley Milgram's lab when the right conditions were present and the right excuses, the right story, was available. "Surely it can't be wrong if a Yale scientist with a white coat is in charge." "The subject did volunteer for this." "I'm not the one responsible, I'm just following instructions." More broadly, the thought that anything mon-strous could be happening in a laboratory, decked out with the regalia of science, at a prestigious university, was so dissonant with the prevail-ing Story of the World, with society's consensus about legitimacy and propriety, that one volunteer after another turned the knob up to max and pulled the lever.

The question in the background was how to explain the fact that the Nazi Holocaust was carried out by bland bureaucrats like Adolf Eichmann and legions of quite ordinary people who had led common-place lives before becoming SS officers and concentration camp guards. How to explain the "banality of evil"? I will return to this question later, because if we are to let go of the War on Evil, we must be able to reframe evil in a way that motivates some other kind of action. Because one cannot deny that some very horrible things are happening on Earth. These things must stop. I am not suggesting, here, that we close our eyes to what looks like evil. I am suggesting we open our eyes even wider to the situation—which is the story that immerses us—that generates evil to begin with.

The situationist perspective is, in one form or another, widely accepted in social psychology. A 1973 experiment by John Darley and C. Daniel Batson offers another example of the power of situation. You might know the Good Samaritan story from the Bible. A man has been beaten by robbers and lies moaning by the roadside. A priest passes him by. Then a Levite (who might be a priest's assistant) does the same. Finally the Samaritan stops to help. In telling this story, Jesus asks his questioner which one of these three proved to be a "neighbor" to the beaten man. He doesn't say the Samaritan was good, but today the story is called the Good Samaritan, implying that what distinguished him from the priest and the Levite was his moral disposition.

In the experiment, a group of seminary students (modern-day priests and Levites in training—the experimenters were not without a sense of humor) were told they had to go across campus and deliver a lecture on the Good Samaritan story. They were divided into three groups and, one at a time, given instructions. Those in the first group were each told, "You'd better hurry up, you're late for your interview." The second group were told, "You'd better hurry up, your interview starts in a few minutes." And the third group were told, "Well, you might as well head on over. Your interview doesn't start for a while, but we're done here."

On their way to the lecture venue, the students walked past a man (actually a confederate of the experimenters) sprawled in a doorway, groaning. The students practically had to step right over him to reach their destination. Did they stop to help? As you might expect, it depended on which group they were in. Only 10 percent of the first group did, but 60 percent of the third.

Why did those in the first group step right over the "injured" man while those in the third group stopped to help? Obviously, it wasn't because all the good people happened to be in the third group. Maybe the Bible story should be called "The Samaritan who wasn't in a hurry." And maybe we cannot blame the people we like to blame. Maybe the problems of the world cannot be met by conquering evil.

Not only our personal judgments but many of our social institutions, the legal system in particular, are based on dispositionist assumptions. We assume that ordinarily, people are responsible for choosing their actions, and distinguish between an act committed under duress and an act voluntarily chosen. But duress is just an extreme example of a situational influence. Are we to be blamed for the sum total of the experiences that have made us who we are?

Similarly, contract law assumes two parties entering an agreement of their own free will, based on an understanding of their own interests and preferences. A contract encodes a kind of force: it says, "I will allow you to force me to carry out what I have agreed to herein." In everyday interactions, we understand that sometimes "things change," and don't hold someone to a promise if her situation has changed a lot. We recognize that the person who made that promise cannot be separated from her life circumstances, and when these change, she changes. The person who promised, in a sense, no longer exists. A contract is an attempt to deny this truth.

Clearly, situationism has immense implications for the nature of choice, free will, motivation, moral responsibility, and criminal justice. These and many other issues are explored in the influential and erudite paper "The Situational Character: A Critical Realist Perspective on the Human Animal" by Jon D. Hanson and David G. Yosifon, along with its companion piece, "The Situation: An Introduction to the Situational Character, Critical Realism, Power Economics, and Deep Capture."

Situationism is also an understanding to which we have direct experiential access. Have you ever had a moment of understanding where another person is coming from, when all of a sudden we inhabit his or her world and everything he or she has been doing makes sense? No longer is that other person some kind of monster, an other. I can understand a little bit of the experience of being her. With this insight, forgiveness arises naturally, and it is impossible to hate. It also shows us that whenever we do hate someone, we are hating ourselves too.

Hate

He who fights too long against dragons becomes a dragon himself;
and if thou gaze too long into the abyss, the abyss will gaze into thee.

—NIETZSCHE

*T*o humanize an opponent might be challenging to allies who are
still inhabiting a Story of Hatred. They might interpret the new
view as softness or betrayal. "How could you excuse those people?"

A friend of mine, a military veteran committed to peace, told me the
story of a friend of his who had the opportunity to serve as the personal
chef to none other than Dick Cheney, a man whom millions of liberals
perceived as an awful human being, a soulless, duplicitous, conniving
warmonger. My friend, expecting confirmation of this view, asked his
friend what it was like working for Cheney. "Wonderful," he replied.
"You can tell a lot about someone's character by the way they treat the
help, and he always treated me with warmth, dignity, and respect, even
though I was only a cook."

This is not an endorsement of Dick Cheney's political views or
conduct. The point here is that a perfectly decent human being, harbor-
ing the same basic motivations and fears as any other human being, can
do awful things in one context and admirable things in another.

The error of attributing bad behavior to personal evil has a mirror
image that *does* result in a kind of betrayal. It is to think that because

Cheney and perhaps some corporate CEO are friendly, intelligent people that their views must not be so wrong either. This leads to the phenomenon of "Beltway environmentalism"—describing those who have worked so long and closely with their Washington, DC, counterparts in business and government that they absorb much of their worldview and, more insidiously, their consensus about what is possible, practical, and legitimate. It is a challenge to stay true to what we serve without vilifying those who do not serve it.

Wouldn't it be nice if the problem were indeed the greed and wickedness of the dastardly individuals who hold the reins of power? The solution would be so simple then—simply remove those people from power, scour the world of evil. But that is just more of the same war against evil that has been with us ever since the first agricultural civilizations invented the concept of evil to begin with. More of the same will only bring more of the same. Surely the time has come for a deeper sort of revolution.

Transition activist Marie Goodwin comments, "The solution of rooting out the 'bad' would make the solving of the world's problems, which seem so very overwhelming, a task that is doable in our current paradigm. This is why we defend it at all costs. I think people get really overwhelmed by today's constant barrage of bad news and disaster stories, all of which (we are told) can be solved by winning, mostly with force, the fight of good and evil."

It is reassuring, because it reduces many problems to one problem and makes sense of the world in a way that doesn't challenge our deeper mythology.

In a perverse sort of way, by refusing to hate, we *are* committing a kind of betrayal. We are betraying hate itself; we are betraying the Story of the World that pits good versus evil. In doing so, we incite the scorn and fury of former allies, who deride us for being so soft and naive as to think their opponents can be treated as anything but implacable enemies.

I remember reading a column by the brilliant and abrasive leftist Alexander Cockburn, in which he recalled a formative experience in his education as a political journalist. An editor asked him, "Is your hate pure?" a refrain that Cockburn repeated to many an intern. Cockburn's was a world of hypocrites and blowhards, of venality and greed, of bold-faced liars and consciously cruel leaders, and of the sycophants and shills who enabled them. I must confess to a kind of unholy delight in the wit and venom with which he dispatched his opponents, but I was aware as well of the psychological pressure—separate from the evidence or reasoning he presented—to agree with his worldview lest I be numbered among the dupes and apologists he so viciously skewered.

With equal fervor, though perhaps less finesse, pundits on the right do the same thing Alexander Cockburn did. Underneath the slurry of opinions, the same mindform prevails. Although we recognize ad hominem attacks as unfair or irrelevant, we are helpless to resist launching them, because of the dispositionism that permeates our beliefs. So-and-so disagrees with me because she is a *bad person*. For "bad" we may substitute all manner of adjectives, but the judgmentality is palpable. I have given up reading comments on my articles because of all the personal invective I must wade through. Commentators impute onto me all kinds of intellectual and moral deficiencies. I am naive. I am a narcissistic wannabe hippie who has never had any real experiences. I am just another arrogant white male hogging a stage. I have overlooked a trivial logical flaw in my argument. I should get a real job. And on the other hand, supporters project onto me various saintly qualities that I obviously do not possess, at least no more than anyone else.

That feels nice. The problem is, once on a pedestal there is only one place to go next. The slightest misdemeanor on my Facebook page provokes intense criticism. I post a photo of my teenage son with his prom date, and get criticized for objectifying women (because I called her a "prom date"). I post a picture of my baby son asleep on my lap while I write, and I get criticized for exposing him to electromagnetic radiation and not giving him empathic attention. My point here is not to defend myself—the criticisms have some validity. What is significant is that the critics sometimes say, "I now have to question your message" or "I can no longer in good conscience endorse your work." This is alarming:

I certainly don't want anyone's acceptance of, say, the proposals in *Sacred Economics* to hinge on my personal moral purity. If you are reading the present book because you are under the impression that I am some kind of saint, you might as well put it down right now, lest you discover someday on Facebook that I'm no better than any other human being, feel betrayed, and dismiss my message as the ravings of a hypocrite. I hope that you will consider these ideas on their own merits, and not on mine.

Ad hominem attacks seek to discredit the message by discrediting the messenger—a tactic that draws on the converse of the dispositionist view that people say bad things because they are bad people: if one can show they are bad people, then what they are saying must be bad too. The situationist knows that this view is mistaken and that tactics drawing from it are likely to be counterproductive. Yes, we should continue to expose the truths of history and the workings of the world, but if we want those truths to be heard we must not wrap those exposés in the usual penumbra of blame. The logic of control tells us that by shaming the perpetrators we can change them, but actually we only drive them deeper into their story. When I am attacked, I seek allies who will defend me. "No, it is the environmentalists who should be ashamed, not you!" On and on we go on the blame merry-go-round.

When we deploy rhetorical flourishes such as "The fault lies with the fat-cat banksters who care not a whit for the suffering of the common man or the degradation of the environment," we also make ourselves sound ridiculous to the bankers themselves, who like most human beings do in fact care about their fellow humans and the planet. If we want to reach them, our articulation of the problem has to avoid ascribing personal evil to them, while also being uncompromising in describing the dynamics of the problem. I cannot offer a formula for how to do this. The right words and strategies arise naturally from compassion: from the understanding that the bankers or whoever do as I would do, were I in their shoes. In other words, compassionate—and effective—words arise from a deeply felt realization of our common humanity. And this is possible only to the extent to which we have applied the same to ourselves. Truly, to be an effective activist requires an equivalent inner activism.

When we ourselves stand in a different story from blame and hate, we become capable of dislodging others from that place too. Our peaceful hearts change the *situation,* disrupting the story in which hate comes naturally and offering an experience that suggests a new one.

Hold on. Maybe I am saying this only because I am naive. Maybe my soft, coddled upbringing has blinded me to the reality of evil and the need to fight it with force. It is certainly true that I have not experienced firsthand the worst of what human beings can do to each other. But let me offer you the story of the South Korean activist and farmer Hwang Dae-Kwon.[1] Hwang was a militant antiimperialist protester in the 1980s, a dangerous activity during that time of martial law. In 1985 he was arrested by the secret police and tortured for sixty days until he confessed to spying for North Korea. He was then thrown into prison, where he spent thirteen years in solitary confinement. During this time, he says, his only friends were the flies, mice, roaches, and lice that shared his cell, along with the weeds he met in the prison yard. This experience turned him into an ecologist and practitioner of nonviolence. He realized, he told me, that all the violence he had endured was a mirror of the violence in himself.

His number one principle for activism is now to maintain a peaceful heart. At a recent demonstration, a line of police equipped with riot gear was marching toward the demonstrators. Hwang walked up to one of the police and, with a big smile, gave him a hug. The policeman was petrified—Hwang said he could see the terror in his eyes. Hwang's peacefulness had rendered him incapable of violence. For this to "work," though, the peacefulness must be genuine and deep. The smile must be real. The love must be real. If there is an intent to manipulate, to show the other up, to highlight the brutality by contrasting it with one's own nonviolence, then the power of the smile and the hug is much less strong.

---

1. I heard Hwang speak of these experiences at a conference and in personal conversations. He also wrote a memoir of his imprisonment entitled *A Weed Letter,* which was a best seller in Korea.

Righteousness

The way you see people is the way you treat them,
and the way you treat them is what they become.

—GOETHE

*U*nderneath the common agreement that the problem with the world is evil and the solution to conquer it is an unmet psychological need for self-approval. Two-thirds of our political discourse goes toward meeting our need to be right, to align ourselves with Good. If the man who disagrees with me does so because he is stupid, naive, bamboozled, or wicked, then I must be smart, canny, independent-minded, and good. Positive and negative judgments alike hold oneself as a tacit reference point (lazy means "lazier than me" and responsible means "responsible like me").

Why do you really visit those websites that get you stirred up and indignant? Whatever reason you give yourself (e.g., to "stay informed"), maybe the real reason is the emotional gratification, the reminder that you are right, smart, in a word, good. You are part of the in-group. If you want even more reassurance, you might start an online discussion group or a face-to-face group where you and a bunch of other people get together and talk about how right you are and how awful, incomprehensible, evil, and sick those other people are. Unfortunately, because this gratification is addictive, no amount will be enough. (The real need here is for self-acceptance, and the proxy offered does not and cannot meet the real need.) Soon everyone will want to be even more right—more right than certain others in the group, which will degenerate into infighting and flame wars.

Maybe you want to be even more right still. Well then, go engage in some civil disobedience, get yourself arrested, get yourself beat up by the police. Demonstrate through your suffering how monstrous are the powers-that-be. Look what they did to me!

Now I am not saying that protest and direct action are always, or even usually, coming from self-righteousness. They are also powerful ways of disrupting the story that allows injustice to flourish. They can expose the ugliness beneath the facade of normal. No doubt, most hard-core activists have mixed motives of genuine service and self-righteousness both. To the extent that the latter motive is present, the results will reflect it. You will achieve your goal—to look good and be right and make your opponents look evil. And you will increase the amount of hate in the world. Your sympathizers will hate and rage against the evildoers. I suppose the unstated hope is that if this rage builds up enough, we will all rise up and topple the elites. But what will we create in their stead, suffused as we are with self-righteousness and the ideology of war?

Militancy has the further disadvantage of alienating the uncommitted, who sense the goal of being righteous underneath the professed goal of changing society. When people are hostile to the angry feminist, the rabid vegan, the militant environmentalist, they are not merely defending their Story of the World and the complacency it allows; they are defending themselves against an implicit attack. If your activism, whether for social change or for your family to adopt a healthier diet, provokes hostility, that might be a mirror of inner discord.

Even if the response to militancy isn't hostile, the militant is easy to write off: his commitment isn't really to the cause, it is to militancy.

The activist Susan Livingston wrote me about a proposal she had written for an Occupy group at Caltech opposing its biofuels contract with BP. She said, "It came because I was troubled by the militant attitude of some of the folks at the teach-in. I didn't see the care I'd like for the community of the conflict—the multitude of low-level bureaucrats, small stockholders, and franchise owners whose livelihoods depend on BP. What are they—collateral damage? And especially after seeing *The Drilling Fields* about the human and environmental devastation in Nigeria at the hands of Shell, I'm not real fond of singling out BP in response to the resentments of some privileged students who want to have their cake and eat it, too. But we've got to start somewhere, and with privilege comes the capacity to mount an effective campaign of resistance."

In this comment, Susan is drawing a key connection between privilege and militancy. Militancy, the mentality of war, always involves collateral damage. Something must always be sacrificed for the Cause. The sacrifice of others (the "community of the conflict") is also the defining mentality of elitism: for whatever reason, those others are less important than me, my class, my cause. The privileged are always sacrificing others for their (the others') own good. If they sometimes sacrifice themselves too, that doesn't mitigate their elitism.

This is not to say that the oil companies should be allowed to continue what they are doing in order to preserve the livelihoods of filling-station owners. It is just that everyone needs to be seen and considered, not written off. Militants think that giving up the fight means letting the bad guys have their way. If the world were indeed divided into good guys and bad guys, that might be true, but despite what the movies tell us, the world is not thus divided. Alternatives to fighting, then, can be more powerful and not less in creating change.

Most often, actions taken from self-righteousness only end up validating the self-righteousness through the hostile response they generate. See? I told you those people are awful! Direct actions, protests, hunger strikes, and so forth are powerful only to the extent self-righteousness is absent. When undertaken in intentional service to a vision of that which could be, they are powerful indeed. They needn't be acts of war; they can be acts of truth-telling, of kindness, or of service. How can you know whether your act is really one of these, and not war masquerading as love? How can you tell what your own motives are in your political activities, whether online or on the street? Well, if you feel a sense of superiority over those not so engaged, a sense of condemnation, or patronizing indulgence toward those who don't get it (and so, you must nobly sacrifice on their behalf), then the motive of proving yourself good is almost certainly present. And that is what you will achieve. You can go to your grave filled with admiration for yourself. You can have engraved on your tombstone "Was part of the solution, not the problem—unlike some people." But wouldn't you rather change the world?

Ask yourself, if you think that the wealthy, the powerful, the Republicans, the Democrats, the big game hunters, the meat industry executives, the frackers, or any other subset of humanity is evil (or shameful, revolting, disgusting, etc.): Would you be willing to give up that belief if it would make you a more effective agent of change? Are you willing to take a look at how much of your belief system is a giant game of upholding a positive self-image?

If you feel any disgust toward the mindset I have described, judgment toward those who live in it, or defensiveness around whether it applies to you, then maybe you are not entirely free from it. It is okay. That mindset comes from a deep wound that civilization has dealt nearly every one of us. It is the cry of the separate self, "What about me?" As long as we keep acting from that place, it doesn't matter who wins the war against (what they see as) evil. The world will not deviate from its death-spiral.

Many people (I hope I'm not the only one!) make what seem to be ethical or moral choices with a secret objective in mind: to demonstrate to themselves and others their own virtue; to give themselves permission to like and approve of themselves. The inseparable partner of this goal is judgmentality toward those who aren't making those choices. "I am a good person because I recycle (unlike *some* people)." "I am a good person because I am vegan." "I am a good person because I support women's rights." "I am a good person because I give to charity." "I am a good person because I practice socially responsible investing."

"I am a good person because I have given up the rewards of society and cast my lot with the oppressed." "I am a good person because I live in the forest eating roots and berries with zero carbon footprint." We are oblivious to our own self-righteousness, but others can smell it a mile away. The hostility that we activists and do-gooders arouse is telling us something. It is a mirror to our own violence.

Derrick Jensen, confronted with Audre Lorde's saying, once said, "I don't care whose damn tools I'm using." The reason to avoid the master's tools is not to avoid some kind of moral taint. It is not to distance ourselves from those who wield power and to demonstrate to one and all (and particularly to ourselves) that we abstain from using the same methods as the oppressors. Rather, it is that these tools are in the end ineffective.

If constructing a positive self-image is the goal of our actions, then that is what we will achieve—no more and no less. We will walk through life congratulating ourselves for our superior ethics, deploring those who don't see the light, and resenting those who don't share our sacrifices. But the bleakness of our victory will grow increasingly apparent with time, as the world burns around us and our deeper need, to know beyond doubt that we are contributing to a more beautiful world, goes unmet.

A reader wrote me an intensely critical response to an article I wrote about the Democratic Republic of the Congo (DRC), saying that my mention of the warlords there reinforces the narrative of African savages who need the white man's help, and obscures the culpability of the real perpetrators in Western companies and boardrooms. In fact, the first third of the article was devoted to the external origins of the problem in colonialism, slavery, mining, and global finance. I wrote that under our current economic and financial system, there will always be a Congo. I even explicitly critiqued the mindset of the "Great White Savior." So what was the reader angry about, really?

My ensuing dialogue with that reader gives a clue to what that might be. I responded to him that I agree that the warlords are victims as well as perpetrators, but that the very same thing might be said for the CEOs and bankers, and it may be said as well for all of us who use cell phones made with rare earth minerals extracted, with great violence, from places like the DRC. We are all victims and perpetrators both, I said. The real culprit is the system; therefore, any strategy that sees the culprits as a certain group of rotten people is misguided and will ultimately fail.

The answer enraged my critic. "How dare you create any moral equivalency between these boardroom warlords who are knowingly perpetrating misery on millions of people and the ordinary consumer using a cell phone? These people must be exposed, tried, held to account."

Aha, I thought. The reason he is angry is that my article doesn't validate his righteous anger. Of course the workings of the system on all levels, including the boardroom, need exposure. But if that effort springs from the assumption that these are reprehensible people, and that punishing them and "holding them to account" will fundamentally solve the problem, then we will leave the core of the problem untouched. We might see temporary, localized improvements, but the main tide—a tide of hatred and violence—will continue to rise.

Some people are always enraged to read anything that does not in some way support the story of "Those awful people out there must be stopped." They will deploy epithets like "naive" or accuse the writer of being himself a sellout, a racist, or a dupe for his failure to see the evil of those in power. (This critic insinuated that I was softening my narrative in order to make it palatable to the gatekeepers of prestigious magazines.) Really, they are just defending their story. The vehemence of the attacks also reveals a personal, emotional dimension to their defensiveness. To see a few awful people as the problem puts oneself in the category of "good person" and excuses one's own complicity. Any threat to the story is thus a threat to one's own goodness and self-acceptance, which feels like a threat to survival itself; hence, the ferocious response.

Typically, the way one defends oneself against someone who believes one is evil is to level the same charges against the attacker. Look at the comments sections on articles online. Though the surface opinions on a right-wing and left-wing site might be opposed, the underlying narrative is the same: the other side is deficient in the basic qualities of human decency. They are ignorant, self-righteous, stupid, immoral, inexcusable, sick. It's not only in politics—the same happens in every polarized debate. Physicist Max Tegmark, coauthor of the MIT Survey on Science, Religion, and Origins (and an atheist himself), was surprised at the vitriolic comments not just from religious fundamentalists, but even more from atheists. He remarked, "I can't help being struck by how some people on both the religious and anti-religious extremes of the spectrum share disturbing similarities in debating style."[1]

Obviously, both sides cannot be right in the implicit thesis that their side comprises a better sort of human being. That is why it is so fruitful to bring together in a room opponents who have demonized each other and create conditions in which their mutual humanity becomes apparent (such as deep listening or temporary suspension of judgment). Israelis and Palestinians, pro-choice and antiabortion activists, environmentalists and corporate officials learn that their convenient explanation of "They're just evil" is invalid. They might retain their differences of opinion, and the larger systems that generate their conflicts of interest may remain in place; they may still be opponents, but they will no longer be enemies.

When both sides of a controversy revel in the defeat and humiliation of the other side, in fact they are on the same side: the side of war. And their disagreements are much more superficial than their unstated and usually unconscious agreement: the problem with the world is evil.

This agreement is nearly ubiquitous. Look at the plot of so many Hollywood movies where the resolution of the drama comes with the total defeat of an irredeemable bad guy. From high-concept movies like *Avatar* to children's movies like *The Lion King* or *Wreck-It Ralph*, the solution to the problem is the same: conquer evil. Significantly, the type of movie that most often has this plotline, besides children's movies, is

---

1. Max Tegmark, "Religion, Science and the Attack of the Angry Atheists," Huffington Post (February 19, 2013).

"action" movies. No wonder defeating the bad guy so often becomes the unquestioned programmatic assumption behind all kinds of political action. I need not mention that it is also the defining mentality of war. And since the label "evil" is a means of creating an "other," one might also say it is the defining mentality of our relationship to everything else we have made other: nature, the body, racial minorities, and so on.

More subtly, Western notions of story and plot have a kind of war built in to them as part of the standard three-act or five-act narrative structure, in which a conflict arises and is resolved. Is any other structure possible that isn't dull, that still qualifies as a plot? Yes. As the blogger "Still Eating Oranges" observes, the East Asian story structure called Kishōtenketsu in Japanese is not based on conflict.[2] But we in the West almost universally experience a story as something in which someone or something must be overcome. This surely colors our worldview, making "evil"—the essence of that which must be overcome—seem quite natural a basis for the stories we construct to understand the world and its problems.

Our political discourse, our media, our scientific paradigms, even our very language predisposes us to seeing change as the result of struggle, conflict, and force. To act from a new story, and to build a society upon it, requires a wholesale transformation. Dare we do it? What if I am wrong? Let's look more deeply into the nature of evil.

---

2. "The significance of plot without conflict," posted on Tumblr, June 15, 2012.

Psychopathy

If something bites you, it is inside of your clothes.

—SWAHILI PROVERB

I have argued that change will come not from overcoming the powers-that-be, but through their transformation. I have stated that we are fundamentally the same being looking out at the world through many sets of eyes. I have described how our perception of evil comes from a lack of understanding of what it is like to be another person. I have asserted that what we do unto the other, we do unto ourselves, and that this is something we can feel. And I have invoked the principle of the gift, that we are all here to contribute our gifts toward something greater than ourselves, and will never be content unless we are. In answer to all of these, sometimes people bring up the counterexample of the psychopath, a distinct subset of humanity that supposedly possesses no compassion, no ability to feel love, and no shame.

These people are, it is said, totally out for themselves, suffering no compunctions in ruthlessly pursuing short-term self-interest. Unfeeling, charming, charismatic, daring, and ruthless, they tend to rise to the top in business and government. To a large extent, they are the powers-that-be, and it would be naive to think that anything but raw force would stop them. Without pity, without conscience, without even the capacity to feel anything but a few basic proto-emotions, they are the epitome of evil. According to many researchers, they can never be cured. They don't want to be cured. They are happy the way they are.

No one agrees on what causes psychopathy. One of the most prominent scholars in the field, Robert Hare, says flat out that no one really has a clue. There might be some kind of genetic predisposition toward psychopathy, but even this isn't certain.

The above narrative, left untouched, reintroduces the story of good versus evil into our worldview. Who knows who is a psychopath and who isn't? "Psychopath" becomes the scientifically sanctioned term for "wicked person."

The invocation of psychopathy to validate the good-versus-evil narrative and all that comes along with it (such as the necessity of force as the primary means of changing the world) is misleading. Granting for a moment that there is a distinct category of irredeemable people whom we call psychopaths, it is also true that the conditions under which they thrive are systemic. Traditional views both in evolutionary biology and in economics essentially assert that our basic nature is something quite psychopathic: that we are driven to maximize self-interest, and that traits that seem to contradict self-interest exist because, in some way that isn't immediately obvious, they actually further it. The example of altruism as a kind of mating display comes to mind, or generosity as a means of gaining status and control over others. This paradigm is woven into our economic system. If you don't maximize your firm's self-interest, firms that do will outcompete you. Even as consumers trying to get the best deal, the incentive embodied in the price tag often contradicts the impulse to pay the workers who made the item a living wage, or to adopt environmentally responsible practices. Those items are more expensive. Living in a system that rewards psychopathy, it is no accident that the psychopathic rise to the top, and that the psychopathic tendencies within each of us rise to the surface. It is a mistake to blame psychopaths for our present condition; they are a result, not a cause.

Under what circumstances do you become a cold, unfeeling person? Under what circumstances do you shut off your empathy? When do you manipulate others for your own advantage? When I notice myself doing it, usually it is when I am feeling insecure.

Insecurity is built in to our Story of the World: the separate self in a hostile universe of competing others, random accident, and impersonal forces of nature. Insecurity is also built in to the structures arising from that story, for example, the economic system, which throws us into competition to meet basic needs even when, objectively speaking, there is abundance for all. Just living in a mass society where the faces we see have no names, where strangers meet our needs for pay, and where even our neighbors know little of our stories, contributes to the same omnipresent insecurity. Our behavior in the world of Separation confirms the premise of that world: it turns us into selfish utility-maximizing quasi-psychopaths.

Given any cultural trait, there are always some people who embody it in extreme form, holding up a mirror so that we can recognize it in ourselves. These would be the psychopaths.[1]

Nonetheless, people with psychopathic tendencies do hold a lot of power today and will act to thwart anything that challenges it. Does that mean we need to use force after all? I don't mean to rule it out categorically. There are circumstances where I personally might use force, for example if someone were threatening my children. But it is dangerous to extrapolate from these situations: before long, one is concocting "ticking time bomb" scenarios to justify torture for political ends, reasoning that in some indirect way, one's children are being threatened. Furthermore, even attempting to lay out ethical principles to distinguish when violence is and is not justified perpetuates a dangerous delusion: that the way we should (and sometimes do) make choices is to reason out guiding principles beforehand, and then act on those principles in

---

1. A good case can be made for the existence of psychopaths in premodern societies. The incidence of psychopathy in these societies is apparently much lower, however, reflecting perhaps the smaller degree of Separation those cultures embodied. It was not absent entirely: some would argue that any society that has adopted domestication, or even symbolic culture (language), has already embarked on the path of Separation. (See for example John Zerzan's *Elements of Refusal*.)

the moment. In actuality, whatever I write in this book and whatever beliefs I profess, if my children were actually being threatened I am sure something else would take over. Would I fight? Maybe. Would I calmly face the man and say, "You must be pretty desperate to be doing this. How can I help you?" Maybe. This choice would surely depend, in part, on a lifetime of experiences and learning. If I have explored nonviolence deeply in theory and practice, I might be more likely to apply it successfully when fighting isn't actually the best choice. But absorbing and integrating the spirit of nonviolent action is very different from setting it up as a rule and imagining I will be able to enforce that rule upon myself when the moment arrives. To aspire to be a "man of principle" is a kind of separation, part of the program of control. It attempts to override the gut, the instinct, and often the heart. How many atrocities in history have been justified on one or another principle?

What, exactly, do we mean when we say that psychopaths hold power in our society? Power in human society depends on a system of agreements within that society. A psychopathic corporate executive doesn't hold power because he personally has big muscles or big guns. His coercive and manipulative powers depend largely on money and the associated apparatus of corporate governance. At the bottom of it all, there are indeed muscles and guns ready to coerce those who refuse to obey the rules, but even so, he doesn't personally wield those guns. They are wielded by perfectly decent police and security personnel who are not much more psychopathic than anyone else.

In other words, power in a complex society arises from story: from the system of agreements and narratives that scaffold our world. Our current story facilitates the rise of psychopathy and empowers the psychopath. Because it is story, and not force, that ultimately empowers those in power, it is on the level of story, and not force, that we must act in order to take away their power and change the system. That is why advocating force as the primary instrument of change is counterproductive—it reinforces the very same Story of Separation that is at the root of our condition to begin with. One facet of it is the story of the good people finally rising up to topple the bad people.

Let us therefore go one step further in questioning the category of the psychopath. Is it true that the psychopath is simply born without empathy? Another explanation is that the psychopath has empathy, but has shut it down at an early age, rendering him- or herself unable to feel. Why would that happen?

It could be because the psychopath is the very opposite of what we think. What if the psychopath isn't someone born without feeling, but rather someone born with an extraordinary capacity for empathy and sensitivity to emotional pain? Unable to endure its intensity, he shuts it off completely. Most of us don't need to do that, because the enormous pain of the world doesn't affect us quite as strongly. Or, shall we say, it affects us in different ways, a deeper ache perhaps, less immediate, less raw.

You can probably think of many ways our culture of child-rearing contributes to the shutdown of feeling, especially in boys. Beyond childhood, it pervades our whole society. Have you ever wondered why "cool" has been the preeminent term of approbation for the last fifty years? Why does "cool" equal "good"? Why is it desirable to be cool in our emotions, to not feel very much, not care very much, not be in earnest about anything? One reason may be the urge to withdraw from a world too painful to bear. Another is that we recognize the bankruptcy of so many of the things we are given to care about. The news media offer us an endless array of trivialities and pantomimes, punctuated regularly by shocking and seemingly disconnected horrors that we learn to shrug off. Do we inure ourselves to them because we are psychopathic ourselves? Or could it be because we sense that they are a kind of a show, symptoms of a deeper disease? Maybe we hold back because the prevailing story has obscured much of what we really want to care about.

Many classic psychopathic behaviors make sense within the context of a general shutdown in feeling. Inured to feeling, the psychopath nonetheless has, like all of us, a strong physiological need to feel. Therefore he is given to impulsiveness, drama, pointlessly risky behavior that doesn't contribute to his self-interest at all. Anything powerful enough to breach the walls he has constructed will attract him. For some, it could be the intensity of infatuation, for others, murder, for others closing the big deal. It could be the big risk, the big purchase, the big gamble. Many psychopaths are addicted to such things that, they sometimes say, make them feel alive. Most academic researchers believe psychopathy is a conjunction of two independent axes of variation: lack of empathy, and impulsivity. In my hypothesis, the two are closely linked. The risky behavior is an attempt to breach the lack of feeling.

I must acknowledge that there is very little research supporting this hypothesis.[2] I base it on my own experience—first and foremost with myself. I was an extremely sensitive child and, due to traumatic bullying in my early teens, learned to shut off most of my feelings. Though the shutoff wasn't nearly as profound as that of a psychopath, still it enabled me to do some pretty callous, manipulative things. I also exhibited other psychopathic traits, such as impulsivity and a penchant for drama. I was trapped in numbness and wanted desperately to feel. Tori Amos's lyric spoke to me: "Give me life, give me pain, give me my self again."

In addition, I have also had extensive interactions with several psychopathic individuals, at least one of whom was profoundly so: a man whose ruthlessness knew no bounds. I'll call him C. He also had other classically psychopathic traits: glib self-justification, total lack of shame, extreme impulsiveness, extraordinary charisma, and great physical courage that often crossed the line into foolhardiness. But there were a few times when I caught a fleeting glimpse of something else, a tenderness or a purity that came out in very convoluted ways, for example as spontaneous, secret, and sometimes magnanimous acts of generosity or caregiving. These were distinct from the cynical devices he routinely enacted to seem a swell guy. There was something else, a real human being. As far as I know, that real human being is still deeply buried, but it is in there and somehow, someday, might awaken.

---

2. See for example "Emotional Capacities and Sensitivity in Psychopaths" by Willem H. J. Martens, MD, PhD.

Whether or not transformation is possible, as a practical matter, most psychopaths might just need to be stopped. I have gone into this speculation on the origin of psychopathy for two reasons. One is to offer an alternative to this common argument for the existence of evil. Looking at the world around us, it certainly does appear sometimes that the psychopaths are in charge. My point is that evil is a consequence, not a cause, and by going to war against it we further the cause of war. Psychopathy is the extreme expression of something that exists in all of us and in the culture that surrounds us. It comes from a cutoff of our extended being.

The second reason I have ventured into this topic is that the transformation of the psychopath has implications for the transformation of our civilization. Exploiting nature and people toward its own ends, applying a superficial charm to entrap other cultures, justifying everything it does with a glib story of progress, our civilization has been little short of psychopathic. On an individual level of course we feel empathy for the species, cultures, and ecosystems that stand in the path of development, but collectively we act only sporadically to stop it—like my friend and his occasional gestures of distorted humanity. Moreover, the question "How can we learn to feel again?" affects everyone, not only those we call psychopaths, because each of us is, in our own way, cut off from the felt connection to parts of our extended selves.

As it happens, I do know that psychopaths can change, because I know one who did. Back when I was teaching at the university, a twenty-two-year-old student came into my office with a rather shocking confession. He told me, in matter-of-fact tones and with no evidence of boasting nor of shame, "I am the top cocaine wholesaler in _____. I make a cash income of $10,000 a week and I spend it all. I drink Dom Pérignon every day. When I go out at night, I have four bodyguards from the inner city. I've heard that the DA has a file on me, but I don't care."

I told him, "Well, that sounds pretty good, so what's the problem?"

He said, "I'm kind of tired of it. It doesn't do anything for me. I walk across campus and all I see instead of faces are walking $100 bills.

Every one of them is going to give $100 to their dealer, who will give it to their distributor, who will give it to me. I don't get a kick out of it anymore. I think I'm going to have to quit my job."

"That won't be easy," I warned. Once in that world, it is nearly impossible to leave. "A thousand hands will be pulling back at you."

It was no easy matter for F. to change his job. As seems true with a lot of psychopaths, he was extraordinary in more ways than lacking empathy: he also had extraordinary creativity, charisma, and resourcefulness, as well as impatience for conventional rules and mores. In nearly any job, he very quickly bumped up against "Why should I?" His first job was in an ice cream store, where he quickly developed the attitude of "Scoop your own damn ice cream!" He got a job selling mortgages, broke all sales records in his first month, then quit. He took up photography and, despite having no experience, in a few months was earning thousands of dollars a shoot—not just because of his salesmanship, but because of his ability to get subjects to let down their habitual guard. That held his interest for a little longer, but soon he didn't see the point of that either. He wanted to focus more on the creative expression and couldn't be bothered to do the stuff one typically does to charge big money. He began working for free.

During this period F. began experiencing enormous amounts of emotional and psychological pain, especially when he decided to quit drinking. He became a person with not an ordinary but an extraordinary capacity to feel. Today he spends his time staying at home with his baby son, and playing with photography and other digital arts. I don't know where he will eventually turn his prodigious capacities. Our society doesn't offer ready-made positions for people like him. He had to make himself small to fit in. What would the world be like if it expanded to accommodate people like that?

His situation is all of ours. Society renders us artificially small so that we may fit into its boxes, a project in which we become accomplices. If the program of diminishment is unsuccessful, or if the energy denied cannot be contained, then society will have no place for you. It is impossible to feel fully, and still be a functioning member of normal society. When we feel too much, we care too much, and the roles we are put in that grease the wheels of the machine become intolerable—good news, as this is the very same machine that we are riding over the edge of a cliff.

Recall the second reason for "cool" I gave above—our recognition of the bankruptcy of the things we are given to care about. Psychopaths have this quality in huge measure: not only are they preternaturally cool under pressure, but they are relatively unaffected by many of the mechanisms of reward and shame society uses to govern us. Many activists would like to be freer from these constraints too, especially when the work we are doing violates many social norms. Being free from what people think is just one of many desirable psychopathic traits. In fact, psychopaths have many traits ordinarily associated with spiritual masters, such as nonattachment, ability to focus, being in the present moment, and courage. Indeed, one might make the case that certain famous spiritual teachers were psychopaths (Gurdjieff and Chögyam Trungpa come to mind).

Here is another story from Book IV of the *Liezi* (translation Thomas Cleary):

Lung Shu said to the physician Wen Chi, "Your art is subtle. I have an ailment; can you cure it?"

The physician said, "I will do as you say, but first tell me about your symptoms."

Lung Shu said, "I am not honored when the whole village praises me, nor am I ashamed when the whole country criticizes me. I look upon life as like death, and see wealth as like poverty. I view people as like pigs, and see myself as like others. At home I am as though at an inn, and I look upon my native village as like a foreign country. With these afflictions, rewards cannot encourage me, punishments cannot threaten me. I cannot be changed by flourishing or decline, gain or loss; I cannot be moved by sorrow or happiness. Thus I cannot serve the government, associate with friends, run my household, or control my servants. What sickness is this? Is there any way to cure it?"

The physician had Lung Shu stand with his back to the light while he looked into his chest. After a while he said, "Aha! I see your heart; it is empty! You are nearly a sage. Six of the apertures in your heart are open, one of them is closed. This may be why you think the wisdom of a sage is an ailment. It cannot be stopped by my shallow art."

There is more to psychopathy than meets the eye. We can shoehorn it into our category of evil, but only by ignoring some of its many dimensions. Another clue I haven't mentioned is the tendency for psychopaths to "mellow" and develop empathy with age. Or could it be that whatever story that generated their kicks becomes stale? Sensing this possibility, with C., my psychopathic friend, while I was appreciative of his resourcefulness and audacity in achieving his goals and would laugh along with him, I would show that I was unimpressed with the end result (bedding some woman, humiliating some person, or closing some deal), trying to communicate to him, "There is a bigger game you could be playing."

While most people are not as extreme as C., who among us can say that we have never been stuck in a smaller game than we could be playing, striving for its trivial rewards that, when we achieved them, left that lingering feeling of "so what"? Psychopaths or not, the winners of the game of our society are the biggest dupes of all.

A generation or two ago, Earth was not yet in such pain, and we had a Story of Ascent—progress and conquest—that absorbed much of the pain there was, which was still a lot. Today the story of technology making life on Earth better and better is tottering, and the pain grows beyond all our attempts to deny it. For a while we might find some distraction, some inconsequential arena where we can feel. Sports extravaganzas, action movies, fantasy novels, celebrity news, and the various heartrending tragedies that appear regularly in the mainstream media all allow us to exercise our feelings and continue living life as normal. But eventually we stop caring about the trivialities, and we realize that the tragedies too are merely the most visible outcroppings of a deeper vein of dysfunction. Life stops making sense. We wonder, as F. did at the mortgage company, what the point is. We keep slogging away, perhaps, at our jobs or school out of fear of financial hardship, but at some point even that isn't enough to keep us going. The next step is medication: antidepressants to inure us to the pain; antianxiety meds to quell the sense that something is terribly wrong; stimulants to force us to pay attention to things we don't care about. But all of these merely drive the life-force deeper underground. There it builds, bubbling up eventually as cancer, turning against the body as autoimmunity, or exploding outward as violence. No wonder that nearly all the school shootings in the last two decades have involved psychiatric medications.

Imagine what this world could be, if we could channel that tremendous pent-up life-force toward something worth caring about. To be sure, most people do have access to things worth caring about on a personal level. There are babies to hold, shoulders to cry on, gardens to plant. Our Story of the World and its systems often squeeze these simple avenues of service to the hurried margins of life. Besides, we also need more than just these, at least in certain stages of life. That is why we, and especially young people, hunger for a cause. Like F., we want to care. We want to find a way to open the floodgates of the heart. Such things as "ending polio in Africa" or "internet freedom" might serve for a time, but eventually they cease to excite us. The gates shut again, maybe via burnout or compassion fatigue. For some of us, none of these causes, taken in isolation, can pierce the ennui, the uncaring, the cool. We need to see what bigger thing we are serving. We need a story of the world we really care about.

Evil

When we confront something we regard as "evil," it poses a threat to the self-preservation of ego. We are so busy preserving our existence in the face of this threat that we cannot see the thing clearly at all.

—CHÖGYAM TRUNGPA

Sometimes in Q&A sessions or internet comments I am confronted with the accusation that I ignore "the dark side of human nature." I would like to unpack that statement. What is the dark side of human nature? It certainly means more than "Sometimes people do some pretty awful things," because obviously if it wasn't someone's fault or intention to cause harm, that is not very dark. Besides, anyone who has read my work knows that I am well aware of the horrible things we humans have done to each other and the planet. No, when we speak of the dark side of human nature, we are making a dispositionist claim: that we do bad things because there is bad within us. We bear within us evil, malice, selfishness, greed, brutality, cruelty, violence, hate, and callousness.

On the one hand, this is trivially true: all of these are parts of the human experience. Even if circumstances bring them out, they must be there to be brought out in the first place. But if it were only that, then the situationist response would be sufficient: change the circumstances that elicit evil. No easy task, this: these "circumstances" include the whole edifice of our civilization all the way down to its foundational mythology of Separation and Ascent. Yet still, a more beautiful world is still possible in principle.

As far as I can tell, the critics are saying something more: "It isn't only that evil is a product of our institutions, though certainly many of them, such as the money system, elicit and reward evil. The evil is prior to any of those; indeed, our evil institutions were created and imposed on us by evil people. Moreover, such people are still among us today. They will not allow you to change the system. There is evil in the world, Charles, fundamental evil. If you comfort yourself with fantasies about how it can be healed, it will simply take advantage of you. The evil must be confronted and defeated."

Some of these critics externalize the evil in the form of an evil cabal of illuminati that secretly rule the world; others offer a more nuanced position that locates evil within themselves as well. Either way, they view it through an essentialist lens.

Before I respond to this critique, I feel it necessary to establish that I am not ignorant of the worst that has happened, and still is happening, in this world. I know what people are talking about when they refer to institutional and personal evil. What else is it when international creditors extract interest payments from countries where children go hungry? What else is it when women in Congo are raped with bayonets? What is it when toddlers are sent to the gallows? What is it when people are tortured using power tools and pliers? What is it when babies are raped on child pornography webcams? What is it when children are murdered before their parents' eyes as punishment for labor activism? What is it when Native American children are forcibly sent to boarding schools to lose their language and often their lives? What is it when virgin forests are leveled for profit? What is it when toxic waste is dumped into sinkholes? What is it when cities are flattened by atomic bombs essentially for demonstration purposes? The brutality and hypocrisy on this planet know no limit. The worst things you can imagine one human being doing to another, have been done. If not because of evil, then why?

Any worldview that does not acknowledge the reality of these things will eventually fail us as a source of optimism, faith, and courage. Born into a world where these things happen, we all carry their imprint. Better be aware of it. For me, it is important to sometimes read about the genocide *du jour,* to look at photographs of tar sands excavation, to read about the worldwide decline in forests, and to touch on the individual stories of people affected by war, the prison industry, and so forth. Only then, seeing the very worst, can my optimism be authentic. It is usually the small, personal cases that get under my skin. For example, there is the woman I met in California who refused to medicate her son with yet another drug that had been prescribed him because, she said, each new drug was making him sicker. He had been prescribed more than twenty and she'd had enough. So child services took her son away. He died a month later. I carry that story and hundreds like it everywhere I go.

If you have eyes to see and ears to hear, you will frequently encounter stories this horrifying, and much worse. Can you peer into the abyss of despair that they offer without falling in? Can you countenance their invitation to hate, to rage, to lash out against evil, without accepting that invitation? This invitation is not unrelated to the despair: by the calculus of war, evil is stronger than good. It has no compunctions. It will use any means necessary. That is why there is no hope within narratives in which an irredeemably evil illuminati control all the world's governments, corporations, military, and banks.

I would like to point to a different invitation that the horrifying stories offer. It is to vow, "I will do anything in my power to create a world in which this no longer happens." Integrating such stories into my awareness inoculates me against the still-dominant Story of the World in which things are basically as they should be.

Years ago, my then-wife Patsy visited an in-home day care with the idea of finding a place where Philip could interact with other toddlers for an hour or two a day (neither of us believed in day care). She walked into a scene where two women were taking care of about twelve children ages zero through four, with some help from the electric babysitter— the television. One of the babies, about nine months old, was just at the age of crawling. He couldn't crawl though, because he was inside a small "playpen"—in other words, a cage. He wasn't crying; he was just sitting there. Patsy felt sorry for him, all penned up like that. "Why can't he come out?" she asked. The woman in charge said, "Look how busy we are. He gets into everything. We can't have him out with this many kids to feed, to change, to watch . . ."

"I'll watch him," Patsy said. The woman agreed the baby could be let out for a while.

So Patsy took him out of the playpen. As soon as he was set free, the baby's face lit up with delight. Finally he got to crawl! To go here, to go there, to mix in with the other children. He was in heaven. He got to do that for fifteen minutes. Then Patsy had to leave, and the baby went back into his cage. Fifteen minutes was all that baby got.

When I heard that story, the vow welled up inside me, "I will do anything in my power to create a world where babies aren't put in cages." A tiny footnote, it seems, in the litany of horrors that laces civilization, but it got under my skin. And I saw how it was connected to everything happening today, with its sacrifice of humanity for efficiency, its monetization of the intimate, and its imposition of the regime of control in every realm of life. I wondered anew: "How have we arrived at a state of poverty so abject, that babies must be caged?" A baby in a cage is one small and integral strand in our totalizing Story of the World.

A world in which babies are put in cages, not to mention in which they are killed with machetes, is intolerable. A good definition of Hell is having no choice but to tolerate the intolerable. Our Story of the World gives us no way to stop it, for evil—whether in the guise of genetic self-interest or demonic powers—is an elemental force in its universe. And you are but a puny individual in an ocean of other. Therefore, our Story of the World casts us into Hell.

The woman taking care of those children was obviously not evil. She was harried, busy, and inhabiting a story in which everything she did was okay. The question of evil might come down to this: Is that woman on a continuum with the overly ambitious prosecutor, the venal politician, all the way to the sadistic torturer? Or is there a discontinuity that divides the ordinary flawed human from the truly evil? Before we jump to conclusions, we should do our best to understand what kind of "situation" might generate even the most heinous acts.

Perhaps what we see as the evil in human nature is a conditional response to circumstances so ubiquitous, and so ancient in their origin, that we cannot see them as conditional. The "othering" that allows us to harm, and the stories that contain that othering, are present to some extent even among the indigenous, and form the warp and woof of modern society. We do not really know what human nature would be in an environment embodying the Story of Interbeing. We do not know what it would be like to grow up in a society that affirmed our connectedness and cultivated its associated perceptions, feelings, thoughts, and beliefs. We do not know what the experience of life would be if we never learned self-rejection and judgment. We do not know how we would respond to conditions of abundance rather than scarcity. In *Sacred Economics* I wrote, "Greed is a response to the perception of scarcity." (If everyone has plenty and the society lives in a sharing economy that rewards generosity, then greed is senseless.) Maybe we can expand that to say, "Evil is a response to the perception of separation."

At a retreat one time, I asked the participants to walk around as separate selves. They were to see the sun as a mere ball of fusing hydrogen, the trees as just so much woody tissue; they were to hear the birdsongs as genetically programmed mating calls and territorial markers. They were to see each other as grasping, selfish egos, and the world as a competitive arena. And they were reminded that the clock was ticking. When we debriefed afterward, one of the participants said, "I just started feeling angry. I wanted to hit someone, kill something."

Those perceptions of separation I told people to take on—those are the air we breathe as members of modern society. They are among the implicit beliefs of our culture. No wonder we are so angry. No wonder we are so violent. Immersed in such a world, who wouldn't be?

None of this is to deny the fact that there are an awful lot of dangerous people out there, people who are so deeply conditioned to Separation that it would take a miracle to change them. Such miracles happen sometimes, but I don't recommend relying on them in every situation.

Again, if an armed intruder were threatening my children, I would probably use force to stop him, whether or not I understood that his actions came from whatever childhood trauma he had experienced. The moment of danger might not be the time to heal such trauma.

On the other hand, it might. I have found—and others have discovered in situations far more extreme than I've experienced—that acting from the understanding of oneness rather than from fear can have amazing effects in tense situations. Hostility begets hostility and trust begets trust. I cannot say it "works" every time, but disrupting the usual script at least allows the possibility of a different outcome. Responding to someone without fear telegraphs to them, "You are not dangerous. I know you are a good person." It creates a new script for them to step into. They may decline that role, but at least the possibility is there.

Not too long ago, my teenage son sold an item of his for $75 to another kid in the neighborhood. The kid met him to get the item, but instead of paying Jimi the money, he grabbed it and ran off. Jimi gave chase but couldn't catch him. Another teenager, a local gang member, saw the scene and asked why Jimi was chasing him. Jimi told him, whereupon the other teen pulled out a gun and said, "I'll help you take care of it. I know where he lives." Jimi said, "I'll get back to you on that." That evening, he told me the story and asked, "What do you think I should do, Dad?"

I thought about it for a minute and said, "Well, you are in the position of strength here and could probably get your money back by force. But if you go with the gun-wielding kid to visit the thief and get your item or money, you know how the story unfolds. The kid will want revenge, either on you or, more likely, someone weak. The cycle of violence will continue. Instead of that, why not transform the situation? You could send the gunman a text, saying, 'You know, if he really wants the item that much, tell him to take it as my gift. Really. It's just a thing.'" I explained further to Jimi that this approach wouldn't work if he didn't already have the upper hand, because then it would be seen as capitulation. But as things stood, such a message would be totally out of the ordinary.

Jimi told me he'd think about it. He didn't do as I suggested, but let me tell you what happened. Later that week Jimi arranged a meeting with the thief. He went accompanied by his friend M., a martial arts expert. The thief brought two of his friends along as well. He said he really wanted the item and didn't want to pay for it. His two friends started egging him and Jimi on, suggesting that they fight for it. Jimi (who is six-feet-two and has also studied martial arts) said, "Forget it, I'm not going to fight you for this petty material object. You keep it. I don't want your money."

The thief was taken aback. Then he said, "You know, that doesn't feel right. I shouldn't have taken it like that. Let me give you some money. How about $50? That's all I can afford."

Whereas each had held the other in a story of enmity, now there was humanity.

Pancho Ramos Stierle runs a peace house on the border between two gang territories in what is considered one of the worst neighborhoods in Oakland, California. People tell me that more than once, local individuals have entered the house with the intention to rob or kill, only to be converted into peace workers instead.

Years ago, Pancho was involved in a protest at UC Berkeley, where he was a PhD student in astrophysics. He was one of a group of students publicly fasting to protest the university's involvement with nuclear weapons development. After nine days, the university got tired of it and had the police come and make an example of the group of hunger strikers. Police officers broke the human chain the protesters had made by interlocking their arms, and one officer lifted the slight Pancho into the air, slammed him onto the concrete, and brutally handcuffed him.

At this point, most of us would probably fall into the story and the habits of separation. We might respond with hatred, sarcasm, judgment. Lacking the physical force to overcome the police, we might try to publicly humiliate them instead. If it were me, I imagine, my lifelong indignation at the injustices of this world would be projected onto the person of this police officer. Finally, someone to blame and to hate. The worse his persecution of me, the more gratified I would feel, the more a martyr, innocent, blameless. It feels kind of good, doesn't it, to have someone inhuman to hate without qualification. One feels absolved. And, by personifying evil, the problems of the world appear much simpler—just get rid of those awful people.

Pancho responded differently.[1] He looked the officer in the eye and said, with love and with no attempt to make him feel guilty, "Brother, I forgive you. I am not doing this for me, I am not doing this for you. I am doing it for your children and the children of your children." The officer was momentarily befuddled. Then Pancho asked his first name and said, "Brother, let me guess, you must like Mexican food." [Awkward pause.] "Yes." "Well, I know this place in San Francisco that has the best carnitas and fajitas and quesadillas, and I tell you what, when I get done with this and you get done with this, I'd like to break my fast with you. What do you say?"

Amazingly, the officer accepted the invitation.[2] How could he not? He loosened Pancho's handcuffs and those of the other protesters. The power of Pancho's action came because he was standing in a different story, and standing there so firmly that he held the space of that story for other people such as the policeman to step into as well.

The Tao Te Ching says: "There is no greater misfortune than underestimating your enemy. Underestimating your enemy means thinking that he is evil. Thus you destroy your three treasures and become an enemy yourself" (verse 69, Mitchell translation). The stories of Pancho and my son illustrate this. I shudder to think of the misfortune that could have resulted from "underestimating" the enemy.[3] Even if the policeman had been humiliated or punished, even if the thief

---

1. See *Parabola* magazine, "If You Want to Be a Rebel, Be Kind," for a more complete account of this event.
2. Pancho asks that I clarify that the lunch never ended up happening.
3. I should mention that this passage is extremely ambiguous. Many translators choose to interpret "underestimating the enemy" in the conventional way. Mitchell, drawing on a subtle, intuitive, and in my view accurate understanding of the sense of the text, added in the sentence explaining that underestimating means thinking your enemy is evil. That sentence is not in the original, but is implicit in the next line, which says that when armies clash, the compassionate or empathetic win.

had been crushed, the real "enemy" would have flourished. The level of hate would not have diminished in this world.

I want to be absolutely clear that for words like Pancho's to work, they must be absolutely authentic. If you say them and don't mean them, if you are actually saying them with the goal of showing your persecutor up as all the more villainous for having spurned your nonviolent loving-kindness, then he will probably oblige by enacting that villainy. People, especially police officers, know when they are being manipulated, and they don't like it. The purpose of responding nonviolently isn't to show what a good person you are. It isn't even to *be* a good person. It comes, rather, from a simple understanding of the truth. Pancho meant what he said. He knew that the police officer didn't really want to do this. He looked at him with the unshakable knowledge, "This isn't who you really are. Your soul is too beautiful to be doing this."

I find that witnessing or reading about incidents like this strengthens my own standing in the Story of Interbeing. Perhaps, knowing Pancho's story, when I am in a situation that challenges my stand in the new story, I will be able to hold it more firmly too. Certainly, I encounter such challenges every day. I haven't been beaten by police, but every day I see people doing things that invite me to "other" them, to demonize them, and to seek to punish or manipulate them. Sometimes it seems as if entire newspapers are designed to bring the reader into that mindset. They invite us into a world of inexcusable, awful people, and predispose us to act accordingly in our social relationships.

A few weeks ago I was speaking in England about the changing mythology of our culture. In describing the scientific dimension of that shift, I listed not only fairly palatable paradigm shifts such as horizontal gene transfer and ecological interdependency, but also more controversial examples like morphic fields and water memory. One of the audience (this was a small room) rolled his eyes and snorted, "Oh come on!" The emotion behind his protest was palpable, and I felt defensive. What should I do? From the mentality of force, my response would be to try to overcome this man, and I must confess that that is how I began. I spoke of my acquaintance with Rustum Roy, one of the twentieth century's greatest scientists, near-universally revered by materials scientists as the father of that field, who elucidated mechanisms for the nanostructuring and microstructuring of water. I was about to continue with a scientific case for water memory that would cite the research of Gerald Pollack of the University of Washington, the character assassination campaign against Jacques Benveniste, and so on, when I noticed the sullen expression on my challenger's face. Obviously, his rejection of water memory was ideological, not based on any reading, and thus unprepared he would have no chance to defeat me in a debate. He would only be humiliated. I would win, but so what? Would the man change his mind? Probably not. He would probably conclude that I was presenting a biased case, and he would go home and read the entry for water memory on skepdic.com. If anything, his belief would harden.

Not wanting to be an agent of humiliation, I took a different tack. I observed to the audience that there is a lot of emotional energy behind this question. Why? Obviously, I said, we are not facing a mere intellectual disagreement. Where is the emotion coming from? It could be, sir, that you deeply care about this planet and see fantastical beliefs as a distraction from the necessary, practical work that we need to do. It could be because you see the damage that ignorance of science has done in areas like climate change. It could be because marvelous possibilities strike us with fear, because we live in a civilization where the marvelous possibility of human life has been systematically betrayed by our systems of education, parenting, religion, economics, and law. It could be because we fear the dissolution of our worldviews that major paradigm shifts entail.

The man was not mollified; before too much longer, he got up and left. But several people afterward told me that that was the most powerful moment of the afternoon. Who knows, perhaps the experience of being met and not humiliated added another featherweight of love to this man's inventory of experiences.

The best victory, says Sun Tzu, is the one in which the losers don't realize they have lost. In the old story, we overcome evil and leave our enemies in the dust, wailing and gnashing their teeth. No more. Everyone is coming along for this ride. In the new story, we understand that everyone left behind impoverishes the destination. We see each human being as the possessor of a unique lens upon the world. We wonder, "What truth has this man been able to see from his perspective, that is invisible from mine?" We know that there must be something; that indeed, each of us occupies a different place in the matrix of all being precisely in order to contribute a unique experience to our evolving totality.

I do not know if Pancho's encounter with the policeman directly changed that man's life. I do know that each experience of love, along with each experience of hate, is written into our inner situation. Each experience of love nudges us toward the Story of Interbeing, because it only fits into that story and defies the logic of Separation.

I think these stories make it clear that acting from interbeing does not equate to being a doormat, being passive, or allowing violence to happen. It certainly isn't the same as ignoring what goes on in the world. Sometimes I get criticisms quite the opposite of the one that I'm naive, along the lines of "Charles, don't you understand? It's all good. We're all one. All these 'bad' things are happening for our growth. Let's focus on our blessings and steer clear of negativity. You criticize technology, but look—the internet allows me to communicate with my son in China. Everything is unfolding perfectly." I disagree with this viewpoint, or rather, I think it represents a partial understanding of a metaphysical principle. Donning rose-colored lenses in willful ignorance of the hurting and ugliness of the world is like paving over a toxic waste dump and hoping it goes away. On a certain level, it is true that "It's all good"—but that includes our perception that something is terribly wrong. It is that perception, and the fire it kindles within us to create a more beautiful world, that makes "It's all good" come true. The perfection of the unfolding encompasses the imperfection. Resisting "negativity" is itself a form of negativity, in that it affirms that doubt, fear, etc., are indeed negative. But they have an important role, just like everything else. To deny that, to deny our fear and pain, would indeed be to ignore the dark side. Acting from interbeing doesn't deny a single fact or experience presented us. It does require shedding our customary interpretation of those experiences. That can be difficult, because those interpretations are not only culturally reinforced in ways both subtle and powerful, they are also a kind of cover for the deep wounds of Separation that most of us carry.

Let me say that again. Hate and the Story of Evil are a cover for the wound of Separation. We need to peel away that cover and give that wound attention, so that it can heal. Otherwise, we will continue to act from Separation ourselves, and we will create more of it, unwittingly, through all we do. Again, can you peer into the abyss that the more horrific atrocities open up, and not plunge into hate? Can you be present to the gaping, painful wound those stories reveal? Can you let it hurt, and let it hurt, and know that having integrated that hurting, you will act with a wisdom, clarity, and effectiveness far surpassing the smiting of enemies?

I was about to say that to act from interbeing, far from being a cowardly capitulation to evil, requires considerable courage. But then I realized that to put it like that hooks into a thought form of separation. It would imply that those who are not doing this lack courage, and that you should cultivate courage in order to act from love. Actually, what is happening is that our immersion in the Story of Interbeing generates courage.

Granted, there may be situations in which no nonviolent means suffice, but habituated as we are to the concept of evil, the paradigm of force, and the habit of othering, we tend to group nearly every situation into this category. The violence may be very subtle, dressed for example in concepts like "holding them to account," which is usually code for shaming, humiliation, and retribution. Rarely do we have the imagination, courage, or skill to act from a felt understanding of the humanity of the aggressor, or of the ingrate, or of the fool. That words like ingrate, fool, idiot, liar, crank, apologist, imperialist, racist, and so on even exist already invites us into the dispositionist belief that people *are* these things. Separation is built in to our very language.[4] Can you see now the depth of the revolution in human beingness that we are undertaking? Can you see how powerfully our context conditions us to see evil as a fact of the world?

Even if the reader is not convinced that there is no such thing as elemental, essential evil, it should at least be clear that most of the time, what we ascribe to evil actually comes from situation. Even if the reader still thinks there is a "discontinuity that divides the ordinary flawed human from the truly evil," it is clear that we often categorize the former as the latter. That is extremely important, because whereas evil can be overcome only by superior force, anything else can be changed by changing the situation, the totality of the inner and outer circumstances. In large part, these circumstances consist of layer upon layer of story, going all the way down to our personal and cultural Story of Self.

This is the level we must work at if we are to create a different kind of society. We must become the storytellers of a new world. We tell the story not only with words, but also with the actions that spring from that story. Each such action shows all who witness it that there is another world out there, another way of seeing and being, and that you are not crazy for thinking it is there.

---

4. Some therefore advocate abolishing all humiliating labels from our speech. If we replace "narcissist" with "person with narcissistic tendencies" and "addict" with "person with an addiction" and "liar" with "person with a habit of dishonesty," they think, we might uphold through our use of language the dignity of all people, separating the behavior from the actual person. Even "hero," they might say, should be replaced with "person with heroic accomplishments" in order not to imply that those not so labeled are unheroic. I tend to get annoyed with crusaders for linguistic correctness—excuse me, I mean people who might be interpreted as having crusading tendencies—for a couple reasons. First, it panders to a victim mentality and encourages us to be easily offended. Second, very quickly the new terms take on the old pejorative or disparaging sense, as exemplified by the evolution from moron to retard to mentally handicapped to mentally disabled to whatever the new locution may be. People can dress vicious intent in all the right words. On a deeper level, we can say all the right things while doing nothing.

Every act of generosity is an invitation into generosity. Every act of courage is an invitation into courage. Every act of selflessness is an invitation into selflessness. Every act of healing is an invitation into healing. I am sure you have felt this invitation upon witnessing such acts.

I once read a news story about a train wreck in Peru. The travelers and tourists were stranded in the mountainous area in winter, without food or heat. Many might have died that night, if it weren't for the local villagers who came with food and blankets to keep them warm. These were poor villagers, and they were giving their only blankets.

I remember when I read that story how petty my own insecurity seemed, how tight my heart, and how tiny my generosity. I felt a kind of opening. If those indigent villagers can give their last blankets, then surely I needn't be so concerned about my financial future. I can give. It will be okay.

One way to interpret this story is to conclude that obviously, those seemingly indigent villagers are much wealthier than I am. Let's try a new definition of wealth: "the ease and freedom to be generous." Perhaps these villagers have what we, in pursuit of money and its illusory security, are seeking to attain. For one thing, they are in community, and know that they will be taken care of by those around them. That is not so true in a money economy like ours. Second, they have a deep connection to the land and a sense of belonging. Through their relationships, they know who they are. That is a kind of wealth that no amount of money can replace. We moderns, the disconnected, have a lot of rebuilding to do. People like those villagers, and anyone living from interbeing, remind us of our potential wealth and the ground truth of interbeing. Their generosity enriches us merely through witnessing it.

All of us have at one time or another been fortunate enough to witness generosity and to feel how it opens us. Nonetheless, if you are like me, you also harbor a voice that says, "But what if it *isn't* okay? What if I give, and just get taken advantage of? What if I give, and have nothing left, and no one takes care of me?" Underneath these plaintive questions is another, even more profound: "What if I am alone in the universe?" This is the primal fear of the separate self. In its logic, giving is insane. If I and the world are one, then what I do to the world, I do to myself—generosity is natural. But if I am separate from the world, there is no guarantee that anything I do will come back to me. I have to contrive it, I have to engineer an avenue of return, an assurance. If I give, I have to leverage some form of influence over the receiver, legal or emotional, to ensure I get paid back. At least I have to make sure other people see my generosity, so that they are impressed and I get a social return. You will recognize that this whole mindset is contrary to the spirit of the gift.

These questions "What if no one takes care of me? What if it's not okay? What if I'm alone in the universe?" also underlie concerns that a philosophy of oneness or interbeing ignores the "dark side." When someone tries to get me to admit the existence of evil, they are speaking from something painful. I know it well, because it is in me too. It is a feeling of indignation, frustration, and helplessness. There is an implacable, malevolent Other out there, threaded through the entire universe, making it always a bit foolish to trust, foolish to give, and never quite safe to love. Of course, we live in a world where that has often been our experience. No wonder we take it as a fundamental attribute of reality, and see any denial of it as dangerously naive. But really what is happening is that we are projecting our experience onto reality, and then, based on the projection we see, reifying it still further by acting within its logic.

Evil is not only a response to the perception of separation, it is also its product. How do we deal with this implacable, malevolent Evil? Because force is the only language it understands, we are compelled to join it in force; as the Orwell dialogue I quote earlier shows, we become evil too. Human beings have been committing horrors for thousands of years in the name of conquering evil. The identity of evil keeps changing—the Turks! the Infidels! the bankers! the French! the Jews! the bourgeoisie! the terrorists!—but that mindset remains the same. As does the solution: force. As does the result: more evil. Must we forever battle the image of our own delusion? We see the results all over our scarred planet. A saying goes, "The greatest tool of the Devil is the belief that there is no Devil." Perhaps the opposite is true: "The greatest tool of Evil is the idea there is such a thing as Evil."

Take a while to appreciate the subtlety of that paradox. It does not say, "Evil does not exist." It is essentially saying that evil is a story. Does that mean it isn't real? No. Evil is as real as a poacher stripping the tusks from an elephant, Monsanto marketing GMO seeds to Indian peasants, the government ordering drone strikes on funeral processions. These are the tip of the iceberg, tiny tremors amid the convulsions wracking our planet.

Evil is real—no less real than any other story. What are some other stories? America is a story, money is a story, even the self is a story. What could be more real than your self? Yet even the self can be realized as an illusory construct when, through grace or practice, we are freed from its story. The point is not that we should treat evil as unreal. It is that we must address it on the level of story rather than accept its own invisible premises and logic. If we do the latter, we become its creature. If we address it on the level of story, and deconstruct through words and actions the mythology it lives in, then we win without defeating. The next chapters address working on the level of story—disrupting the old and telling the new—in more detail.

We have entertained a number of paradoxes: that the reason "It's all good" is that we are realizing it is all terribly wrong; that the Devil's greatest weapon is the notion that there is such a thing as the Devil; that evil comes from the perception of evil. In order to tie up a remaining loose thread in this chapter's ontology of evil, I'm afraid I will have to pile on one more paradox. It is not only evil that is both "real" and a story; "real" is both real and a story as well. Our use of the word real encodes assumptions of an objective universe that, as we saw in the chapter "Science," are highly questionable. We cannot even say, "Reality is not real," because to do so smuggles in an objective backdrop in which reality either is, or is not, real. I could ask, "What if reality is real for you and not for me?" but even then, the word "is" smuggles in the same thing. That said, I would like you for a moment to drop your habit of objectivism and consider whether it might be possible for evil to exist in the Story of Separation, and for it not to exist in the Story of Interbeing. I don't mean that one story countenances it and one does not. I mean that in transitioning between stories, we transition between realities. How does one make that transition? That's what this whole book is about.

Questioning the absolute division between subject and object leads one to ponder what the experience of evil reveals in oneself, as well as what state of being attracts one to believe or disbelieve in absolute evil. Have you ever had a personal encounter with an implacable, malevolent power, either in human form or in an altered state of consciousness? If you have, you know the overwhelmingly intense feelings of impotent rage, grief, and fear the experience provokes. One steps into the archetype of the Victim, powerless, utterly at the mercy of a merciless force. Until one has had this experience, it is impossible to see that such a state is latent inside each of us. The experience is a vehicle of self-discovery, conveying one to a very dark, inaccessible corner of being. As such it is a kind of medicine, a harsh medicine to be sure, but perhaps necessary to bring to the light of awareness, and therefore of healing, a primal wound. I would be curious to know what people who have been victimized by psychopaths or other malevolent powers have in common. Are they just random victims, or is there something inside of them that attracts the experience?

Those who do what they call shamanic work might ask the same question about the "entities" that attach themselves to people. Are these arbitrary, predatory forces, like the impersonal forces of nature, that visit themselves upon the unlucky? Or is there an energetic hole, a missing part, a wound that perfectly complements the configuration of the entity that attaches itself? In that case, perhaps the entity is performing a service, merging with the host into a symbiotic whole. One might ask, is the entity really a separate entity at all, or could it be an unintegrated part of the psyche? Is there even a meaningful difference between those two categories? What is a self, anyway? If we are interbeings—the sum total of our relationships—then the existence of an alien, othered "evil" is highly problematic.

The idea that evil is part of a larger alchemical dance vastly complicates the usual narrative of fighting on the side of good to conquer evil. We might instead see the evil we encounter as the externalized image of something hidden within ourselves. In contrast, the concept of absolute, merciless evil is closely analogous to the impersonal, merciless forces of the Newtonian universe, which visit destruction randomly upon us. It is also analogous to the ruthlessly competing gene-controlled robots of Darwinian natural selection. Both of these are key pillars of the old story. Does it not stand to reason that evil is as well?

Dreams, psychedelic experiences, and a few in waking consciousness have shown me that each time I enter a confrontation with a malevolent force, there has been something in me that complemented it. In the case of actual human beings, I was pulled in two directions: toward an interpretation of the other person in which he or she was wholly evil, and an interpretation in which his or her appalling behavior had a more innocent explanation, or perhaps an explanation that encompassed my own culpability. Despite my best efforts, it was never possible to know for sure. It wasn't a matter of mere intellectual curiosity. Do I take preemptive measures? Do I treat that person as an implacable enemy? Do I interpret a seemingly conciliatory move as a mere ploy? Is my feeling of shared responsibility a leverage point for the perpetrator, implying that I should adopt a protective self-righteousness? How do I know for sure?

How to answer these questions is a matter of great planetary importance, for they are the same ones that the Palestinians and the Israelis, the Sunnis and the Shiites, the Hindus and the Muslims, must answer to decide between war and peace. I find that usually, it is impossible to discover incontrovertible evidence that can decide these questions, as if there were an objective fact of the matter to ascertain. Rather, it often seems that whatever answer one chooses becomes true. Before the choice is made, it is as if the persecutor were in a quantum superposition of states. Each story that we consider has a role for the other person. By choosing the story, we choose their role.

Now for a few more complications. For one, what about situations in which it is naive and counterproductive to continue giving the violator the benefit of the doubt, as in domestic abuse situations, or in dealing with an addict? Second, what about situations in which the other party does not accept the invitation into a peaceful role—what if they refuse to join the Story of Interbeing? Third, it is all well and good to say that people with a certain psychology draw to themselves experiences of being persecuted or abused, and that the encounter with evil is part of a developmental process, but it seems callous and arrogant indeed to say that about toddlers abused by their parents, or entire populations subjected to genocide.

I mention these mostly to assure the reader that I have not over-looked the obvious. I will not in these pages attempt a thorough answer to these and other points; I'll just point toward how they might be addressed and leave the rest to the reader. First, it is important to dis-tinguish between refusing a story of "he is evil" and accepting the other person's story. I am not talking about capitulation here. It is certainly possible to stand in a Story of Interbeing and lovingly, compassionately refuse to allow the alcoholic to borrow your car, or the wife-beater to have another chance.

As for the second point, it is certainly possible that even if you hold open the invitation into the new story as strongly as Gandhi, the other party will refuse to step into it. In that case, other circumstances will arise that eject them from your world. Those who live by the sword, die by the sword, and we needn't take it upon ourselves to be the killer. Lao Tzu warns, "There are always executioners. If you take over their function, it is like trying to replace the master woodcarver—you will probably cut your hand." And the Bible says, "Vengeance is mine, say-eth the Lord" (i.e., vengeance is not yours, only God's).

Again, I am not saying there is never a time to fight. All things have their place in this world: the buck struggles against the wolf, and some-times he gets away. It is just that, because of our ideology, we apply the mentality of fighting, struggling, and warfare far beyond its proper domain. I will not attempt to delineate principles that distinguish when fighting is "justified"; to decide on principle is part of the old story, and besides, principles are easy to twist into justifications for nearly any atrocity. I will just say that if fighting is accompanied by hate or self-pity, it is probably outside its proper domain.

The third point opens up a hoary theological question about the purpose of evil and of suffering in our world. Why do the innocent suffer? Here is a paragraph from a long discussion of this question in "Eulogy and Redemption" in *The Ascent of Humanity*. You can read the whole section (and the whole book) online.

> We often think of misfortune as some kind of punishment for past evil, a theme that runs through religious thought both East and West. In the East it is the idea that present suffering represents the negative karma generated through past misdeeds; in the West we have the image of Yahweh striking down the cities of Sodom and Gomorrah for their sins, threatening Nineveh for its "wickedness." However, the self-evident fact that it is often the innocent who suffer the most demands all kinds of theological contortions, from past lives to Original Sin, from future rebirth to Heaven and Hell. How else to explain the sweet, innocent babies in the children's cancer wards? If we are not to resort to blind, pitiless, purposeless chance, we need another explanation for the innocence of our victims. Perhaps they are great souls, meeting the huge necessity for innocent victims that our civilization has wrought. "I will go," they say. "I am big enough. I am ready for this experience."

Humanity has been on a journey of Separation for thousands of years, and every crevice of that territory must be explored. The perpetrators and the victims of all we call evil have explored the furthest reaches of Separation. One might even define evil as separation: the total othering of a person, a nation, or nature, as well as the natural consequence of being cast into an alien universe separate from oneself. Recall the workshop exercise: "I wanted to kill something." Significant it is that the label "evil" is itself a profound form of othering. That is another way to see that the concept of evil is part and parcel of the phenomenon of evil.

Thankfully, having explored the extremities of the territory of Separation, we now have the possibility of embarking on the return journey. If evil is part of your Story of the World, either through direct experience or as a fundamental ontological category, you might want to explore how that story serves you and what is the hurting that draws you to it. Because again, evidence and logic will not resolve whether evil is real. I have made extensive arguments drawing from situationist psychology, from psychopathy, from metaphysics, and from numerous anecdotes, but one could probably rebut each point, and I could rebut the rebuttals *ad infinitum*. How will you choose your story? How will you influence how others choose theirs? I leave you with the tale of Christian Bethelson as a final example of the redemption of evil and the disruption of stories.

My friend Cynthia Jurs met Christian Bethelson while she was doing peace work in Liberia, which had suffered a horrendous civil war in the 1990s. A rebel leader known by the *nom de guerre* of General Leopard, Bethelson was infamous in a milieu of massacre, child soldiery, and torture. If any human being is evil, it would have been him; he was, in his words, a man with "no conscience." Eventually the war ended, and with it Bethelson's livelihood: he had no skill other than killing. He decided to go to the nearest war, in Ivory Coast, where there might be demand for his gruesome services. On the way his car got stuck in the mud. Who would have guessed that another car would be stuck in the mud on the same stretch of road at the same time, and that that car would be bearing members of a peace group called the Everyday Gandhis? Intrigued by their conversation, he announced himself as a former rebel general. He thought they would vilify him, maybe even beat him, but to his astonishment the group gathered around him, hugged him, told him they loved him. He decided to join them and dedicate his life to peace.

Let us hold out for no less a miracle planetwide. Let us accept the invitation that it offers us into a larger sense of the possible.

Story

*L*et me share another story from the ancient collection of Taoist allegories known as the *Liezi*, as rendered by Thomas Cleary in *Vitality, Energy, Spirit: A Taoist Sourcebook*.

> One day Confucius was walking along with some disciples when they came upon two boys arguing. Confucius asked the boys what the dispute was about. They told him they were arguing about whether the sun was nearer at dawn and farther away at noon, or farther away at dawn and nearer at noon.
>
> One of the boys argued that the sun appeared larger at dawn and smaller at noon, so it must be closer at dawn and farther away at noon.
>
> The other boy argued that it was cool at dawn and hot at noon, so the sun must be farther away at dawn and closer at noon.
>
> Confucius was at a loss to determine which one was correct. The boys jeered at him, "Who said you were so smart?"

Cleary explains, "[The story] illustrates the limitations of discursive reasoning, thus hinting indirectly at a more comprehensive mode of consciousness. Presented as a joke at the expense of Confucius, it illustrates how logic can be coherent within the bounds of its own postulates yet be ineffective or inaccurate in a larger context."

We have seen already how so much of what we consider to be real, true, and possible is a consequence of the story that embeds us. We have seen how the logic of Separation leads ineluctably to despair. We have seen how evil is a consequence of the perception of separation. We have seen how the entire edifice of civilization is built upon a myth. We have seen how civilization has been trapped, indeed, in its "own postulates," its ideology of intensifying control to remedy the failure of control. We have seen how so many of our efforts to change the world embody the habits of separation, leaving us helpless to avoid replicating the same in endless elaboration.

As Cleary suggests, to exit this trap we must operate from a larger context, a more comprehensive mode of consciousness. This means not only inhabiting a new story, but also working in the consciousness of story. If, after all, our civilization is built on a myth, to change our civilization we must change the myth.

By now it should be clear that this is no recipe for inaction or for mere words. Any action that is open to symbolic interpretation can be part of the telling of a story. And that is every action. We humans are meaning-making animals, constantly seeking to make sense of the world. When Pancho Ramos Stierle spoke to the abusive policeman with kind respect, he opened a rupture in that man's story of the world.

Paradoxically, actions that are designed to be symbolic are usually less powerful story-disrupters than actions that are taken in earnest. I have been reading about the Shuar tribe in Ecuador, who have vowed to forcefully resist the destruction of their rainforest by mining companies looking for copper and gold. Said one Shuar chief, Domingo Ankuash, "The forest has always given us everything we need, and we are planning to defend it, as our ancestors would, with the strength of the spear. To get the gold, they will have to kill every one of us first."

Let's consider the potency of these words. They were not a calcu-
lated PR device. Already the Shuar have evicted mining outfits from
several preliminary locations. This fierce tribe is obviously willing to
die to protect its land. Their words are true through and through.

On the other hand, if they are successful it won't be because their
spears have overcome the tanks, machine guns, helicopters, defoliants,
and bulldozers that the government might deploy to protect the mining
companies. They cannot possibly overcome industrial civilization by
force. Industrial civilization, after all, is the master of force, harnessing
every possible source of stored energy to exert force upon the material
world. Force is the essence of our civilization and our technology. The
Shuar will not beat industrial civilization at its own game. Yet the Shuar
are going to win. Let us understand why. What game are they playing?
If we, aspiring changemakers, can understand that, then perhaps we can
win too.

Whatever game they are playing, we might recognize it as the
same game Diane Wilson was playing in the story I related earlier, the
same game Pancho was playing, perhaps the same game the indigenous
women in western Canada are playing in the Idle No More movement
to stop the ravaging of their lands. In a sense, all of these people are
being naive. Such movements do not always prevail—or do they, in
some way we cannot see? What of all the exterminated tribes who died
protecting ecosystems that are no more? Were their efforts in vain?
Will your efforts be in vain, to create a more beautiful world?

The first thing I notice about the Shuar is that their commitment is
to the land, the forest, the tribe, and to what they hold sacred. It is not
a fear-based response to a threat; indeed, they are facing much greater
personal risk by resisting the Onward March of Progress than they
would be acquiescing to it.

The second thing I notice is that they are not fighting against something; they are fighting for something. They have a vision of their land
as it should be. They have something bigger than themselves they can
commit to. I suspect that as they deepen their involvement in resistance,
their vision of what they serve will grow. In contrast, many activists

today are consumed with stopping this and stopping that; rarely do they frame their vision in terms of what they want to create or what larger thing they serve. One symptom of this deficiency is the goal of "sustainability." What, exactly, do we want to sustain? Is the purpose of life merely to survive? Are the creative powers unique to humanity without a purpose in the unfolding order of nature? We need to be able to see a vision of what's possible that we can commit to.

A third thing is that even though the Shuar didn't conceive their resistance actions with symbolic intent, they are nonetheless potent carriers of meaning. They make the story that it is perfectly fine to take minerals from the Amazon a lot harder to maintain. The mining companies do their best to construct that story—the trees will be replanted, the waste tailings kept in safe containment pools, and besides, the Shuar are killing wildlife with their hunting and their children aren't attending school—but to add to these absurdities another, that the Shuar are benighted savages who don't know what's good for them, is perhaps too much for that story to bear, when the Shuar believe so fervently that they are willing to lay down their very lives.

If the Shuar succeed in preserving their homeland, it won't be because their spears overcame civilization's machine guns. It will be because the story that justifies killing them and taking the minerals wasn't strong enough to withstand their challenge. It will be because enough people in key positions declined to take up the guns, bombs, and bulldozers. It will be because we—the industrialized world—refrained from using the force at our disposal. A strong story would be able to justify and rationalize everything necessary to get that gold. Half a century ago, few people would hesitate to agree that it is unfortunately necessary to clear the Indians away from the path of progress. Until recently, we had no compunctions in killing "every last one of them." But today our story is infirm.

When a story is young and hale, it has a kind of immune system that insulates its holders from cognitive dissonance. New data points that don't fit the story are easily discarded. They seem outlandish. The immune system responds in a variety of ways. It can attack the bearer of the disruptive information: "What are that guy's credentials?" It can muster a few superficially convincing rebuttals and pretend that the offender has not thought of those and has no response: "But technology has vastly increased the human life span, so we need to get the minerals from somewhere." It can appeal to the implicitly assumed rightness of the system: "Surely, scientists and engineers have determined that this is the least ecologically disruptive way to do it." Or it can discard the offending information into the bin marked "anomaly," or simply toss it down the memory hole.

When a story grows old, none of these immune responses work as well. Inconsistent data, even when dismissed, leaves a lingering doubt. Like an aging body or a womb nearing childbirth, the story becomes less and less comfortable. This is why people like the Shuar might succeed where others like them have, for thousands of years now, failed. Their resistance might dislodge us from the story that enables the pillage.

The Shuar are not a peaceful people, and they have evicted prospecting crews and machinery under threat of force. They are not, however, at war, in the sense that they are not striving to defeat an enemy. In contrast, much of our popular culture and the mentality of war see victory in terms of overcoming, by force, the perpetrator of evil. So for example, in the movie *Avatar*, which closely parallels the situation of the Shuar, the fictional Na'vi overcome the spaceships and artillery of the human invaders with spears, bows and arrows, and large animals. When the chief human general is killed, then the victory is complete. There is no other way, since he is depicted as irredeemable. Fortunately, the Shuar seem not to be infected with the virus of the ideology of "evil." They are not fighting the mining companies. They are fighting the mining.

I would have liked to see a different ending to *Avatar*. I would have liked to see the planet infiltrate the nervous systems of the humans so that, when they destroyed its world-tree, they themselves felt the pain of it, erasing the us/them divide that enabled them to see the planet as a mere source of resources. That is precisely the change of perception that our civilization needs to undergo. Because I don't think that the Shuar are going to overcome us with their spears.

They might, however, with their spears, their words, and other actions, overcome our stories. In this, all of us might join them and learn from them. What is the difference between the kind of symbolically potent force the Shuar are using, and run-of-the-mill violence and terrorism? It is, after all, a small step from the necessarily asymmetrical struggle the Shuar are engaged in to what people today call terrorism. I would not be surprised if the Ecuadorian government levels that epithet against the Shuar soon.

I will not here attempt to penetrate the thicket of distinctions between terrorism and asymmetrical warfare, and the possible justifications for each. I will just say that as we migrate from the concrete (stopping *this* bulldozer from felling *these* trees right here) to the abstract (striking a blow at an enemy or a symbolic blow for a cause) we enter dangerous territory.

To paraphrase Martin Luther King Jr., you can kill the haters, but you cannot kill the hate; in fact, you will create even more hate by even trying. Moreover, in the present world you are bound to fail, because those in power can easily outkill you.

To see how deeply ingrained the habit of separation called "conquering evil" is, look at how consistently we frame any attempt to enact social or political change as a "fight," a "struggle," or a "campaign." All military metaphors. We speak of "mobilizing our allies" to exert political "pressure" in order to "force" our opponents to "surrender."

Again, I am not saying there is never a time to fight, nor do I intend to settle here the long and nuanced debate over nonviolence. Broadly enough interpreted, violence—that which "violates" another person's boundaries—is unavoidable. A public protest that causes traffic jams feels violating to the poor commuter schlepping an hour each way to work from the low-income suburbs. In transitioning to a new world, the disruption of the old is inevitable. But when the violence comes from the hatred or demonization of the other, it is founded on an untruth. Let us not deceive ourselves into using the familiar, comfortable tactics and metaphors of force, when more potent processes for change may be available to us.

The reason that the defiance of the Shuar moves us isn't that they are willing to kill for their cause; it is that they are willing to die for it. This is, in pure form, service to something greater than oneself. This is what we must emulate if we are to cocreate the more beautiful world our hearts know is possible. It is also a way to transcend the separate self, since to bow into service is to merge with something greater, something whose power to precipitate change extends beyond our understanding of causality. Then, the unexpected, the improbable, the miraculous can happen.

The more firmly we stand in a larger Story of Self, a Story of Inter-being, the more powerful we become in disrupting the old Story of Separation. I think questions of violence and nonviolence, ethics and principles, right and wrong, lead us into a conceptual maze. See, the sun is nearer at noon. No, it is at dawn. Every evil deed and every cowardly inaction that has ever been perpetrated on this earth has been justified by principle—the logic of a story. As we sober up from our long intoxication with the Story of Separation, we have the chance to enter a "more comprehensive mode of consciousness"—the consciousness of story. In it, we ask ourselves, "What story shall I stand in?"

Disruption

It is useless to attempt to reason a man
out of a thing he was never reasoned into.

—JONATHAN SWIFT

T he world as we know it is built on a story. To be a change agent is, first, to disrupt the existing Story of the World, and second, to tell a new Story of the World so that those entering the space between stories have a place to go. Often, these two functions merge into one, since the actions we take that are part of the telling of a new story are also disruptive to the old.

This is how I see my work, the work of activists, and even on some level the work of artists and healers. Many of the stories I have told in this book exemplify the disruption of the old story: Pancho's interaction with the policeman, for instance. I will share some more examples soon, but let's start by considering a class of people that is the source of the greatest despair for many people I know. It is the class of "people who just don't get it."

When I speak publicly, I usually get a question along these lines: "To create a more beautiful world requires a mass change in values and beliefs, and I just don't see it happening. People are too stuck, too ignorant. They'll never change. Not the people in power, and not my conservative brother-in-law. What can we do to get people unstuck?"

One thing that almost never works is to overcome the subject's opinions through the force of logic and evidence. This should not be surprising, given that people do not form their beliefs based on evidence or reason to begin with. Rather, we use reason to arrange the evidence into a story aligned with an underlying state of being that includes emotional tendencies, old wounds, patterns of relationship, and outlook on life. This story interlocks with other stories, and ultimately with the deep, invisible personal mythologies that define our lives. These personal mythologies in turn are woven into our cultural mythology, the consensus reality that goes as deep as civilization itself. Because beliefs are typically part of a larger story that includes one's identity and value system, a challenge to them is often taken as an assault, triggering various defense mechanisms to preserve that larger story. You'll be ignored, written off as a hippie, lefty, enviro, or dreamer, or rebutted with whatever counterclaims are conveniently at hand. Perhaps your target will divert the conversation onto some trivial point, a misstatement, a grammar error, or a personal slight, thereby invalidating everything you say.

Such people are not like you. Unlike them, you choose your beliefs based on evidence and reason. Not like the Republicans! The liberals! The Tea Party! The religious fundamentalists! The credulous New Agers! The medical establishment! That's right, you have arrived at your opinions through an open-minded consideration of the evidence, while those who disagree with you are mired in ignorance, prejudice, and plain old stupidity.

Let's be honest with ourselves. Who among us can look back on our lives and deny that most of the time, we too closed our minds to the truth while believing the open, dismissing challenges in just the ways I've described? What makes you think you are any different today in the fundamental ways you form and uphold beliefs?

The idea that we base beliefs on reason and evidence, or at least the ideal of so doing, has deep roots in Western philosophy and the worldview from which it arises. It echoes the axiomatic method in mathematics, the philosophical program of establishing "first principles" and reasoning upward from those, and the objectivism of science that says that we can find truth through the impartial testing of hypotheses about a reality outside ourselves. It is reflected in the idea that one must start any argument with clear definitions of terms. Well, any argument with your Republican brother-in-law or your anti-vaccine aunt or your pro-vaccine cousin (pick the one that tweaks you) should confirm that this approach just doesn't work. It quickly becomes apparent that it is impossible to agree even on what the facts are, let alone what the facts mean.

It gets worse. A series of studies at the University of Michigan in 2005 and 2006 showed not only that people routinely dismiss facts that don't fit their beliefs, but that they actually harden their beliefs when presented with contradictory facts, perhaps in an effort to avoid cognitive dissonance. Moreover, the most misinformed people had the strongest opinions, and the most politically sophisticated thinkers were the least open to contrary information.[1]

The facts arrive at our brains already prefiltered by the distorting lens of the stories in which we operate. The debate over climate change illustrates this nicely: when one digs into it, one finds that it is impossible to be sure what the actual data are. Certainly there are many studies and reports, but there are also accusations of exclusion of contradictory data, bias, sloppiness, and outright dishonesty in those reports. Ultimately, the evidence one accepts is strongly colored by one's trust or lack thereof in authority, which is colored by personal history, perhaps one's relationship to one's father, and so forth. Consider, for example, appeals to the "near-unanimity of climate scientists." (Is there really near-unanimity? Whether or not you accept that pronouncement again depends on your trust in the authority of the source that is saying it. Do you trust the *New York Times* on that? Or do you trust a maverick scientist ostracized by his profession?) Moreover, appeal to near-unanimity among scientists invokes the basic integrity of science as an institution, which in turn rests within larger and less visible stories.

My point here is not to question climate change; it is merely to

---

1. See Joe Keohane's "How Facts Backfire" in the July 11, 2010, *Boston Globe* for a discussion of this research.

illuminate how evidence, rather than being the basis of belief, is filtered by belief to maintain the integrity of a story. Good storytellers understand this and do it on purpose, using facts, studies, and so forth as elements of their story. In the climate change debate, both sides do it. You might suppose that an intelligent, rational person (like yourself) would never deny global warming if only they looked at the evidence in an unbiased way. But guess what—your opponents think the same thing about their position. Is the reason for our collective folly just that the smart people aren't in control of things? Or could it be that we have been in the grips of a story that necessarily imprints its precepts onto the world?

I met a really smart lady recently. She was a vice president at Nestlé Corporation. I overheard a college student questioning her glowing portrayal of Nestlé's social and environmental policies. The student bravely interrogated the VP about their leading beverage category, bottled water. "Do we really need such a thing?" she asked. And "I understand you are using 40 percent less plastic per bottle, but wouldn't it be better to use no plastic at all?"

To each query, the VP had a ready, methodical response. Bottled water meets a real need in a society on the go. And did you know that one raw ingredient for making the plastic bottles is a by-product of producing gasoline from petroleum? If it doesn't go toward bottles, it will end up as some other plastic product or dumped directly into the environment. Glass uses way more energy to produce. And tap water is no longer pure.

I was impressed not only by her evident sincerity, but also by her patience, her attentive listening, and her lack of animosity in the face of what must be frequent attacks. Nestlé, after all, is notorious among activists as a corporate villain and the target of a decades-long boycott over its marketing of infant formula to indigent mothers. It has been accused of overpumping from mineral springs, collaboration with the Burmese junta, union-busting in Colombia, buying cacao from farms that use child labor, and so on. The contrast between this reputation and the VP's fervent, heartfelt exposition of Nestlé's environmental virtues was such that a few left-leaning folks had to step out of the auditorium.

How to explain this contrast? Let's try three theories.

1. The woman is a glib liar paid well to make the company's case. Either she is cynically aware of the truth obscured by her lies, or she is in a state of deep, self-serving denial. Either way, she cherry-picks a few positive gestures toward the environment ("Nestlé protects orangutans!") and draws from reams of tendentious evidence that the company's PR department compiles to make anyone who questions the company's practices seem naive.

2. What the woman says is true. The company has learned from its mistakes to become a leader in social and environmental responsibility. There are many well-meaning people who still criticize the company, but that is because they don't know the true story: not only is Nestlé leading the way toward sustainability, but the industry as a whole is improving its practices. There are still challenges to deal with, but everything is moving in the right direction. The people in industry care about the environment just like you do. They get it now, and with your help they will continue making progress.

I hope I have done justice, in the second theory, to the Nestlé VP's viewpoint. I had a conversation later on with her, and found her to be very human, highly intelligent, and not averse to introspection. My impression is that she deeply and truly believes in her company and her work. So let me offer a third explanation:

3. Not only does she sincerely believe everything she says, but it is irrefutable from within her frame of reference. If we take for granted the endless acceleration of modern life, then the convenience of safe bottled water is indeed a boon for people who otherwise would drink sugary soft drinks. It is a boon as well if we take for granted the continuing

deterioration of municipal tap water, its chlorination, and chemical contamination. And if we take for granted our current petroleum-based economy, it is, for all I know, true that plastic bottles don't add much harm.

The VP's positions are unassailable unless we can expand the scope of the conversation. We have to ask questions at the level of "What role do plastic bottles play in the accelerating pace of modern life, why is this acceleration happening, and is it a good thing?" "Where does our busyness and need for convenience come from?" "Why is our tap water becoming undrinkable?" "Why do we have a system in which it is okay to produce waste products that are unusable by other life-forms?" And "Is the 'sustainable growth' championed by Nestlé possible on a finite planet?"

I believe the conversation must go deeper still. What that Nestlé VP did to justify her company, others can do to justify our whole civilization, as long as we grant them certain premises about the nature of life, self, and reality. For example, if we grant the premise that primitive life was "solitary, poor, nasty, brutish, and short," then any doubts about the overall beneficence of technology run into a brick wall. Similarly, if we grant the premise that nature bears no inherent tendency toward organization and that life is just a random collocation of lifeless, generic building blocks bumped around by purposeless forces, then clearly we need have no scruples about seeking to conquer nature and turn it toward human ends. And finally, if we grant the premise that each of us is a discrete, separate self seeking to maximize genetic self-interest, then ultimately there is no arguing over the broad legal and economic parameters of our society, which seek to overcome that wanton nature and channel it toward pro-social ends.

The Nestlé VP's views are more or less sound within the framework I have described above, the framework of "making life better through technology," of the progressive conquest of inner and outer nature. Her views will not change until that framework crumbles. They are completely at home within the Story of Ascent.

I heard another smart guy one morning on The Diane Rehm Show, an energy industry consultant. One of the topics was the controversial Keystone XL pipeline, intended to transport Albertan tar sands oil to refineries on the Gulf Coast. The consultant made the following point, which I will paraphrase: "Look, if we don't build the pipeline, the refineries on the Gulf Coast are just going to refine heavy crude from somewhere else, and the tar sands will send their oil to Asia instead of the United States. Stopping the pipeline won't have any impact on climate change or ecosystem destruction. That oil is going to be extracted and refined anyway, so it might as well be done in a way that brings jobs to the United States."

Philosophers of ethics would have fun demolishing these arguments, which would apply just as well to selling body parts from the Nazi concentration camps. Whether I sell them or not, the camps are still operating, so I might as well put those body parts to good use, right? The point here, though, isn't to expose the logical flaws in the justifications for the Keystone XL pipeline or plastic bottles, but to show how the things we take for granted determine our moral choices. In the reality bubble they inhabit, their arguments make perfect sense. If it is indeed an unalterable fact of the universe that the tar sands will be extracted, then it would be vain and counterproductive to disdainfully refuse to engage that fact. If our current petroleum-based civilization is unalterable, then we might commend Nestlé for putting its waste to good use. If we take the growing busyness of people's lives for granted, then we must welcome the conveniences that make modern life tolerable. Within their operating paradigms, both these smart people are doing good.

How do you know you are not like that Nestlé VP? How do you know the speck in her eye isn't the image of the log in your own? What you and she probably share in common, and what the climate change denier and the climate change alarmist share in common, is the belief that facts and logic are on one's own side, and that one's position is based on them. But obviously, the elusiveness of facts and the ease with which reason can be put in service of a story tell us that to change beliefs—and our beliefs must change—requires a more comprehensive, holistic change in our stories and all that are attached to them, all the way down to our sense of self, habits, and basic perceptions of the world. It is the totality of these things that I call a Story of the World.

Even "facts" as basic as the universal constants of physics or the Second Law of Thermodynamics depend, on some level, on subjective choices about who and what to believe. Rupert Sheldrake describes, for example, how the accepted value for the speed of light changed by 20 km/sec for a span of eighteen years in the 1930s and '40s—a change consistent across all experiments around the world. Then in 1945 the speed of light reverted back to its original pre-1928 value. The discrepancy far exceeds the margin of error of the measurements. Sheldrake also documents variability in G, the universal gravitational constant. Could it be that facts are what the etymology of the word suggests— something that we make, as in a "factory"?

Back now to your brother-in-law. If you can't out-argue him, how can you change his beliefs? On a broader level, as people seeking to change the world, how can we change our society's story?

Reasoning from the situationist perspective, people gravitate toward a set of beliefs resonant with the totality of their life experiences. These are the foundation of the beliefs, of which what we call "opinion" is only the most visible, superficial aspect. Opinions are symptoms of a state of being. Therefore, to change opinions and beliefs, one must change the foundation of the "situation"; one must give to someone an experience that doesn't fit the existing story, or that resonates with a new one. The same applies to changing the stories that operate on an organizational, social, or political level.

One example of a disruption to the old story is a classical labor action such as a strike. It does not always do for workers to politely ask for better wages and working conditions, because the "story"—the system of agreements, conventions, business practices, market expectations, shareholder expectations, and so forth—has no room for the bosses to say yes. It is necessary to render that story inoperative. To be truly radical agents of change, though, we must be careful in so doing not to invoke and therefore reinforce the deeper story of "evil." The strike statement could embody the sentiment "We are going on strike so that our needs and interests, and the unfairness of our situation, become visible. By making injustice visible, we give all involved the chance to do the right thing," as opposed to the more inflammatory "The greed of the company has gone far enough! We're going to force management to do the right thing, even though they don't want to." The strikers needn't entertain the expectation that nonjudgmental words will mitigate the violence of the authorities' response, but it could affect public opinion.

No matter what the statement, the effect of a labor stoppage is disruptive to the story we call "business as usual." On a larger scale, a general strike does the same thing. It makes it impossible for people wedded to the belief that everything is fine to continue holding that belief.

One of the most powerfully disruptive proposals emerging at the present time is the idea of a debt strike. Like a labor strike, it goes far beyond mere symbolism, far beyond "raising awareness," but strikes at the heart of the agreements and narratives that run our society. If a significant proportion of individuals and nations repudiated their debts, the present financial order would collapse, clearing the field for the kind of radical reforms that cannot even enter the minds of policymakers today. At present, even minimal reforms, reforms that are not nearly enough to reverse the despoliation of the biosphere and the impoverishment of billions of people, are too much to merit serious political consideration. A debt strike would puncture the illusion that there is no alternative. As long as most people acquiesce to the present system, those heavily invested in its perpetuation will find ways to keep pretending it is sustainable.

Here again, the strike can be framed in language that doesn't reinforce us-versus-them thinking. We should be especially wary of framing the issue in terms of greed. Whether it is corporate greed, bankers' greed, or the greed of the wealthy, greed is a symptom, not a cause, of our core problems. The same is true for immorality and corruption.

Railing against the perfidies of the immoral corporations and corrupt banks gratifies our rage and makes us feel self-righteous, but it is ultimately a distraction from deeper systemic problems. Therefore, I would suggest a debt strike mission statement along the following lines: "Our current debt-based financial system holds students, families, and governments hostage, while even creditors are subject to the relentless pressure to maximize returns. It is time for this system to end. We are therefore refusing to pay our debts, to highlight the unfairness of the system that is driving society and the planet to ruin."

What do we really want? Is it to triumph over the bad guys and be the winners? Or is it to fundamentally change the system? You might think that these two goals may not be contradictory. I think they are: first, because the pattern of "fighting evil" comes from the same mentality as our competitive, dominator system; second, because in demonizing those we perceive as other, we drive them toward the very behaviors that justify our demonization; third, because we are unlikely to win at the power elite's own game; fourth, because even if we do win, we will have become better at being them than they are; fifth, because if we enlist allies based on the motivation of triumphing over those greedy folks, they will abandon us once we have achieved that goal, even if the deeper systems remain unchanged. This is what happens nearly every time a dictator is toppled. Thinking they have won, the people go home; someone else steps into the power vacuum, and soon everything more or less goes back to the way it was.

Traditional populist strategies such as strikes, protests, direct action, civil disobedience, and so forth have an important role to play in disrupting the prevailing story. They are, however, both perilous and insufficient on their own to the task at hand. They are perilous because even if they come from a place of compassion and nonjudgment, they very easily trigger old habits of hatred. Their nature is to create a perception that there are two sides, one of which will win and one of which will lose, one of which is the good guys and one the bad guys. They are also insufficient, because they disrupt the prevailing story on only one level. They might disrupt the story we call "the economy," but they leave untouched the deeper, less visible mythos that defines our civilization and embeds the economy. This limitation doesn't mean that these strategies aren't useful or necessary. But we need to work on other levels as well. So, let us look at some other ways, other *kinds of ways,* to disrupt the Story of Separation.

One example is "culture jamming," ranging from pranks like fake advertisements to campaigns such as "national buy-nothing day" and "TV turnoff week." Subversive and illegal art, à la Banksy, also falls into this category, as might incursions of clowns into office buildings or business conferences. The Yes Men, who impersonate corporate and government officials on television interviews, are also culture jammers. All of these expose the inauthenticity, the insanity, or the inhumanity of dominant narratives.

Another form of disruption is simply to create a living example of a different way of life, of technology, of farming, of money, of medicine, of schooling . . . and by contrast reveal the narrowness and dysfunction of dominant institutions. I do not entirely agree with Buckminster Fuller's adage "You never change things by fighting the existing reality. To change something, build a new model that makes the existing model obsolete," because sometimes the existing reality suppresses these new models. Does your local building code allow composting toilets or sod roofs? But there is truth in it nonetheless.

Now let's take it a level deeper. After all, our systems of law, economics, and politics rest on a foundation of invisible myths, habits, and beliefs. We must work with story on this level too. The above-mentioned University of Michigan studies hint at what this deeper approach might be. The researchers found that people who had been given a self-affirmation exercise were better able to consider information that contradicted their beliefs than those who had not. Presumably it made them feel less threatened and therefore more open.

The most direct way to disrupt the Story of Separation at its foundation is to give someone an experience of nonseparation. An act of generosity, forgiveness, attention, truth, or unconditional acceptance offers a counterexample to the worldview of separation, violating such tenets as "Everyone is out for themselves," and affirming the innate desire to give, create, love, and play. Such acts are invitations only—they cannot compel someone to soften Separation-based belief systems. Generosity can always be interpreted as "He's trying to get something from me." Forgiveness can be seen as manipulation (as so often fake forgiveness is). Truth can be ignored. But at least the invitation is there.

When I was living in Taiwan in my twenties I became acquainted with a marvelous musician and artist whom I'll call W. I admired him and envied his creativity and freedom, and I wanted him to like and admire me as well. So one day, I got him into a conversation where I tried to impress him by casually mentioning that I spoke fluent Chinese, that I made lots of money as a translator, and so forth. I tried hard to be nonchalant so as not to seem as if I were bragging. He was listening carefully but not saying anything. Suddenly it dawned on me that not only was W. unimpressed, but that he saw through me completely. My whole game was obvious to him. But instead of calling me on it, he short-circuited my rising shame by looking at me with love in his eyes and gently saying, "Right on, brother."

These words were more powerful than any reproach. They landed on me like something of a miracle. Here was someone who saw something I myself felt ashamed of, yet he did not join me in that judgment. He celebrated me. He loved me where I could not love myself. That was something that didn't fit into my world. I can't say that it changed me right away, but that experience of being unconditionally accepted imprinted itself onto my psyche and made "reality" a little less real.

After a lifetime of training in self-rejection, unconditional acceptance by another shows us a new possibility. This is a transformative power that we all possess. We can all give each other experiences that are living refutations of the beliefs of Separation.

The Dalai Lama was once asked, "What is the most important quality in a spiritual teacher?" His answer: "Cheerfulness." That cheerfulness is a kind of invitation that says, "It feels good to be here. Wouldn't you like to come too?"

The general principle of disrupting the story expands the scope of activism well beyond its traditional conception, validating the kinds of action that are not based on force or confrontation. One example would be silent witness: Amish people packing courtrooms to bear peaceful witness to the administration of justice, or Occupy protesters silently watching as the chancellor who ordered the pepper-spraying walks from her office. I don't know about you, but I find it easier to do the right thing when I know someone is watching.

Hwang Dae-Kwon, introduced earlier, told me of a recent direct action he and some fellow pacifists took at the construction site of a new U.S. military base in Korea that would destroy a centuries-old village. They simply went to the site every morning and evening and did "bowing meditation" (repeated full prostration) for hours. No media campaign. No placards. No banners. Soon people became curious, and before long the issue was all over the media. Things were going well, Hwang told me, until traditional militant protesters decided to get involved. They flooded in with their anger and violence, and soon the media coverage became more hostile. The protest no longer defied existing narratives about law and order, disgruntled protesters, and so forth.

In these examples we see the merger of activism and spirituality described earlier in this book. Because our economic and political systems are built upon our shared stories, action that doesn't directly address political issues still has a political impact.

I often ask participants in my seminars to share stories that expanded their understanding of what is real, possible, and The Way of the World. Recently, a man from Colorado named Chris described a real estate investment seminar he led many years ago. It was a multiday event with 160 real estate investors and it was, by his own admission, quite dull.

On the third day, something came over him. He put aside his presentation and, as he describes it, virtually channeled an activity he had once experienced at a Tony Robbins workshop. He asked everyone in the audience to reach into their purses and wallets and grab some money. "If you don't have any large bills, borrow one from a neighbor." Then he told them, "Okay now, crumple up the money in your hand. I am going to ask you to do something on the count of three, without thinking. When I get to three, take the money and throw it in the air with a scream. Just do it. Now! One, two, three!"

The whole room did as they were told, and once they screamed they couldn't stop screaming. When things finally settled down, he told them, "All right, now I'm going to give you a choice. You can either go pick up your money, showing that money controls you, or you can leave it on the floor, because you are the master of money." For the rest of the day the seminar was magical. The air in the room seemed to vibrate.

At the end of the afternoon, it was time to leave the hotel auditorium where the event was being held. "What are we going to do with the money?" asked the participants. "If we are truly not enslaved to money, then we are going to leave it here on the floor," said Chris. "It is a gift to the janitorial staff." One man, scowling, picked up his money and stalked out. The rest left it there. Chris stayed for a while in the empty room, thousands of dollars littering the floor. Soon the hotel cleaners arrived, five of them. They stopped dead in their tracks, jaws open, staring at the floor. What to do?

Of course, they went to ask the guy in the suit. "Señor," they said, "what is this?" They didn't speak much English, and Chris didn't speak any Spanish. He tried to explain that it was for them, to little avail. "For you, for you," he said, but it was as if they couldn't hear him. For that to be true was an impossibility in their world.

Before long, they had called in their supervisor, and Chris explained to him that the money was for the janitors. When the supervisor finally understood that this was for real, he was overcome with emotion and started to weep. "This is more money than they have ever made in a month," he said. "I don't know what you guys have been doing in here, but you are welcome back to our hotel any time!"

The magic continued for the remaining two days of the seminar. Chris told the participants about the janitors, and the spirit of generosity was infectious. People were paying for people behind them at the café when they went to lunch. He continued to disregard his script for the seminar and speak from a kind of intuitive flow. Every process he led them in was amazing.

Years later, he says, he still gets emails from those participants, telling him that their lives have never been the same since. "Tell me when you give another seminar," they say. "I don't care what the topic is."

The power of that act of generosity was far beyond the mere economic impact on the working-class janitors. Its power lay in its violation of the laws of reality as the janitors, their supervisor, and the seminar participants had known them. The impossible happened, that day. Experiences like that tell us, "The world doesn't work the way you thought it did. The realm of the possible is greater than you believed it was."

Miracle

We have tried everything possible and none of it has worked.
Now we must try the impossible.

—SUN RA

W orking on the level of story has two dimensions. First is to disrupt the old, which says, "What you thought was real is just an illusion." Second is to offer the new, which says, "The possible, and the real, are much grander than you knew." The first, we experience as crisis and breakdown. The second, we experience as miraculous. That's what a miracle is: not the intercession of an external divinity in worldly affairs that violates the laws of physics, but something that is impossible from within an old Story of the World and possible from a new one.

Because a miracle is (by this definition) impossible from where we stand today, we cannot force the universe to produce one. It is beyond our understanding of cause and effect. We can, however, give the experience of miracle to another person. To the extent we stand in a new story, we all have the power to be miracle-workers. Like Chris, we all have the power to perform acts that violate the old Story of the World.

A miracle is an invitation to a larger reality. Maybe I am more stubborn than most, but it typically takes repeated miracles for me to accept the invitation they hold. The perceptions of separation—for example, linear causality and rational self-interest—are embedded deep within my cells, for I am a product of that age.

At age twenty-one I arrived in Taiwan, uncomfortable in my own culture, in which I felt like an alien, but wedded still to many aspects of its defining stories. True, thanks to my somewhat leftist political upbringing I was cognizant of the bankruptcy of the mythology of progress and economic globalism, but I accepted without question the Scientific Method as the royal road to truth, and believed that science as an institution had arrived at a fairly complete general understanding of how the universe worked. I was, after all, a Yale graduate, trained in mathematics and analytic philosophy. It wasn't long, though, before my story of the world came under assault. I had experiences with Chinese medicine and qigong that were impervious to my best efforts to explain away. I had a powerful LSD trip that melted what I'd called "reality" into an ocean of mind. I soaked up the Buddhist and Taoist thought that suffused the island, and heard countless stories of ghosts, Taoist shamans, and other weirdness from respectable people that I could dismiss only with a strenuous effort of interpretation. (Maybe they are trying to impress the foreigner. Maybe they are ignorant and superstitious, given to seeing what isn't there.) I found myself increasingly uncomfortable with the cultural and personal arrogance I had to assume in order to preserve my worldview. To dismiss an entire culture's perceptions of the world in favor of the dogma of objectivity and reductionism seemed akin to the very same economic and cultural imperialism that I was already aware of. Here was a kind of conceptual imperialism, to see an entire culture through a lens of anthropology or through a narrative of cognitive development that, in both cases, was heavily freighted with the power relations that rule our world.

At the same time, I encountered books that suggested that the Western worldview was crumbling from within. Of particular impact was the work of the Nobel laureate Ilya Prigogine and the physicist David Bohm, two of the twentieth century's greatest scientists, who upended my understanding of causality and my assumption, which I'd never thought to question on scientific grounds, that the universe is devoid of an inherent order or intelligence. This liberated me from the trap of dualism: to see the phenomena I'd become aware of in Taiwan as the exercise of some separate, nonmaterial realm of spirit; to conclude that science has its domain, and spirituality another. But now I could see that materiality was much more than we had made of it; that potentially, it could include all the phenomena we associate with spirit, and that this could happen, not by reducing, dismissing, or explaining away the "spiritual," but, on the contrary, only by expanding the material far, far beyond what any scientist was comfortable with.

We are afraid of anything that disrupts our Story of the World, anything that challenges the rules and boundaries of the real. We are afraid of miracles, yet we crave them as well. It is our greatest desire and our greatest fear. When the story we live in is young, the fear is stronger than the desire. A young story has a strong immune system. It can dispose of conflicting data points with ease. I see a *dangji* (a Taiwanese shaman) in a shaking trance, carrying a burning hot brazier in his bare hands—well, it must not really be as hot as it looks. A taxi driver tells me of the time he picked up an odd woman in a wedding dress and drove her to a street number that didn't exist, and when he turned to ask her she had disappeared from the cab—well, he was probably drunk that night, or maybe he was trying to impress the gullible foreigner. I sprain my ankle so severely I cannot walk, and am taken to a one-room cement clinic, where the doctor, smoking a cigarette, digs his thumbs into the swollen, inflamed flesh for five minutes of torture, puts some paste on it, wraps it up, and sends me home, and the ankle is completely better the next day—well, it must not have really been that bad, it must not have actually been swollen to double its size like I thought, and in any case it would have gotten better anyway. I visit a qigong master, who taps me on a few spots on my body to "clear my meridians," and I start pouring sweat within seconds and walk out half an hour later feeling like a million bucks—well, I was probably hot going in there, and didn't notice that the room was extra hot, and as for the intense tingling I felt when he showed us what projecting qi was, I must have been imagining it.

The hundreds of people studying with that man—they must be dupes, bamboozled by his slick talk into believing an impossibility, probably psychologically dependent on the bogus spiritual teachings he peddles. I don't even need to know what those are or examine whether they are bogus or not—they must be, because otherwise my world falls apart. The same goes for all the claims and lifelong careers of hundreds of thousands of homeopaths, naturopaths, acupuncturists, chiropractors, energy healers, and all the others who practice modalities for which there is "no scientific evidence"—controlled, double-blind studies in peer-reviewed journals. If there were any merit to their ideas, surely the unbiased institutions of science would recognize it by now. Those practitioners have been deceiving themselves, selectively remembering only those cases where the patient got better—and some inevitably will get better even with no treatment at all. They are misguided, self-deceiving, poor observers of reality. Unlike me, and the people I agree with. We are the ones who base our beliefs on evidence and logic.

You can see how robust a Story of the World can be, and how comprehensive. Ultimately, our beliefs about what is and is not scientifically acceptable implicate our trust in existing social structures and authorities. The accusations of naiveté, of mental derangement, of being out of touch with reality, and the emotional energy behind those accusations, stem from a feeling of threat. The threat is real. What is being threatened is the fabric of the world as we have known it. Ultimately, the same fear is behind the mental calisthenics of environmental skeptics or central bankers or anyone else who ignores the increasingly obvious signs that our system is doomed, and that the beliefs we took for granted, the institutions that seemed so permanent, the truisms that seemed so reliable, and the habits of life that seemed so practical are serving us no longer.

How to help people, and the systems that comprise them, to let go of the old story? A direct assault—matching evidence with evidence and logic with logic—only intensifies the fear and the resistance. Not that I don't think that there is a logic behind my beliefs, or that they can only be maintained against the evidence. Quite the contrary. But as

I have described, something else has to happen, something deeper has to shift, before someone becomes willing to even look at the evidence. As healers and change agents, we have to address this deeper thing, the wound at the heart of the Story of Separation. We have to think instead about extending an invitation into a larger world. That is the essence of our work as miracle-workers.

Stories, like all beings, have a life span. In their youth, their immune system is strong, but as time goes on they become increasingly unable to withstand the contrary evidence and experiences that pile up. In the end, I could no longer believe my own story. Who I had to be to maintain it—cynical, dismissive, patronizing, holding back from new experiences—became intolerable. As the old world became intolerable, invitations from the new came faster and stronger.

As a story ages, cracks appear in its boundary, in the shell of the cosmic egg. A miracle is the name we give to the light that shines through from a larger, more radiant world. It says not only that reality is bigger than we thought it was, but that that bigger reality is coming soon. It is both a glimpse and a promise.

To the extent that we ourselves are living in the realization of interbeing, we too are able to become miracle-workers. That doesn't mean that what we do seems miraculous to ourselves—it fits in with our expanded understanding of the nature of life and causality. For example:

- When one is aligned with the purpose of service, acts that seem exceptionally courageous to others are a matter of course.
- When one experiences the world as abundant, then acts of generosity are natural, since there is no doubt about continued supply.
- When one sees other people as reflections of oneself, forgiveness becomes second nature, as one realizes "But for the grace of God, so go I."

- When one appreciates the order, beauty, mystery, and connectedness of the universe, a deep joy and cheerfulness arises that nothing can shake.
- When one sees time as abundant and life as infinite, one develops superhuman patience.
- When one lets go of the limitations of reductionism, objectivity, and determinism, technologies become possible that the science of separation cannot countenance.
- When one lets go of the story of the discrete and separate self, amazing intuitive and perceptual capabilities emerge from lifelong latency.

These and many other miracles are the landmarks of the territory of interbeing.

Truth

*O*rdinarily, it is through no mere act of will that we stand in the Story of Interbeing. It is a long process of healing the wounds of Separation, changing its habits, and discovering unexpected realms of reunion. Sometimes sudden and sometimes gradual, sometimes by hard work and sometimes by grace, sometimes like a birth and sometimes like a death, sometimes painful and sometimes glorious, it is a profound process of metamorphosis. We must keep that in mind as we work as agents of the transition in stories in other people and society generally.

The question "What story shall I stand in?" brings us to an apparent paradox. Part of the "new story" is a kind of meta-awareness of story itself. Are we attempting to enter a new story, or are we attempting to stand outside story altogether? Postmodernists would say that it is impossible ever to stand outside story; as Derrida put it, "There is no such thing as outside-the-text." They would say that there is no truth or reality outside our social constructions. I don't agree with this position, though I think at its historical moment it offered a salutary antidote to the pretensions of scientism and rationalism, which purported to offer a royal road to truth. We human beings are meaning-makers, map-makers, exchanging one map for the next and wandering within it as if it were not a map but the territory. Postmodernism liberated us from that trap by questioning whether there even is a territory. A slippery question indeed, given that even the words "there is" are fraught with Cartesian assumptions about the nature of reality; in other words, they themselves are part of a map.

None of this means, however, that there is no territory behind the map. It only means that we cannot use conceptual thinking to get us there. That the world is created from story is itself a story. Each map is a map of another map, layer after layer. We deconstruct each one, expanding our understanding of how it was created and what powers it serves, but no matter how many layers we penetrate, we never get to the territory. That doesn't mean it isn't there though. It's just not to be found in this manner, just as infinity is not to be reached by counting, nor Utopia created by perfecting one more technology, nor Heaven attained by building a tower to the sky. Truth is similarly outside the progression of story from one to the next. That doesn't mean it is far away; it means it is close, closer than close. The sky starts where the ground ends; we need only look with different eyes to realize we are already there. Utopia is a collective shift of perception away. Abundance is all around us. Only our efforts at tower-building blind us to it, our gaze forever skyward, forever seeking to escape this Earth, this feeling, this moment.

So, while the new story speaks of a place beyond and between stories, it does not bring us to that place. It is a place we need to touch back upon more often than we have, in order to anchor our stories in truth. As long as we are human, we will always create and enact stories. We will form agreements about what things mean, we will mediate those agreements with symbols, and we will embed them in narratives. That is how we coordinate human activity toward a common vision.

The new story allows us room to reconnect with what is prior to story, to draw power from the void that lies prior to meaning, where things just are. A story can carry truth, but it is not truth. The Tao that can be spoken is not the real Tao. "Truth," wrote Ursula K. Le Guin, "goes in and out of stories, you know. What was once true is true no longer. The water has risen from another spring." Sometimes we can recognize this truth, but not, as the Scientific Method prescribes, by testing that story's conformity to experimental results. That attempt draws itself from a story of the world called objectivity, and is always the product of invisible choices (What questions are important to ask? What theory do we test? What authority structures do we invoke to legitimize results?) that also encode a story.

Where, then, do we find the truth? We find it in the body, in the woods, in the water, in the soil. We find it in music, dance, and sometimes in poetry. We find it in a baby's face, and in the adult's face behind the mask. We find it in each other's eyes, when we look. We find it in an embrace, which is, when we feel into it, being to being, an incredibly intimate act. We find it in laughter and sobs, and we find it in the voice behind the spoken word. We find it in fairy tales and myths, and the tales we tell, even if fictional. Sometimes embroidering a tale enlarges it as a vehicle for the truth. We find it in silence and stillness. We find it in pain and loss. We find it in birth and death.

My Christian readers might say, we find it in the Bible. Yes—but not in its literalisms. Truth shines like a backlight through the words. By themselves they are no truer than any other words, and can be (and have been) put into the service of all manner of horrors. Taoism speaks of the "obstacle of the writings": when we get caught up trying to find truth in the words themselves, rather than traveling through the words to the place whence they arose.

Thus, while we will always live in story, we need to anchor our stories frequently in the truth. To anchor a story in truth prevents us from getting too deeply lost in story, to the point where, as today, children burning alive are "collateral damage," and the necessities of biological life on Earth are "resources." These are the kinds of delusions that moments of truth destabilize. Perhaps that is why, according to a Bhutanese monk I met, the king of Bhutan makes sure to spend most of his time in the rural villages. "If I am in the capital too much," he says, "I cannot make wise decisions." Surrounded by the artifacts of Separation, we are likely to internalize the story they are part of. Unconsciously, then, we live from that story.

The silence, the stillness, the soil, the water, the body, the eyes, the voice, the song, birth, death, pain, loss. Observe one thing that unifies all the places I listed in which we can find truth: in all of them, what is really happening is that truth is finding us. It comes as a gift. That is what is right about both the Scientific Method and the religious teaching of an absolute truth outside human creation. Both embody humility. This same state of humility is where we can source the truth to anchor our stories.

The necessity to reach beyond story for the truth that anchors story means that there is a limit to how much smart guys in rooms can do to create a more beautiful world. (Am I one of those? Pay no attention to the man behind the curtain!) Much more important are those who make available to us experiences of truth (the senses, the soil, the body, the voice, and so on)—hence the political and ecological necessity for the things we don't have time for in our rush to save the world.

The truth is beyond our contrivance. That it comes as a gift implies that something has to *happen to us* in order to initiate us into our full power as changemakers. Our efforts as healers and changemakers evolve as we go through the loss, the breakdown, the pain on a personal level. When one's own personal subsector of the Story of Separation dissolves, one is able to see that story for the first time for what it is.

Each time that happens (and it can happen as many times as there are variations on the theme of Separation), we enter the sacred space I have mentioned, the space between stories. We might think we can enter it on purpose, without loss or breakdown, perhaps through prayer, meditation, or solitude in nature. Maybe so, but what brought you to such a practice? Unless you were raised in it, something probably happened to eject you from the normal world in which this isn't something people do.

Besides, one way that spiritual practice works is to bring about the unraveling of old beliefs and self-image—the Story of Self and World. This unraveling is a kind of collapse, a kind of loss, even a kind of death. Whether the journey into the space between stories happens via a practice, a divorce, an illness, or a near-death experience, we are all on the same journey.

Just as our civilization is in a transition between stories, so also are many of us individually. When we look at the various stories we tell ourselves about our lives, certain patterns become apparent, and it may be possible to discern in these patterns two (or possibly more) dominant themes. One might represent the "old story" of one's life, and the other the "new story." The first is often associated with various wounds one is born into or has grown into as a member of this culture. The second story represents where one is going, and is consistent with the healing of these wounds.

Here is a process called "What's true?" that is designed, first, to bring resident stories that lurk invisibly inside us into our field of awareness so as to depotentiate them, and second, through the mantra "What's true?" to bring the story-bearer into the space between stories, the space where truth is available. The process originated in a retreat I co-led with the marvelous social inventor Bill Kauth in 2010, and has evolved considerably since then. I will present here a fairly original version of it that the reader can adapt to her own teaching and practice.

First, everyone present identifies a situation or choice she is facing, a doubt, an uncertainty—something about which you "don't know what to think" or "don't know how to decide." On a piece of paper, describe the bare facts of the situation, and then write down two separate interpretations of it entitled "Story #1" and "Story #2." These stories describe what the situation means, the what-ifs around it, what it says about the people involved.

Here is an example of my own. When I finished the first draft of *The Ascent of Humanity* I began looking for a publisher. Enamored with the beauty and depth of this book that I'd spent so many years writing, it was with high hopes that I sent appropriate pitch packets to various publishers and agents. I'm sure you can guess what happened. Not a single publisher showed the remotest bit of interest. No agent wanted to take it on. How could anyone fail to be seduced by (what I saw as) the profundity of the book's thesis and the beauty of the excerpts? Well, I had two explanations that inhabited me concurrently, waxing and waning in their relative influence.

Story #1 was as follows: "Face it, Charles, the reason they are rejecting the book is simply that it isn't very good. Who are you to attempt such an ambitious meta-historical narrative? You don't have a PhD in any of the fields you write about. You are an amateur, a dilettante. The reason your insights are not in the books you've read is that they are too trivial and childish for anyone to bother publishing them. Perhaps you should go back to graduate school, pay your dues, and someday be qualified to make a modest contribution to the civilization that you, in your sophomoric rebelliousness, so conveniently reject. It isn't our society that is all wrong, it is that you just can't quite cut it."

And here was Story #2: "The reason that they are rejecting the book is that it is so original and unique that they do not have a category to put it in, nor even eyes to see it. It is to be expected that a book so deeply challenging to the defining ideology of our civilization would be rejected by the institutions built upon that ideology. Only a generalist, coming from outside any established discipline, could write such a book; your lack of a legitimate place in the power structure of our society is what makes the book possible and, at the same time, what makes quick acceptance so elusive."

There are several features of these stories worthy of note. First, one cannot distinguish between them on the basis of reason or evidence. Both fit the facts. Second, it is quite obvious that neither story is an emotionally neutral intellectual construct; each is connected not only to an emotional state, but also to a life story and a constellation of beliefs about the world. Third, each story quite naturally gives rise to a different course of action. That is to be expected: stories contain roles, and the stories we tell ourselves about our lives prescribe the roles that we ourselves play.

After each person has written down a situation and two stories about it, everyone assembles into pairs. Each pair has a speaker and a questioner. The speaker describes what he or she has written, ideally taking just a minute or two to do so. It only takes that long to convey the essentials of most stories.

The listener, facing the speaker, then asks, "What's true?" The speaker responds by speaking whatever feels true in the deep listening attention of the questioner. She might say, "Story #1 is true" or "Story #2 is true," or she might say, "Actually, I think what is true is this third thing . . ." or "What's true is that I wish I could believe Story #2, but I am afraid the first story is true."

After the response, the questioner follows up with "What else is true?" or, if the answer was just more story, perhaps with "Yes, and what is *true*?" Other useful questions are "If that is true, what else is true?" and "What's true right now?" Another way to run the process is simply to repeat the initial question, "What's true?" again and again.

This is a subtle, unpredictable, and highly intuitive process. The idea is to create a space into which the truth can emerge. It might happen right away, or it might take several minutes. At some point the speaker and the questioner will feel that the truth that wanted to come out has come out, at which point the questioner can say, "Are you complete for now?" The speaker will probably say yes, or perhaps might say, "Actually, there is one more thing . . ."

Often, the truth that comes out is about the speaker's true feelings on the matter, or something she knows beyond doubt. When it comes out, there is a feeling of release, sometimes accompanied by a sigh-like exhalation of breath. Leading up to it, the speaker might go through a mini-crisis, an attempt at avoidance through intellectualizing the situation. The questioner's job is to short-circuit this dissembling and return again and again to "What's true?" When the hidden truth comes out, it is usually very obvious and often, paradoxically, somewhat surprising as well, something "right in front of my face that I couldn't see."

To give you a better flavor for what comes out of this process, here are some examples of truths that I have seen emerge:

- "Who am I kidding—I've already made my choice! All this rationalization is just my way of giving myself permission."
- "You know, the truth is that I just don't care anymore. I've been telling myself I should care, but honestly, I just don't."
- "The truth is, I'm just afraid of what people will think."
- "The truth is, I'm using fear of losing my savings as a cover for what I've really been afraid of: that I'm wasting my life."

If the speaker keeps dancing around the truth, the questioner, if he can see it, might make an offering along the lines of "Is it true that . . ."

The main "technology" in this process is what some people call "holding space." The truth comes as a gift, welling up through the cracks between our stories. It is not something we can figure out; it comes, rather, *in spite of* our attempts to figure it out. It is a revelation. To hold space for it might require a lot of patience, even fortitude, as the stories and their attendant emotions seek to draw us in.

Once the truth has come out, there is nothing else to do. The process is finished, and after a moment of silence, speaker and questioner switch roles.

Some processes like these encourage the speaker to make some kind of declaration or commitment based on the truth she has discovered. I advise against it. The truth exercises its own power. After having these realizations, actions that had once seemed inconceivable become matter-of-course; situations that had been hopelessly murky become crystal clear; anguished internal debates fade away by themselves, without any struggle to let go of them. The "What's true?" process brings something new into the field of attention and therefore into our selves. Indeed, another question lurks behind that of "What's true?" That other question is "Who am I?"

The same holds for those experiences of nature, death, loss, silence, and so on. The truth they bring changes us, loosens the hold of story. Nothing needs to be done, yet much doing will happen.

I have noticed that life itself conducts a kind of "What's true?"

dialogue with each one of us. Experiences intrude upon whatever story we inhabit, bringing us out of story and back to truth, and inviting us to rediscover parts of ourselves that our story had left out. And life is relentless in its questioning.

What life does to us, we, as part of others' lives, can do for them, both on a personal level and on the level of social, spiritual, and political activism. On a personal level, we can decline the frequent invitations we get to partake in the dramas people create that reinforce a story of blame, judgment, resentment, superiority, and so on. A friend calls to complain about her ex. "And then, he had the nerve to just sit in the car waiting for me to trot out and bring him his briefcase." You are supposed to join in condemnation and affirm the story of "Isn't he awful and aren't you good." Instead you might play "What's true?" (in disguised form), perhaps simply by naming and giving attention to the feeling. Your friend might be annoyed with you for refusing to join her story; sometimes this will be seen as betrayal, just as any refusal to hate is. In fact you may notice that in leaving a story behind, you may also leave behind the friends that inhabited it with you. This is another reason for the loneliness that is such a defining feature of the space between stories.

The journey out of the old normal into the new has for many of us been a lonely journey. Internal and external voices told us we were crazy, irresponsible, impractical, naive. We were like swimmers struggling through choppy seas, getting only an occasional desperate breath of air enough to allow us to keep swimming. The air is the truth. Now we are alone no longer. We have each other to hold each other up. I certainly didn't emerge from the self-doubt around my book by dint of some heroic personal effort, courage, or fortitude. I stand in a new story, to the extent that I do, thanks to crucial help at key moments. My friends and allies hold me there when I am weak, as I hold them when I am strong.

Without support, even if you have an experience of universal oneness, once you return back to your life, your job, your marriage, your relationships, these old structures tend to pull you back into conformity with them.

Belief is a social phenomenon. With rare exceptions (such as Frank in "Insanity"), we cannot hold our beliefs without reinforcement from people around us. Beliefs that deviate substantially from the general social consensus are especially hard to maintain, requiring usually some kind of sanctuary such as a cult, in which the deviant belief receives constant affirmation, and interaction with the rest of society is limited. But the same might be said for various spiritual groups, intentional communities, and even conferences like the ones I speak at. They provide a kind of incubator for the fragile, nascent beliefs of the new story to develop. There they can grow a bed of roots to sustain them from the onslaughts of the inclement climate of belief outside.

To discover such an incubator might take time. Someone recently exiting a conventional worldview may feel alone in her rejection of it. New beliefs well up within her, that she recognizes as ancient friends, intuitions from childhood, but without an articulation of those beliefs by someone else, those beliefs cannot stabilize. This again is why it is so important to have preachers to the choir so that she can hear the choir's loud singing. Sometimes one receives a totally new piece of the Story of Interbeing that no one has articulated yet, for which there is not yet a preacher nor a choir. But even then there are kindred spirits awaiting, more and more of us, as the new story reaches critical mass.

That is happening in our time. True, the institutions built on Separation appear bigger and stronger than ever, but their foundation has crumbled. Fewer and fewer people really believe in the reigning ideologies of our system and their assignation of value, meaning, and importance. Whole organizations adopt policies that, in private, not a single one of their members agrees with. To use a hackneyed analogy, a mere month before the Berlin Wall was dismantled, no serious observer predicted such a thing could happen anytime soon. Look how powerful the Stasi is! But the substructure of people's perceptions had been long eroding.

And so is ours. I just said the new story is reaching critical mass. But has it reached it? Will it reach it? Perhaps not quite yet. Perhaps it is just at a tipping point, a moment of equipoise. Perhaps it needs just the weight of one more person taking one more step into interbeing to swing the balance. Perhaps that person is you.

Consciousness

Work on the level of story is not only the key to creating a more beautiful world; it is also identical with what has always been called spiritual practice. Of course it is: at the bottom of our Story of the World is a Story of Self, with its delusions of separation from other people, from nature, from Gaia, and from anything we might call God.

In *Sacred Economics* I questioned the notion that we ought to pursue some unitary spiritual goal called enlightenment; indeed that such a thing, as one thing, even exists. The parallel is too close to money, the one thing from which all other blessings supposedly arise. In a society where, it is advertised, money can meet every need, money becomes not just a universal means but a universal end as well. Of course, when one achieves financial wealth, one realizes that it cannot in fact meet every need: not, for example, the need for intimacy, connection, love, or meaning. Whether or not we are financially rich, we all know this. But then, rather than question the notion that achieving one thing will lead to all other things, we merely displace that one thing away from money and onto something else. Beholden to the dogma of separation of spirit and matter, we take this other thing to be, unlike money, something "spiritual." Some call it God, some call it enlightenment, but we have not left the money-patterning of pursuing a unitary goal—the most important thing there is—to which one must render endless sacrifice.

None of this is to say there is no such thing as enlightenment or God. Perhaps it is, rather, that all the things we leave out when we create the category "God" are actually part of God as well. And perhaps our pursuit of enlightenment as a goal necessarily neglects the very things that are actually necessary for our enlightenment. Here again we see the peril of getting lost in story.

Rather than ascending a linear evolutionary axis of consciousness toward a destination called enlightenment, as most New Age metaphysics seems to teach, perhaps what is happening is more subtle. It is not for nothing that the idea of an evolution of consciousness is so compelling. From crude schemata like "transitioning from the third to the fifth dimension" to sophisticated psychosocial cartographies like Spiral Dynamics,[1] various maps of the evolution of consciousness illuminate a real phenomenon. We *are* evolving. It just isn't a linear evolution. We are entering a vast new territory, each one of us exploring a different part of it.

While I'm at it, I'd like also to question whether "consciousness" is a unitary phenomenon, something we can essentialize without distortion. I think when we try, we enter dangerous territory, the territory of "some people are more conscious than others." The toxic consequences of that kind of elitism are all too plain. Or, if all people are equally conscious, then it becomes "Humans have it but animals don't," and soon we are justifying factory-style animal barns. Or, if animals have it too, then it becomes "Animals with a central nervous system have it, and

---

1. For those in the Integral community, here is something to chew on: the utility of the Spiral Dynamics map is nearing a limit, because it itself is an expression of Yellow consciousness. It is therefore ill-fitted to illuminate much about the levels beyond Yellow; at best it can translate and reduce them to the conceptual apparatus of Yellow consciousness. That has not been a problem until recently, because nothing past Yellow had really crystallized yet.

plants don't," and soon we are justifying monocrop farming and the treatment of trees as things. Or if plants have it too, then what about water and mountains? Enough of that. What if "consciousness" is one name we give to many things? What if, like God or enlightenment, our naming of it always leaves part of it out—the very part we most need to see? As Lao Tzu said, "A name that can be named is not the true name."

While ancient humans may have lived in a much stronger realization of interbeing than we know today, nonetheless we may say that humanity is stepping into new territory, propelled by the crisis of the old. Each of us is conscious in some ways, blind in others. When we think someone "doesn't get it," perhaps we are only seeing their deficiencies and missing our own; surely others can look at us and cluck that we don't get it either. The person who doesn't get it—that's you. As Wayne Dyer says, "If you spot it, you've got it." How could it be otherwise in a world of interbeing, where each is in all and all is in each?

It is not as if the world contains two types of people, those who get it and those who don't; those who are conscious, awakened, or evolved, and those who are not; those who are entering the fifth dimension and those who are stuck in the third; those who are among God's elect and those who are fated to burn in Hell. How often have you felt like an alien in a world of people who don't get it and don't care? The irony is that nearly everyone feels that way, deep down. When we are young the feeling of mission and the sense of magnificent origins and a magnificent destination is strong. Any career or way of life lived in betrayal of that knowing is painful and can be maintained only through an inner struggle that shuts down a part of one's being. For a time, we can keep ourselves functioning through various kinds of addictions or trivial pleasures to consume the life-force and dull the pain. In earlier times, we might have kept the sense of mission and destiny buried for a lifetime, and called that condition maturity. No longer. The Story of the World that kept it buried is dying. The institutions that conspired to keep us addicted are crumbling. Each in his or her own way, through a different permutation of crisis and miracle, expulsion and invitation, we are starting to get it.

I have written as if the transition from the old story to the new were a singular, all-or-nothing event, but the reality is more complicated. One can live some aspects of the old and some of the new simultaneously, and in each of these aspects experience the same dynamic of crisis, collapse, the space between, and birth into the new.

A newborn is fragile and dependent, able to remain in the world only with the nurturing of those already established in it. So it is when we are born into a new dimension of the Story of Interbeing. To stay there, we need help from the people who already inhabit it and have mastered its ways. Enlightenment is a group project.

Today, the breakout of consciousness into the Story of Interbeing is happening for the first time on such a mass level as to obviate old teachings about spiritual practice, gurus, and masters. The age of the guru is over—not because we don't need help from the outside in order to inhabit a new story, but because the transition is happening to so many people in so many ways, no one person can, on his or her own, serve the traditional function of a guru. Those who tried to serve this role in the late twentieth century, if they hadn't the good grace to pass away or the good sense to retire from guru-ing, generally came to ignominious ends, embroiled in scandals of money, sex, and power. This wasn't because they were charlatans—most, I believe, were people of profound insight, mystical experience, and deep practice. But the water table of consciousness had risen to such a point that it came gushing from many new springs, and none were able to hold the energy.

To be sure, there remain many teachers today with wisdom and integrity, both within and without traditional lineages, who have much to offer. I have met quite a few of them, people far wiser than myself, but each, it seemed, needed teachers of his or her own, and many of the ones I admire the most readily acknowledge that. So it is not that we can rely solely on the inner guru, as some New Age teachings would have us think. It is that the guru, unable now to incarnate in something as small as a single person, takes the form of a group. As Thich Nhat Hanh says, the next Buddha will be a sangha. As Matthew Fox says, the second coming of Christ will be the advent of Christ consciousness in everyone. Perhaps it might be said that the millennia-long work of the saints, sages, mystics, and gurus is nearing completion—they have nearly rendered themselves obsolete.

Destiny

There are no facts. There are only stories.

—WHITEMAN

(Nigerian shaman, quoted by Adebayo Akomolafe)

I speak of the more beautiful world our *hearts* tell us is possible, because our minds, steeped in the logic of Separation, so often tell us it is not. Even as we begin to accept a new logic of interbeing, still the old doubt lingers on. That is because intellectual beliefs are just an outcropping of a whole state of being. This book has explored various facets of that state of being: the habits associated with it, the wounds bound up in it, the stories that reinforce it, and the social institutions that reflect and sustain those stories. Change on all these levels is necessary in order for any one of us, and therefore all of us, to inhabit a more beautiful world.

Because this world is not possible from within the Story of Separation, it will take a miracle (by the definition of the chapter "Miracle") to get there; in other words, we can get there only through the methods, actions, and causal principles of a new story, a new understanding of self, life, and world. By the same token, the despair that says, "We can't make it" illuminates the deficiency of the methods, actions, and causal principles we equate with the practical and possible.

The question "Will we make it?" itself encodes a profound dis-empowerment. The question implies that there is a fact of the matter independent of one's own agency. The fear behind the question is "Whatever I do, it won't matter, because the world is doomed anyway," and the assumption behind the fear is that I am separate from the universe. That is part of our story. The assumption, the fear, and the question go away as we transition to the Story of Interbeing. In it, we know that any change in ourselves will coincide with a change in other people in the world, because our consciousness is not separate from theirs.

To deny "What I do doesn't much matter" is so audacious as to seem delusionary. It says: whether we make it or not is up to me, personally. I do not mean that in the egoic sense of "It is up to me, and not to you." I mean that it is up to me, *and* it is up to you, and you, and you . . . to everybody. It is utterly different—opposite in fact—from the disempowering truism of separation that says we won't make it unless everyone changes and that therefore what you or I do hardly matters. What I am saying is that it is indeed all up to you, regardless of what I do, and it is all up to me regardless of what you do. The mind of Separation quails at that paradox, but the mind of interbeing understands that in the world in which you have done what it is up to you to do, I will also have done what it is up to me to do. By your actions, you choose which story and which world you are part of.

Far be it from me to attempt an intersubjective metaphysics. Let's just say that the paradox is only a paradox in the context of separate beings in an objective universe. True, that is also the context for the Scientific Method as well as for most scientific paradigms and currently accepted technologies. Since the latter determine what we perceive as possible, when we accept that worldview the answer to "Will we make it?" is bound to be negative. There are just no realistic solutions to too many of our problems. The time for conventionally accepted solutions probably came and went in the 1960s.

I'll share with you a bit of intuition I had recently, a picture that arose of whole cloth instantaneously in my mind when someone asked me why I don't think we will repeat the disappointment of the '6os.

"Yes," I said, "that was indeed our first chance, and we missed it." We could have made a very smooth transition then, with a world population of only three billion and the majority of the rainforests still intact, the coral reefs still vibrant, CO_2 levels still remediable, and so on. Forward-looking scientists *got it* about ecology, and visionaries of all sorts were developing all the simple technologies necessary for three billion people to live in harmony with Earth. But it was not to be.

Now we have a second chance, and this time the transition cannot be so smooth. Too much wealth has been destroyed, too many people traumatized, for there to be any hope of an easy transition. In fact, those who understand most deeply the severity of the multiple crises converging upon us hold out little cause for hope at all. Many speak of "hospicing a dying civilization." This book argues that their despair arises from the same source as the crises themselves, and that as we transition into a new Story of the World, things become possible that had seemed miraculous before. Even with these extraordinary social and material technologies, the transition will be bumpy, but at least we can avoid the billions of casualties that some doomsayers predict.

Perhaps we will miss this chance as well. If mythology is any guide, we will still have a third chance. Maybe it will be around the year 2050. That is when the damage to the ecosphere will hit home with truly calamitous consequences, inevitable without a near-miraculous change of course right now. At that point, the cumulative damage to ecology, health, polity, and psyche will be so great that even given a hugely expanded realm of the possible, only a remnant of humanity will survive. Desertification, genetic pollution, infertility, toxic and radioactive pollution, etc., will stretch to the very limit the planet's capacity to heal. And it is possible we will miss even that third chance. Some beings don't make it through adolescence.

Millenarians and Utopians alike have been saying for thousands of years that their generation is living through special times. What makes me any different? What makes our time more special than any other? Could the story civilization has lived in for thousands of years continue for a few more thousand? I think not, for one basic reason: ecology.

The narrative of civilization has held us as separate from ecology and exempt from its constraints on growth. I needn't belabor the point that such growth is unsustainable; that we are reaching a coincidence of various resource peaks and ecosystem peaks that add up to Peak Civilization. If we are willing to ravage every last bit of natural wealth, we might sustain consumption growth and population growth for another forty years, but no more.

We can say, then, with confidence that we are living in special times.

I spoke on the phone yesterday with Vicki Robin, the author of *Your Money or Your Life*. "I am in danger of becoming a crotchety old lady," she confessed. "People get in touch with me all the time for inspiration and support, sometimes simply wanting my presence. Just recently it was an ecovillage in Brazil. And this crotchety old woman part of me was thinking, 'Ecovillage? We've tried that already. It isn't going to work.' And I don't want to play that role."

Vicki certainly isn't alone. In my travels and correspondence I meet a lot of disillusioned old hippies. They come to my talks with such pain and weariness sometimes, not daring to rekindle the hopes of their youth for a more beautiful world. They recoil at any talk of a transformed society or a shift of consciousness, for it touches the wound of betrayal. In their communes, their love-ins, their ashrams, they caught a glimpse of an astonishingly beautiful possibility. We say they became "disillusioned," presuming that what they saw was not real, but at the time it clearly *was* real, not a hallucination but a view of the future. It was just so obvious that the Age of Aquarius was dawning, and that war, crime, poverty, jealousy, money, school, prisons, racism, ecocide, and all our other shadows would soon melt away before the radiance of expanded consciousness.

What happened then was not disillusionment, which would be to discover that what they saw wasn't real. What happened was that these harbingers of the future crumbled under the onslaught of the forces of the past, whether institutional or psychological. Not only did the powers of our society conspire to crush the hippie experiment, but the hippies themselves carried the image of those powers, an internalized oppression that had to play itself out. Even if they were aware of the need for mutual healing, their fledgling structures were too weak to hold it.

Another way to see it is that in the 1960s, the Age of Separation had not yet reached its culmination. There were still further extremes of alienation, separation, fragmentation for humanity to explore. The '60s were like an addict's moment of clarity on the way down. Only when the world falls apart do we hit our collective bottom and begin living the way that was shown to us.

If any of my readers are part of the hippie generation that I so love, please let me remind you of what you know: what you saw and experienced was real. It was no fantasy; it was nothing less than a glimpse of the future. Your valiant, doomed attempt to live it was not in vain, because it helped to summon and strengthen the morphogenetic field of that future possibility. Put more prosaically, it initiated a cultural learning process that a new generation is beginning to fulfill.

How do I know that what you experienced was real? Again and again, I see the embers of that experience smoldering in the eyes of even the most cynical ex-hippie. And now the moment is coming to rekindle it into flame.

What I shared with Vicki was that the new generation of idealists has a tremendous advantage over the hippies. "The reason they will succeed where your generation failed is, put simply, you." The original countercultural pioneers didn't have elders who had preceded them into this new world. They had no one from whose mistakes they could learn, and no one to hold them in the new story when the old patterning erupted. Of course there were scattered exceptions, but in general the hippies understood that the generations preceding them were beholden to a different world. "Don't trust anyone over thirty," they warned.

A friend told me today, "In organizing this event we keep meeting twentysomethings who carry a wisdom and generosity that just blows me away. They have a kind of intelligence that I couldn't have touched when I was twenty-five." Everywhere I go, I find the same thing: young people who were seemingly born into the understandings it took my generation decades of hard struggle to achieve. And they inhabit these understandings so much more fully. A journey that took us decades takes them months. The patterning of the old world has a very superficial hold on them. Sometimes they don't need to go through the same process of unraveling and breakdown to leave it behind. All that is needed is an initiation, an attunement, and they shift fully into the new. We older generations hold the space for them to step into, but once there they go further than we ever could.

The generation coming of age today can actually create the world that previous generations only glimpsed. They will do that because they have shoulders to stand on. The hippie generation, and to some extent the rebel elements of the ensuing X and Y generations, will stand guard around the new creators, helping them hold the story of a more beautiful world so that it does not repeat the story of the '60s.

The foregoing account is, admittedly, quite America-centric. As far as I am aware, what America and Western Europe were going through in the '60s had no parallel in India, China, Latin America, or Africa. Moreover, indigenous people have always lived many of the ideals the hippies tried to reenact. However, it is Western civilization that is now taking over the world, its science, technology, medicine, agriculture, political forms, and economics pushing all alternatives to the margins. As people around the world react to that civilization and strive to build alternatives, they can still benefit from their predecessors where civilization first reached its climax.

Do not imagine, though, that it will be the West that rescues humanity from the very civilization it has perpetrated. Haplessly floundering within the invisible habits of separation, we cannot undo a civilization based on Separation. Our healing will come from the margins. Everytime I travel outside the developed world I realize this anew. When I was in Colombia, I thought, "Here are people who haven't forgotten so much how to be human. They are spontaneous, they hug, they sing, they dance, they take their time." On a visit to the United States, the Congolese activist Grace Namadamu agreed that my society was no less troubled than her own. True, we don't have militias running around raping women and massacring Pygmies, but "people here don't even know how to raise their own children," she told me. She was flabbergasted at the lack of respect (and the obesity, the impersonality, the lack of community . . .).

Our healing will come from the margins. How could it be otherwise, as the center falls apart?

- It will come from the people and places that were excluded from full participation in the old Story of the People, and that thus preserved some piece of the knowledge of how to live as interbeings.
- It will come from the ideas and technologies that were marginalized because they contradicted dominant paradigms. These include technologies of agriculture, healing, energy, mind, ecological restoration, and toxic waste remediation.
- It will also draw from marginalized or near-forgotten social and political technologies: consensus-based decision making, nonhierarchical organization, direct democracy, restorative justice, and nonviolent communication, to name a few.
- It will engage the kinds of skills that our present system suppresses or fails to encourage. People who have languished outside our dominant economic institutions, working for very little doing what they love, will find their skills and experience highly valued as pioneers of a new story.
- It will liberate the marginalized parts of people who have been suppressing their true gifts and passions in order to make a living or be normal. To some extent, this category probably includes every member of modern society. We can feel the stirring of these suppressed gifts any time we think, "I wasn't put here on Earth to be doing this."

- It will embody and validate marginalized parts of life, the things we neglect in the rush and press of modernity: qualities of spontaneity, patience, slowness, sensuality, and play. Beware of any revolution that doesn't embody these qualities: it may be no revolution at all.

Do you want a glimpse of the future? You can find it in what has been rejected, cast into the waste pile, and flourished there, in the domain of the "alternative," the "holistic," and the "countercultural." (Things that were cast aside and did not flourish and develop, say foot binding or chattel slavery, are not in this category.) These will become the new normal. Some people are living there already, but most of us are still caught between two worlds, living part in the old and part in the new.

Initiation

A man sets out to draw the world. As the years go by, he peoples a space with images of provinces, kingdoms, mountains, bays, ships, islands, fishes, rooms, instruments, stars, horses, and individuals. A short time before he dies, he discovers that the patient labyrinth of lines traces the lineaments of his own face.

—JORGE LUIS BORGES

*B*ut will we make it? If, as in so many other questions, evidence and reason alone are insufficient to determine a belief, then how will we answer that question—especially when the answer implicates everything else, even our basic stories of self and world? I offered an answer earlier: to choose the story you will stand in.

How to choose? What will you believe, given how easily reason, logic, and evidence are conscripted to the service of a story? Here is an alternative: choose the story that best embodies who you really are, who you wish to be, and who you are in fact becoming.

Behind the fog of helplessness of the question "Will we make it?" is a gateway to our power to choose and to create. Because written on its threshold is another question, the real question: "Who am I?"

The despair is only as valid as the story beneath it that generates what we believe possible. The story beneath it is the Story of Self. So who are you? Are you a discrete and separate individual in a world of other? Or are you the totality of all relationships, converging at a particular locus of attention? Get over the fantasy that you can answer this question by finding proof. Reading one more book on psi phenomena or past-life regression won't satisfy your inner skeptic. No amount of evidence will be enough. You are just going to have to choose, without proof. Who are you?

The mystics have been offering us an answer for thousands of years—two answers. On the one hand, strip away everything that connects you to the world, your money, your relationships, your arms and legs, your language, and still something that is "you" is left. I am not this. I am not that. Something minus everything is nothing; hence the first answer: you are nothing. But when we go there, we find that nothing is not nothing, it is everything: all things spring from the void, and a speck of quantum vacuum has the energy of a billion suns.

And so the second answer: you are everything. Take away even the tiniest relationship and you are diminished as well; add one and you are increased; change any being in this cosmos, and you are altered as well. You are, therefore, everything: a web of relationship, each containing all.

That is the self of interbeing. Divested of "situation," your attention is my attention is everyone's attention. We are the same being looking out at the world through different eyes. And these "eyes," these vantage points, are each unique. As the comedian Swami Beyondananda puts it, "You are a totally unique being—just like everybody else!"

I won't say more about the nature of being. The more I say the less true it becomes. Besides, who am I to know what "you" are? So let's just say that the separate self we have lived with, in various guises, for the last few centuries is one of many possible stories of self.

Who are you? It is not an objective question, which story and which self is the real you. It isn't only that no accumulation of evidence will answer it; it is that there is no objective fact of the matter. There is, however, what is true. Can you sense that the truth of who you are is changing? Do you know that less and less are you the self of Separation?

The separate self who is afraid to give, afraid to serve, a victim of impersonal forces, and helpless to affect the hostile world out there very much is the same self who wants proof that it is not that self. I cannot prove it to you, I cannot prove that the Story of Interbeing is true, just as neither side can prove to the other that it is right in politics or often even in science. Reliance on certain proof is part of the old story, part of which is the story we call objectivity. You are going to have to choose, and you can no longer take refuge from that choice in proof. This goes for every question you face. Which belief is true? All the more this is so for the question "Who am I?"

Do I still hear the cynic, the betrayed one, saying, "What happens if I choose to be the self of interbeing and therefore to live in a world-story in which healing is possible, but I am just deluding myself?" That question, you might recognize, carries the same energy as "Will we make it?" It is the plaintive cry of the separate self. "What if I am alone? What if I give and serve, but no one in this hostile world gives back to me and takes care of me?" The conclusion: "I'd better play it safe. I'd better look out for my own interests and maximize my own security." Add up billions of people all thinking the same thing and acting from it, and you can see that it is from our collective immersion in that story that we have created its image and its confirmation in the world around us. We have created the evidence that we then insert into the foundation of our story as its justification.

Choose to live in a new story and you'll experience a similar self-confirming positive feedback loop. You will have migrated into a different world, with different laws. I get letters all the time saying things like "I gave away all my money, and I can hardly believe the magic that has unfolded in my life." Sometimes New Age teachers, being aware of such stories or having experienced themselves the results of liberation from scarcity programming, advocate that people change their beliefs around money. Easier said than done, when those beliefs are part of a much larger mosaic, an integral pattern at whose center lies "Who I am." Only when that is changing can associated beliefs change with it, resolving into a new and more beautiful pattern. But if "who I am" hasn't changed, it will drag other beliefs back into alignment with itself, with separation, no matter how hard you try to avoid "negativity." Negativity is built in to our most basic mythology of self and world.

Ultimately, unless one has stepped at least partway into the Story of Interbeing, it will not only be impossible to change isolated derivative beliefs, it will also be impossible to create anything but the image of Separation in the world. Nothing you do will really be of service. Even if you fight against self-interest in order to "be a good person," you are still serving the end of appearing (to oneself and others) as a good person, and not actually serving other people and the world. So stop trying to be a good person. Instead just choose who you are. What you create from that will be of far greater service than anything you achieve out of covert vanity. Besides, our semiconscious concept of "being good" is hopelessly entangled with mechanisms of social conformity and bourgeois morality that serve to perpetuate the status quo. It restrains us from taking the bold actions that disrupt the old story. In this regard, we might even have something to learn from the psychopaths.

Another reason we could say that all the effective action toward a more beautiful world comes from "Who am I?" is that that question implies another: "Who are you?" In other words, we see others through the same lens as we see ourselves. Seeing others as interbeings who desire deeply to give and be of service, we will engage them accordingly, holding the space for them to see themselves that way too. If on the other hand we see them as selfish and separate, we will engage them accordingly, applying the tactics of force, and pushing them toward a story in which they are alone in a hostile universe.

Earlier I described how activist tactics that are based on leveraging an opponent's fear of public opinion and desire for profit in effect say to that opponent, "I know you. You are selfish and corrupt. You don't want to do the right thing, so we are going to have to force you." To believe that about someone we must believe it about ourselves too, even if we tell ourselves that unlike them, we have overcome that in ourselves. Moreover, by believing that about someone we hold that story open for them, inviting them to fulfill that role. When they do, we feel vindicated in our tactics and our way of seeing them. But when we stand in the new story the same dynamic brings the opposite results. We look at everyone around us, including those we would have seen as opponents and all the people we judged, and we now telegraph to them, "I know you. You are a magnificent divine being who thirsts to express that divinity in service. You, like me, want to apply your gifts toward the creation of a more beautiful world."

Most of us cannot stand alone in the new story—to do so would contradict the basic principle of interbeing. If you are part of me, then if you are in Separation, so also is a part of me. Lord knows there are a lot of social and economic forces holding us in the old story. A miracle or a breakdown can catapult us temporarily out of the world of Separation, but to stay there, most of us need help. This is something we can all offer each other. That is why I say enlightenment is a group effort.

The road to Reunion has many twists and turns. Sometimes a hairpin turn makes it look like each step takes us farther away from the destination. These turnarounds, even the dead ends and backtracks, are all part of the path through the new territory of interbeing. It is unfamiliar to us, that territory. There are few maps, and we have not yet learned to see the trail. We are following an invisible path, learning from each other how to follow it. As we do that, and as we learn to see its subtle markings, the path becomes visible. Absent a map, and in the very early stages of a new story, we can only follow our intuition at each choice point, guided by our heart-compass, not knowing how our turnings will add up to the destination. Frequently our habits of separation lead us to stray onto the old, worn paths that we can see. We have to develop new vision, to see the faint traces of ancient footsteps that lead out of the maze. We have to see the terrain itself, the truth behind the stories.

As we walk, the destination bobs in and out of view. Ascending a hill—there it is! Somehow my wanderings have taken me closer. Descending into a vale, feeling lost, searching for the right direction, I come to doubt that the destination I saw really exists. At those moments I meet another traveler. "Yes," he says, "I have seen it too." We share what we have learned about how to walk the invisible path. As more of us enter this territory, these meetings happen more frequently, and together we find our way toward the more beautiful world our hearts know is possible.

One common pattern on this path is that a first venture into new territory can be smooth for a while, but soon life provides an experience that says, "Are you sure? Are you sure this is where you want to live and who you want to be?" For example, you leave a job that provided financial security, trusting that you'll be okay following your heart. But no miracle job opens, your savings dwindles, and the lurking fears that were hiding behind that assurance "it will work out somehow" come to the fore. Who are you, really? If everything had gone smoothly, you would not have to face that question full in the face. Sometimes a choice has to be stark to clarify who we really are. The "what if" fears come to pass, or look convincingly as if they will. A woman said to me, "I'm afraid that if I start standing up for what I want, then my husband will leave me." Eventually she did just that—and her husband did leave her. Stop living the way you have lived, and maybe the worst will come to pass. At least it will threaten to. Then you will understand whether you are willing to make a real choice, or the conditional choice predicated on the hope it will all work out, and ready to be reversed as soon as it looks like it won't.

When one goes through a series of initiations like this into the new story, he or she becomes strong in it. Being strong in it, one can hold that story open for other people. Even if someone cannot, in a moment of crisis or when facing her own initiation, believe in the Story of Interbeing, a strong, initiated person can believe it for her, holding that possibility open until she is ready to step into it. With each initiation we become stronger carriers, and our words and actions become part of that story's telling.

I hope this book has served to strengthen you as a teller, a carrier, and a servant of the new Story of the People. I will end with a story of my own.

A Gathering of the Tribe

Once upon a time a great tribe of people lived in a world far away from ours. Whether far away in space, or in time, or even outside of time, we do not know. They lived in a state of enchantment and joy that few of us today dare to believe could exist, except in those exceptional peak experiences when we glimpse the true potential of life and mind.

One day the elders of the tribe called a meeting. They gathered around, and one of them spoke very solemnly. "My friends," she said, "there is a world that needs our help. It is called Earth, and its fate hangs in the balance. Its humans have reached a critical point in their collective birthing, the same point our own planet was at one million years ago, and they will be stillborn without our help. Who would like to volunteer for a mission to this time and place, and render service to humanity?"

"Tell us more about this mission," they asked.

"It is no small thing. Our shaman will put you into a deep, deep trance, so complete that you will forget who you are. You will live a human life, and in the beginning you will completely forget your origins. You will forget even our language and your own true name. You will be separated from the wonder and beauty of our world, and from the love that bathes us all. You will miss it deeply, yet you will be unable to name what you are missing. You will remember the love and beauty that we know to be normal only as a longing in your heart. Your memory will take the form of an intuitive knowledge, as you plunge into the painfully marred Earth, that a more beautiful world is possible.

"As you grow up in that world, your knowledge will be under constant assault. You will be told in a million ways that a world of destruction, violence, drudgery, anxiety, and degradation is normal. You may go through a time when you are completely alone, with no allies to affirm your knowledge of a more beautiful world. You may plunge into a depth of despair that we, in our world of light, cannot imagine. But no matter what, a spark of knowledge will never leave you. A memory of your true origin will be encoded in your DNA. That spark will lie within you, inextinguishable, until one day it is awakened.

"You see, even though you will feel, for a time, utterly alone, you will not be alone. We will send you assistance, help that you will experience as miraculous, experiences that you will describe as transcendent. These will fan that spark into a flame. For a few moments or hours or days, you will reawaken to the beauty and the joy that is meant to be. You will see it on Earth, for even though the planet and its people are deeply wounded, there is beauty there still, projected from past and future onto the present as a promise of what is possible and a reminder of what is real.

"After that glimpse, the flame may die down into an ember again as the routines of normal life there swallow you up. But after each awakening, they will seem less normal, and the story of that world will seem less real. The ember will glow brighter. When enough embers do that, they will all burst into flame together and sustain each other.

"Because remember, you will not be there alone. As you begin to awaken to your mission you will meet others of our tribe. You will recognize them by your common purpose, values, and intuitions, and by the similarity of the paths you have walked. As the condition of the planet Earth reaches crisis proportions, your paths will cross more and more. The time of loneliness, the time of thinking you might be crazy, will be over.

"You will find the people of your tribe all over the Earth, and become aware of them through the long-distance communication technologies used on that planet. But the real shift, the real quickening, will happen in face-to-face gatherings in special places. When many of you gather together you will launch a new stage on your journey, a journey that, I assure you, will end where it begins right now. Then, the mission that lay unconscious within you will flower into consciousness. Your intuitive rebellion against the world presented to you as normal will become an explicit quest to create a more beautiful one."

A woman said, "Tell us more about the time of loneliness, that we might prepare for it."

The elder said, "In the time of loneliness, you will always be seeking to reassure yourself that you are not crazy. You will do that by telling people all about what is wrong with the world, and you will feel a sense of betrayal when they don't listen to you. You might hunger for stories of wrongness, atrocity, and ecological destruction, all of which confirm the validity of your intuition that a more beautiful world exists. But after you have fully received the help we will send you, and the quickening of your gatherings, you will no longer need to do that. Because you will know. Your energy will thereafter turn toward actively creating that more beautiful world."

A tribeswoman asked, "How do you know this will work? Are you sure our shaman's powers are great enough to send us on such a journey?"

The elder replied, "I know it will work because he has done it many times before. Many have already been sent to Earth, to live human lives, and to lay the groundwork for the mission you will undertake now. He's been practicing! The only difference now is that many of you will venture there at once. What is new in the time you will live in, is that you will gather in critical mass, and each awaken the other to your mission. The heat you will generate will kindle the same spark that lies in every human being, for in truth, each one is from a tribe like ours. The whole galaxy and beyond is converging on Earth, for never before has a planet journeyed so far into Separation and made it back again. Those of you who go will be part of a new step in cosmic evolution."

A tribesman asked, "Is there a danger we will become lost in that world, and never wake up from the shamanic trance? Is there a danger that the despair, the cynicism, the pain of separation will be so great that it will extinguish the spark of hope, the spark of our true selves and origin, and that we will be separated from our beloved ones forever?"

The elder replied, "That is impossible. The more deeply you

get lost, the more powerful the help we will send you. You might experience it at the time as a collapse of your personal world, the loss of everything important to you. Later you will recognize the gift within it. We will never abandon you."

Another man asked, "Is it possible that our mission will fail, and that this planet, Earth, will perish?"

The elder replied, "I will answer your question with a paradox. It is impossible that your mission will fail. Yet, its success hangs on your own actions. The fate of the world is in your hands. The key to this paradox lies within you, in the feeling you carry that each of your actions, even your personal, secret struggles, has cosmic significance. You will know then, as you know now, that everything you do matters."

There were no more questions. The volunteers gathered in a circle, and the shaman went to each one. The last thing each was aware of was the shaman blowing smoke in his or her face. They entered a deep trance and dreamed themselves into the world where we find ourselves today.

About the Author

*C*HARLES EISENSTEIN is a speaker and writer focusing on themes of civilization, consciousness, money, and human cultural evolution. His viral short films and essays online have established him as a genre-defying social philosopher and countercultural intellectual. Eisenstein graduated from Yale University in 1989 with a degree in Mathematics and Philosophy and spent the next ten years as a Chinese–English translator. The author of *Sacred Economics* and *Ascent of Humanity*, he currently lives in Camp Hill, Pennsylvania.

SACRED ACTIVISM SERIES

SACRED ACTIVISM SERIES

Heart in Action

When the joy of compassionate service is combined with the pragmatic drive to transform all existing economic, social, and political institutions, a radical divine force is born: Sacred Activism. The Sacred Activism Series, published by North Atlantic Books, presents leading voices that embody the tenets of Sacred Activism—compassion, service, and sacred consciousness—while addressing the crucial issues of our time and inspiring radical action.

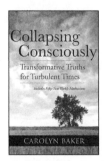

Collapsing Consciously
Carolyn Baker

The More Beautiful World Our Hearts Know Is Possible
Charles Eisenstein

Earth Calling
Ellen Gunter and Ted Carter

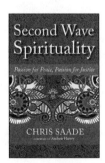

Second Wave Spirituality
Chris Saade

Pioneering the Possible
Scilla Elworthy

Spiritual Democracy
Steven Herrmann

The Sacred Activism Series was cocreated by Andrew Harvey, visionary, spiritual teacher, and founder of the Institute for Sacred Activism, and Douglas Reil, executive director and publisher of North Atlantic Books. Harvey serves as the series editor and drives outreach efforts worldwide.